Higher education governance between democratic culture, academic aspirations and market forces

Jürgen Kohler and Josef Huber (eds.)

Sjur Bergan, Series editor

Council of Europe Publishing

Cover design: Council of Europe Graphic Design Workshop
Layout: H. Mourreau/Hciligenberg

Council of Europe Publishing
F-67075 Strasbourg Cedex
http://book.coe.int

ISBN 978-92-871-5957-1
© Council of Europe, April 2006
Reprinted November 2007
Printed at the Council of Europe

Table of contents

Preface

Governance as a sine qua non of higher education policies

A word from the series editor

Sjur Bergan

Welcome to the fifth volume of the Council of Europe higher education series. We are proud that only a year and a half after launching the series in December 2004, the Council of Europe can already present its fifth substantial contribution on higher education policies and practice in Europe.

The Council of Europe higher education series aims to present issues of concern to higher education policy makers in ministries, higher education institutions and governmental and non-governmental organisations as well as to all those interested in and concerned with the further development of higher education in Europe. We hope that the higher education series will continue to be of interest to higher education policy makers and practitioners all over Europe – and beyond.

Where does a volume of higher education governance fit in this picture? Firstly, the higher education series reflects the commitment of the Council of Europe – and also of the European higher education community – to the basic values of democracy, human rights and the rule of law. The Council of Europe is dedicated to good governance, based on democracy, human rights and the rule of law. It is one of the very positive developments of Europe that this mission now unites 46 countries as members of the Council and 48 as party to the European Cultural Convention.

In 2005, we completed the celebration of the 50th anniversary of the European Cultural Convention. The year 2005 also marked the 50th anniversary of the Higher Education and Research Committee, which has been through a number of organisational incarnations but which has always remained focused on developing higher education policies for Europe. Furthermore, 2005 was the European Year of Citizenship through Education (EYCE). No short formula can better describe this key aspect of education, and the present publications, as well as the higher education forum on which it is based, are important contributions to the year and to making sure that its core concerns will be on the agenda well after the year itself is over.

Beyond this, governance is what in current language is often referred to as a "transversal issue" in higher education policies, an issue that cuts across political and administrative devices like action lines, specific objectives, log frames and immediately quantifiable "deliverables".

Higher education governance is a key aspect of maintaining and developing the democratic culture without which democratic institutions and democratic legislation cannot function. The importance of democratic culture was recognised by the heads of state and government in the action plan they adopted at the 3rd Council of Europe Summit held in Warsaw in May 2005.

At the same time, higher education is crucial to developing the knowledge, skills, values and attitudes that modern societies need. It is crucial to enabling higher education institutions and systems to address the core issues of higher education. The Council of Europe higher education series aims to explore higher education policies with regard to the full range of purposes of higher education, which we, in the second volume of the series,[1] described as:

- preparation for the labour market;
- preparation for life as active citizens in democratic societies;
- personal development;
- development and maintenance of a broad, advanced knowledge base;

and to put them in their proper context.

Higher education governance is also at the heart of the Bologna Process, in which governments, higher education institutions, students and other partners aim to establish a European Higher Education Area (EHEA) by 2010. Put simply: this endeavour is unthinkable without good higher education governance.

As with most complex topics, there are a few pitfalls along the road, and I would like to mention six.

Firstly, we are dealing with higher education governance as a whole. Student and staff participation in governance is of supreme importance – and it was already addressed in the first volume of this series[2] – but there is more to the topic. Institutional governance is also vital, but there is more to the topic – system governance, for example. Democratic participation is essential, but again there is more to the topic – such as the ability to make decisions, the ability to implement them and the time and effort we invest in doing so. Participation by actors within the higher education community is important, but there are other considerations such as the role of the wider society.

Secondly, as members of the academic community or as policy makers with a close affinity to it, we understand the need for basing systems and actions on sound theory. What is perhaps less evident is the need for theoretical underpinnings when taking action. Our deliberations must be theoretically sound – and

1. Weber, L. & Bergan, S. (eds.), *The public responsibility for higher education and research*, Council of Europe higher education series, No. 2, Council of Europe Publishing, Strasbourg, 2005.
2. Bergan, S. (ed.), *The university as* res publica, Council of Europe higher education series, No. 1, Council of Europe Publishing, Strasbourg, 2004.

they must lead to practical policy recommendations. Ultimately, higher education policies and the governance arrangements and procedures that define and adopt them will be judged on their practical and political value.

Thirdly, and closely linked to the first two topics, the term "higher education governance" is both complex and somewhat fuzzy. It is perhaps more widely used than understood. The issue is real: this is not an easy topic. I hope that one of the virtues of this book will be a clearer picture of what higher education governance entails. We do not aim for a common model for governance but we should try to move toward a common language.

Fourthly, decisions once made and strategies once defined must be implemented. Today, many academics complain about the time they spend on governance bodies and committees, and probably rightly so. Yet, they are often unwilling to delegate the implementation of their strategies to professional administrators, and in some systems there may even be a lack of adequately qualified administrators. For our purposes, it seems important to consider the line to be drawn between governance and management. Perhaps it is not always easy to draw a neat line, but if we do not attempt to draw one at all, we may easily be confused.

Fifthly, the 3rd Summit refers to the importance of democratic culture, and we are, as already mentioned, contributing to the EYCE. Governance is important in this respect, and not only because of the composition of the governance bodies. Rather, governance should also be thought of as a set of practices and attitudes that encourage transparency, participation, interest and commitment on the part of all members of the academic community. As such, good governance will help develop not only skilled representatives but a much wider group of committed, interested citizens who will feel that their contribution to society matters.

Sixthly, higher education governance has a purpose. It is an instrument to help us, as academics and policy makers, fulfil the goals of higher education. While the temptations of single issue politics and policies are numerous, we must think of governance in terms of the full range of purposes of higher education as well as the context of society as a whole.

Modern society is characterised not only by a high degree of complexity, but also by an extent of bewilderment and lack of overview. In societies like ours, characterised by technological complexity as well as wide participation, the ability of political decision makers to guide and steer the overall development of society is far less obvious than it was a generation or two ago. If there is competition or tension between centripetal and centrifugal forces, the latter often seem to gain the upper hand. This has both positive and negative consequences, but one of the negative consequences is a general disrespect – not to say disdain – for those who embark on a political career.

The issue is, of course, more complex than can be expressed in a paragraph or two, and most readers will have no shortage of examples of politicians who have fully earned the disrespect with which they are treated. When disrespect is turned from individuals who deserve our scorn rather than our admiration to our political processes and systems as a whole, there is, however, every reason to stop and think, because this touches at the core of democratic society. "Politics" is hardly a term of endearment in modern parlance, a fate it shares with the term "bureaucracy". Like bureaucracy, however, politics is essential to democratic society. Max Weber, one of the foremost theorists of bureaucracy, underlined[3] that a true bureaucracy makes impartial decisions according to transparent procedures, based on facts, and with predictable outcomes once the facts and procedures are known.

Politics is about how societies are governed and – in its democratic variety – about how decisions are made, legitimised and accepted. No society can function without politics, and the ones that have tried to be "apolitical" are not ones we would wish to emulate. Scorn of politics and politicians, therefore, ultimately challenges democracy itself.[4] Politicians should of course behave in such a way that they earn the respect of their fellow citizens, but higher education institutions can also do much to develop democratic culture. Higher education governance is an important part of what institutions can do, for teaching the values of democracy does not lend credibility unless they are also reflected in the practice of governance.

When people ask me whether higher education is politically important, I sometimes answer by asking how many governments have had to resign in the face of student protests. Luckily, the question is normally treated as a rhetorical one, which saves me from actually trying to find the answer.

There are, however, much deeper reasons why higher education is politically significant. Perhaps the most important is that higher education plays a vital part in developing the kind of society in which we would like future generations to live. Can we really imagine that society as:

- one *not* built on high quality education and the advancement of knowledge?

- one that does *not* seek to combine economic development with democratic achievement?

- one *not* built on the premise that intellectual discovery is of intrinsic value and that learning is one of our greatest pleasures?

- one that does *not* value the individual as well as the community?

- one that does *not* take education to be a lifelong endeavour about which nobody can speak from the perspective of a fully accomplished learner?

- one that does *not* value coherent prose and institutions that by their very nature take the longer view, but that lives by sound bites alone?

- one that does *not* combine the need for speedy reactions and rapid results with longer term reflections on who we are and a principled view of the pur-

---

3. In *Wirtschaft und Gesellschaft*, originally published in 1922.
4. As one example among several, see Augusto Pinochet Ugarte, *Política – politiquería – demogagia*, Editorial Renacimiento, Santiago de Chile, 1983, written while the author held political office as President of Chile.

pose of what the Swedish author Wilhelm Moberg called "your time on earth"[5]?

If we cannot imagine this kind of society, we urgently need good higher education governance.

I hope you will enjoy this fifth volume of the Council of Europe higher education series.

Sjur BERGAN

Strasbourg, 20 March 2006

---

5. *Din stund på jorden* (Stockholm, 1963: Bonniers).

A word from the editors

Jürgen Kohler, Josef Huber

This book on higher education governance, the fifth volume of the higher education series published by the Council of Europe, is not only the direct result of a conference on higher education governance held in Strasbourg in September 2005, but also the outcome of a project launched in 2003 by the Council of Europe's Steering Committee for Higher Education and Research, in response to the strongly felt need to address and publicly discuss an issue which although underlying much of the current debate on higher education reform has not been fully discussed at an international level.

The publication attempts to depict features and to highlight current challenges of governance matters in higher education and to link them to basic issues debated in society at large and to the Bologna Process in particular. In doing so, the publication intends to contribute well-founded arguments to a necessary ongoing discussion rather than to present finite conclusions. Furthermore, this discussion is bound to gain in importance and relevance as the transformation process of the EHEA is intensifying and issues of sustainable governance of change will move up the agenda.

It is to be seen as part of a continuum of issues currently debated in the same context, thus following the recent publication *The public responsibility for higher education and research* (Council of Europe higher education series No. 2, 2005), the previous investigation in *Concepts of democratic citizenship* (Council of Europe Publishing, 2000), and the EYCE, but ultimately it is intent on providing a solid base for further investigation, namely with regard to questions concerning interdependencies between public responsibility, governance, management, quality and quality assurance, and recognition.

Higher education governance as a topic requires definition of scope, identification of issues and among these particularly of values and necessities, and assessment of opportunities and risks. Last but not least, the topic demands limitation of ambition as far as tackling the vast array of its features, connotations, practices, choices, value judgments, economic and political environments and demands, challenges of fact finding and of methodological approaches is concerned. That is why this book cannot be expected to be a comprehensive and exhaustive manual of good practice which could be seen as providing a blueprint ready for copy in order to 'manage' – good – governance of higher education.

Instead, this publication offers a survey of topical approaches to governance issues related to higher education on the backdrop of a blend of concrete practical experience and of more systematic and theoretical analysis. Bearing the complexity of the issue and the diversity of backgrounds of contributors to the debate in mind, this publication tries to find an optimal balance between integration of different approaches, completeness of survey, concreteness of dealing with issues, in-depth scrutiny, and clarity of message, in order to facilitate further exploration. Finding a common language for future debate and exploration is an essential step forward, and we hope that this publication contributes to it.

Dealing with higher education governance in the framework of the Council of Europe promises to be particularly rewarding due to the fact that its committee on higher education and research, under whose auspices the project leading to this publication was launched, is composed both of representatives of governments and of members of the academic community, and that there is stakeholder representation on the committee. This made the debate more comprehensive in that various perspectives could be included. In addition, it was obvious that matters of governance in higher education had to be, and were in fact, considered as issues of steering at institutional, at systems – national or regional –, and at international, particularly European, levels, including multi-faceted approaches and interests that reflect the multitude of roles of those involved.

The inclusion of political interests also meant that the proceedings were not only concerned with a mere analysis of higher education governance per se but also tried to put emphasis on identifying elements, core principles of what might constitute 'good' governance, without attempting to come up with "one-size-fits-all" notions of best practice to be copied all over Europe.

Finally, an assembly representing the full array of those involved in higher education policy making in Europe, and indeed in some cases beyond Europe, makes sure that the full span of the topic is covered, both without neglecting issues and without focusing on just a few issues, thus trying to sketch – rather than fully elaborate – an all-embracing picture of the matter at stake.

This overall approach has transformed into a subdivision and aggregation of contributions leading from an initial outline of the issues in an introductory chapter by *Jürgen Kohler* (co-editor) to setting the scene by placing the issue of higher education governance into a wider societal context of change with contributions by *Pavel Zgaga*, *Luc Weber* and *Virgílio Meira Soares*.

The second chapter sets out to illustrate and clarify concepts of higher education governance thanks to the review and discussion of the relevant literature by *Jochen Fried*, and contributions by *Dijana Tiplič*, *Robin Farquhar* and *Josef Huber* (co-editor).

This is followed by a chapter on studies of concrete cases gathered from Georgia by *Aleksander Lomaia*, Estonia by *Jaak Aaviksoo*, Serbia and Montenegro by *Radmila Marinković-Nedučin*, and the University of Uludağ, Turkey, by *Erdal Emel*.

The final part is devoted to the conclusions and suggestions for further development containing the general synthesis and report of the September 2005 conference by

Martina Vukasovic and the concrete considerations and recommendations adopted by the participants at the conference.

Put in a nutshell, the view of good governance of higher education, which underlies much of the contributions and discussions, could be described as follows:

> *Good governance in higher education could be seen as a method of reaching agreement on valid objectives and orientations of higher education (fitness of purpose) and of developing strategies and instruments to implement them in practice (fitness for purpose). In order to accomplish this aim, it should offer a space for the negotiation of interests of the diversity of stakeholders respecting the multiple mission of higher education to best serve the interests of the whole of society and should be a participative process as well as a model of and preparation for life as an active citizen in a democratic society. Such a process should be based on transparent procedures and tasks and contain the capacity to reach, win acceptance for and implement decisions (legitimacy and efficiency) and be sufficiently flexible to adapt to diverse contexts on the basis of common principles.*

The articles in this publication speak for themselves. At this stage there may be just one observation concerning the article "What does it really mean? – The language of governance". Unlike the other contributions, this article has emerged as a direct spin-off from the conference, reacting to the observation that the meaning and accompanying notion of the English term 'governance' is not necessarily easily understood in, or transferable into, other European languages. Fortunately, the presence of people with a great variety of languages not only highlighted this difficulty but also made it possible to gather possible modes of translation, which indeed are modes of understanding, on the spot, even though the findings do not pretend to be all-embracing or valid research into the language complications involved.

This publication, or indeed the conference, on higher education would not have been possible without the valuable support of a number of people. Above all, sincere thanks are extended to all those who contributed by providing presentations for the conference and ultimately articles for this book. In addition, throughout the project's duration and during the preparation of the conference, the working party underwent a period of intense reflection on the content of the issue and the format that seemed feasible for dealing with it within the limited scope and timeframe provided by the conference. This also applies to the staff of the Higher Education and Research Division of the Council of Europe, namely Sjur Bergan, Can Kaftancı, Sophie Ashmore and Mireille Wendling, who have facilitated the preparatory work and support for the conference and for this publication. Particular thanks go to Sjur Bergan, Head of Division, who has made invaluable contributions to the content of this project. Last but not least, special thanks are owed to Martina Vukasović, who has been a tremendous help both with preparing the conference, while working within the Council of Europe, and later for accepting and brilliantly mastering the challenging role of general rapporteur of the conference.

The editors hope that this publication will serve as a useful thought-provoking and stimulating source of reference in the context of the continued debate on higher education governance in Europe. If this has been achieved, this publication has met its purpose.

Jürgen KOHLER and Josef HUBER

Greifswald/Germany, and Strasbourg, 30 January 2006

Setting the scene

Higher education governance –
Background, significance and purpose

Jürgen Kohler

I. Higher education governance:
significance of the issue and confusion of words and emotions

Higher education governance is an issue permeating almost all matters of higher education dealt with both by higher education and research institutions, but no less by state authorities involved in higher education and research. Catchwords such as optimising institutional structures, internal and external participation and communication, democratic, legal and monetary steering mechanisms, public responsibility and autonomy, ensuring quality while minimising cost, to name just a few of the hotly-discussed topics concerning higher education governance, determine much of the current debate in higher education and research. This indicates that higher education governance is indeed seen as being crucially important both at institutional and systems level.

However, issues of higher education governance are not necessarily explicitly and coherently debated under this very headline and name. Instead, in many a case there is a piecemeal approach to addressing issues of higher education governance which, in order to enhance full comprehension of the structural and procedural overlaps, should rather be viewed under a common headline which denotes the interdependence of all the issues mentioned. There are several reasons for this observation of a significant shortcoming: the term itself, or an equivalent, may not even exist in a number of languages, and so the entire concept seems strangely outlandish. The notion of higher education governance appears to be hard to understand. It is seen as being complex and abstract. Rightly so; and yet, as mentioned, it shows itself in very concrete forms and modes of cultures and techniques to be found with regard to autonomy and external stewardship, to internal leadership and steering, to communication and inclusion, to collectivism, stratification and individualism, be it in relation to political setup, administration, decision making, implementation, or monitoring of higher education institutions and their activities.

There may be a deeper reason for not fully addressing the issue of higher education governance as such which reaches beyond sheer linguistic non-existence of the concept and intellectual capitulation in view of complexity. Arguably there is also an emotional barrier to taking up the term unequivocally in the context of higher education since it smacks of belonging to the realm of politics and business management. For many an academic, governance in higher education may be seen as an intrusion of a different world into the sanctity of academia. The term seems to hail the arrival of entrepreneurial outlook on universities, and of the intervention of non-initiated stakeholders in matters of academic expertise. So, possibly, approaches to higher education governance under this very name, particularly when identified or confused with "higher education management" only, could be seen as a threat to traditional values and cherished styles of collegialism or individualism rather than a positive challenge.

Bearing in mind the significance of the higher education governance issue on the one hand, but also on the other hand both the vagueness and the implicit cultural challenges of notions which go along with the term and subject matter, this publication is intended to shed light on the ever-present yet not necessarily fully understood or even fully appreciated notion of higher education governance.

1. Multiple purposes: a survey

What does this rather general statement encompass in more concrete terms? In short, the answer is: this publication is meant to address a number of purposes behind, and related to, the notion and the value of higher education governance, and it is about clarifying the concept of higher education governance with a view to promoting what could be considered to be "good" governance.

Subsequently, and this may be called the overriding purpose, the publication is about formulating visions of good governance in view of our understanding of the mission, cultures and even, if one may say so, of the "mechanics" of three aspects: higher education and research per se, higher education and research from the viewpoint of the institutions dedicated to them, and the – local, regional, national, and international – political systems within which they operate and which expect them to serve, i.e. to be "useful" in as many ways as possible. Obviously this endeavour encompasses the need to first of all lay open our preconceived notions of the concept, of which there will be a number of different kinds due to differences of national traditions and political creeds.

These purposes, and their expected outcomes, can roughly be summarised and specified under the following three main categories:

- One set of purposes behind scrutinising the issue of higher education governance relates to the need to identify the link between this issue and both current and permanent political contexts, agendas, cultures, traditions, or perhaps mere trends or even fashions. A suitable headline to summarise this aspect could be 'contextuality'.

- Furthermore, a major driving force and purpose behind investigating the notion of higher education governance is the need to explore the practical "hands-on" elements of the issue and its long-term effect, such as understanding the characteristic substance of "good" higher education governance as well as the qualitative and procedural challenges of implementing adequate higher education governance in a given environment. If there was to be a summative line for this facet, it might be: "understanding and implementing 'good' governance".

- Last but not least, dealing with higher education governance is intended to answer pressing practical issues of policy design with regard to sharing roles and responsibilities between higher education institutions and national governments, between central institutional steering and decentralisation, and between higher education institutions and their members and stakeholders; in the end, the basic understanding of the role of higher education and the principles steering higher education institutions is essentially at stake here. This aspect, finally, might succinctly be put under the caption "job sharing between state, institution, sub-institutional structures, and the individual".

All these aspects, if not more, appear to be essential when dealing with higher education governance. They should, therefore, be scrutinised more closely, while the sequence in which they are dealt with hereafter does not indicate any kind of priority in importance.

2. Purpose I – Proper sharing of roles and responsibilities: identification of demands, choices and their challenges

a. Understanding the core of the issue

To start with the latter aspect: the question of proper job sharing is about investigating the buzzwords of legal, political or economic gravity fields shaping higher education policy debates. In that respect there are a number of archetypal questions and choices on the table which make dealing with higher education governance a burning issue. In essence, they revolve around models of institutional steering, and these are largely concerned with different ways of attributing responsibilities inside a complex system of tasks. Discussions on "autonomy" and "public responsibility", "overall institutional orientation" and the "principle of subsidiarity", the role of "central planning" and of "individual freedom of research, teaching, and learning", fuel the debate here at the level of traditional terminology.

The overarching issues behind all these items of formal structuring of responsibilities and rights are, in terms of substance, the perennial questions of "regulation" versus "independent choice", of "competence" versus "representativity", and of "efficiency" versus "legitimacy and consensus". This may be said at this stage irrespective of whatever these notions may really mean. However, it may even at this stage be fair to assume that the term "versus" between these buzzwords should rather be replaced by the word "and" in the course of any substantial debate on the governance issue, and that the quest for a fitness-for-purpose approach towards a properly blended balance of these concepts of would-be extremes should appear to be the actual job to be done.

b. Multitier differentiation of roles and their (traditional and new)
institutionalisation

When considering these buzzwords, at least at this stage, it becomes obvious that the entire governance debate needs to address the issue from a multitier approach laid out along the lines of types and purposes of the major actors in the field. There are at least two traditional and perhaps two more recent tiers which must be identified as such for the purpose of understanding the issue, although the real challenge lies in bringing them together by moving from a fragmented understanding of duties and rights to an integrative concept of facing a joint responsibility and effort.

Traditionally, and hence first of all, the debate needs to differentiate between higher education governance issues and viewpoints related to steering higher education and research institutions at their individual level, and to those related to steering entire higher education and research systems. Both worlds may consider the challenges more or less differently, and findings of relevance to one level may not necessarily translate into relevance to the other. That is why this differentiation of institutional and system levels will have to be borne in mind throughout the governance debate, as well as the need to define the interfaces in order to avoid confrontational attitudes and to proceed to fruitful co-operation.

Moreover, there certainly is another tier structure underlying this traditional set-up, and it applies to both system and institutional levels. The emergence of the so-called civil society – stakeholders of various kinds – must be considered here, not just as a menacing challenge but also from the angle of the potential gained from integrating the civil society and its representatives into higher education governance; the issue of addressing the role of boards and private funding of activities fits into this category. Last but not least, inclusion of internal partners is at stake and still a challenge in various ways across Europe; the issue of student participation is the major, but not necessarily the only item to consider here.

Bearing this stratification of roles and viewpoints in mind, the following outline of choices to consider may be useful to operationalise the proceedings of the debate along concrete models and challenges.

c. Typology: traditional archetypology – and more choices?

From a more organisational viewpoint, but essentially reflecting the issues behind this terminology, Burton Clark's taxonomy comes to mind first when labelling types of governance along the line of basic choices, and the balance of choices within his well-known triangle may well become a focal point of the ensuing debate. In essence, the questions thus raised are: is there a preference for the "entrepreneurial university" versus the "collegial" type versus the "externally, state-run bureaucratic" higher education institution? In fact, what do these terms as such, as opposites or in a reality of various crossovers, really mean, what are the pros and cons, what could be a wise and workable amalgam of these different types – if there is any choice left? Why, in fact, do these questions of choice arise?

More radically, and with a view to having more choices, or at least to finding more models in reality: are these questions really a true picture of fact, or should there be a closer look at the role of the individual vis-à-vis the institution, in as much as to say that there is a fourth type of higher education institution hiding behind the so-called collegial type? Such a possible fourth type might be the anarchic agglomeration of individuals gathered in "freedom and solitude", as Wilhelm von Humboldt used to put it, and bound together not by a sense of institutional ownership and institutional responsibility of "true republicanism" but merely, as has been said jokingly, by a common heating system. And will this type of higher education institution survive, despite of or because of the prevalence of individual freedom and the absence of joint policies and institutional governance?

Finally, what about a fifth type of higher education institution, which might be called a university of stakeholders or a civil society university, superseding the traditional role-sharing between institutions and governments? The speedy arrival in very recent times of boards in universities outside the Anglo-American universities heralds a type of higher education institution which might either be welcomed as a sign of new openness to society or condemned as falling prey to partisan interest groups ready to make use of higher education institutions for their individual benefits only.

3. Purpose II – Correlating the governance issue with its political context

Challenging traditional role models of higher education institutions as such and of the actors therein takes the debate back to identifying the first purpose mentioned above, which is: to connect the debate on higher education governance with the current political context. There are substantive and perhaps more procedural answers to that aspect of the governance topic.

a. Elements of the Council of Europe agenda

The procedural aspect of this debate on higher education governance, i.e. its linkage to overriding general themes of policy, is the easier one. The issue of higher education governance blends into Council of Europe policy fields and action lines. This is obviously true for the present Council of Europe project "European Year of Citizenship through Education"(EYCE), resuming the previous Council of Europe analysis of universities as sites of democratic citizenship.[6] More basically, matters of higher education governance are strongly connected to the Council of Europe's key missions, i.e. to protect and enhance human rights, democracy and the rule of law, it can relate to the Council of Europe's activities in the Legislative Reform Programme,[7] and it links on to the previous Council of Europe exploration of the issue of higher education being a public good and a public responsibility.[8] Last but not least, and probably most importantly so, it may be fair to say that in effect higher education governance should contribute to meeting the objectives of higher education in general, which the Council of Europe has formulated so poignantly into four items: maintaining and advancing a solid knowledge base, being relevant to society at large, including making provision for employability, contributing to personal development and to active

---

6. Reference is made in particular to articles in: *The university as* res publica, *Higher education governance, student participation and the university as a site for citizenship*, Bergan, S. (ed.), Council of Europe higher education series, No. 1, Council of Europe Publishing, Strasbourg, 2004.
7. The Legislative Reform Programme was a project conducted by the Council of Europe from 1991 to 2000. It provided support for reform of higher education legislation in countries of central and eastern Europe.
8. Reference is made in particular to articles in: *The public responsibility for higher education and research*, Weber, L. & Bergan, S. (eds.), Council of Europe higher education series, No. 2, Council of Europe Publishing, Strasbourg, 2005.

citizenship in democratic societies, and that ultimately matching these objectives is the proper yardstick for what could be called "good" governance.

b. Exploring the concept and implementation of democratic citizenship

However, despite all these links, why is there an "EYCE" in the first place, and why link the issue of higher education governance to it? Trying to answer this question necessarily takes the debate back to the substantive political issues, of which there are at least the following three items: democratic citizenship as an educational issue in general, and institutional participation in particular; facets of the Bologna Process; general political paradigm shifts and evolution of circumstantial challenges such as mass education, the advent of the knowledge society, development strategies and funding.

The most obvious political issue connecting higher education governance to democratic citizenship is participation of university members – students in particular, but not only them – as "university citizens" in governing "their" institutions. This is a long-standing debate, a lot has been said and achieved, be it on paper or in reality, and yet there may be need for more to come in a number of countries. The specific question of integrating minorities actively into university life would be an additional facet to that debate.

At a more subtle level, however, safeguarding "democratic citizenship" and preparing for active citizenship in democratic societies should be considered to be a major objective of higher education itself. The Council of Europe has been advocating this educational purpose for years, and it is now explicitly recognised in the Bergen Communiqué too, when stating that each level of the three cycles serves to prepare, *inter alia*, for active citizenship. This approach to specific learning outcome turns the challenge of how to integrate preparation for joining and steering social processes, i.e. politics and policy making in the realms of administration and government as much as of governance in a wider sense, into a meaningful learning experience of higher education. Here the quality issue of higher education as such overlaps with the governance topic.

The political context relating to higher education governance is also present in the discussions pertaining to the Bologna Process even as it stood before the Bergen conference, which addresses another substantive point of the current higher education debate. Although the term has not yet been covered extensively as such in the Bologna documents,[9] it is an underlying theme of all aspects of the Bologna Process – namely of the issues of participation and the social dimension, but no less of quality and quality assurance –,[10] and it may require to be addressed more

---

9. Governance issues have, however, been dealt with in the Bologna seminar on "Exploring the social dimensions of the European Higher Education Area" in Athens early in 2003, and in the Bologna seminar on "Student participation in governance in higher education" organised by the Norwegian Ministry of Education and Research in mid-2003.

10. As for the participatory element of the governance issue, the Prague Communiqué states that ministers affirm that "students should participate in and influence the organisation and content of education at universities and other higher education institutions", which the Berlin Communiqué seconds by stating that students are full partners in higher education governance. With regard to the issue of quality assurance, the Berlin Communiqué recognises that quality assurance is the prime responsibility of institutions, thus making the establishment of elements and procedures of quality and quality assurance cultures and mechanisms a governance issue at institutional level.

explicitly and coherently in the Bologna Process in future.[11] In essence and above all, governance issues are inseparably intertwined with the Bologna Process due to the fact that the latter, whatever objectives and tools it entails in detail, is about change – hopefully, in the sense of improvement – and hence are about a culture of change and about change management, both of which undoubtedly are an essential part of governance.

In addition, the notion of higher education being a public good and a public responsibility has been highlighted explicitly again and again in the Bologna documents at least since Prague,[12] and there is no denying that this topic is closely linked to higher education governance, at least in that matching the demands which public responsibility makes on higher education provides an indispensable yardstick for identifying "good" governance.

c. General paradigm shifts in the public sector

Finally, the most blatant political impulse in the debate on higher education governance brought about by real political context is the intertwining of paradigm shifts pertaining to the entire public sector with new demands on higher education and research as such.

As for embeddedness of the higher education world in the public sector, it must be noted that the sector as a whole has been undergoing a rearrangement – or at least a debate – under the heading "New Public Management" (NPM). In essence, it may be said that this approach is characterised by a switch from traditionally legalistic steering mechanisms of top-down implementation of normative formulae to a more economically driven steering system based on contractual consent on objectives to be achieved. Autonomy, as seen from the perspective of this approach, can be understood as part of a management concept of freedom to negotiate which, however, needs to be correlated to a strict understanding of accountability in all its facets, not in the least economically. Despite leaving aside the question as to where the roots of this development can be found, whether it is a workable and fruitful concept, and what happens in reality, it may be fair to assume that this undercurrent is shaping the more specific area of higher education governance, and probably justifiably so since a more consensus-based steering mechanism which leaves room for local adaptation of devices is more in tune with modern understanding of democratic state operations, with its trend towards decentralisation, and towards enhancing motivation at grass-roots level.

This undercurrent blends into specific new challenges to higher education and research which give rise to reconsidering adequate governance at institutional

---

11. There may be a starting point in the Berlin Communiqué which states that "ministers accept that institutions need to be empowered to take decisions on the internal organisation and administration".
12. The Prague Communiqué of 2001 states that "higher education should be considered a public good and is and will remain a public responsibility". The Berlin Communiqué of 2003 underlined this once again by stating that "the need to increase competitiveness must be balanced with the objective of improving the social characteristics of the European Higher Education Area, aiming at strengthening social cohesion and reducing social and gender inequalities both at national and at European level. In that context, Ministers reaffirm their position that higher education is a public good and a public responsibility."

level and at national, or even European, systems level. One of these challenges is funding, which is brought about both by the advent of an "open access" policy and subsequent mass education paralleled by enhanced demand on quality and by research expenses, while funding has not been keeping pace adequately. "Doing more with less" has become a significant slogan steering the higher education governance debate from the viewpoint of effectiveness and efficiency, the idea being that new approaches to governance may be the answer to matching funding deficiencies and added tasks at the same time. Looking at the case from this angle, governance is seen as creating a "money machine" or at least a savings bank, which is also a way of interpreting the notion of entrepreneurship in higher education. Internationalising higher education and putting higher education into a widely open unprotected market place of services, namely known under the term "commodification" newly coined in the context of including higher education in GATS, lends extra drive to a competitive-oriented outlook on higher education operations where "output" may be more important than "outcome", efficiency more important than quality in absolute terms, and speed of innovation rather than extensive deliberation on quality may have become a new essential.

The same, basically economic, motivation and objective, i.e. the drive for effectiveness and efficiency, may be at the root of readdressing governance issues with a view towards turning higher education institutions into "job machines", which could yet be another way of understanding the term "entrepreneurial university". Modern emphasis on the human capital factor, the notion of the knowledge-based society, awareness of total competitiveness around the globe, makes the general public and governments in particular expect miracles from higher education institutions, thus turning the governance issue into a centre-stage affair of affluence and social peace which requires higher education governance either to adjust or else to be adjusted in order to "deliver".

d. Malfunctioning, misunderstanding, distrust?

At the same time there are many places in Europe where the aspiration of higher education institutions to gain substantial autonomy, the preparedness to identify challenges and the ambition to meet these effectively and efficiently do not match the actual ability to "deliver", while the question is open as to whether this is in fact true or merely false perception. On the other hand and in return, in a number of cases higher education institutions feel that the interventionist role of external public or private institutions, mainly executed via financial constraints and ethical demands which may at times be seen as executing mere "political correctness", is on the increase, despite all rhetoric endorsement of the notion of autonomy. So there is a certain element of distrust, or of misunderstanding or doubt at least, between actors. Mutual frustration in view of growing demands may be diagnosed, while ever-increasing expectations on conflicting objectives such as quality, cost-effectiveness, open access, democratic participation, and instant reaction to new requirements nourish the debate.

Thus a debate on the issue of governance may be advisable to prevent distrust and frustration by finding out how to solve any such problems by means of wise, or wiser, governance at all levels concerned. This may be one of the major purposes of a multi-level debate on governance issues in higher education. In that respect, the Council of Europe's composition, which provides a forum for both public authorities and the higher education sector, is the best forum for the debate indeed.

e. A word of caution: do concepts of governance really have an impact on higher education institutions?

Eventually, however, when correlating the issue of higher education governance to its political context – and when understanding "political" in the wider sense of national, institutional and personal cultures, traditions, and habits – there is reason to ask to what extent a conceptual approach to governance will actually work in higher education institutions. Institutions of higher education, but in many a case no less ministries of education, show a tremendous amount of inertia, tend to be at least mentally fragmented organisations with a high degree of anarchy, working on what looks like the principles of fuzzy, if any, logic. That is why planning and "constructivism", which tend to be the traditional approaches to issues of governance, have failed more often than they have succeeded in matters of higher education. Higher education institutions have seen many a governance philosophy or management scheme come and go. In fact it may be argued that the element of disorganisation characteristic of higher education institutions is part of their talent for survival in view of many an ill-conceived, wrongly politicised and hence short-lived concept of governance.

Bearing this in mind, the essence of the message is two-fold. First, that there is reason to be humble as for any belief in swift and lasting change by means of external introduction of governance concepts. And finally, and no less, that the reality of governance in higher education institutions and in systems will only be seen when thinking in at least two distinct layers: the outer organisational structure and operations, and the meta-level, or perhaps rather the undercurrent, of live attitudes and patterns of behaviour which tend to survive, resist and prevail, largely due to the type of independent minds which a good higher education institution prefers to attract as its staff in order to foster innovation, i.e. to break new – unplanned – ground.

4. Purpose III – Exploring the concrete issues of higher education governance: a survey

Beyond these political contexts, implications and aspirations, and bearing the notion of cautious self-constraint with regard to expectations of success in mind while nevertheless not abandoning a "constructivist" approach to the issue of higher education governance, there is a wide array of permanent and substantive debates on the notion and contents of higher education governance. This is, so to say, the expert level of the issue which is bothered with the small print of the nitty-gritty questions of what might be called "doing – good – governance". In essence, this debate is centred around the following, which admittedly is a brave attempt to summarise a complex issue into one question around one formula.

a. An approximate definition – a basic question

If – good – higher education governance may be roughly defined as:

- that institutional set-up and those processes at strategic level of both higher education and research institutions and of national and international systems

- which are concerned with the identification, validation, and realisation of those prerequisites and consequences and of that culture and those steering devices which pertain to institutional autonomy and individual freedom in their contexts with public responsibility of the institution to be governed,

- and which must be described and developed for the sake of maintaining and enhancing benefits

- with regard to the well-being of individuals and society, traditional and more recent academic values and objectives,[13] quality and quality assurance, institutional positioning, effectiveness and efficiency of mass higher education and advanced research in democratic societies

- based on expert competence, on inclusion and participation, on the rule of law, on the freedom of ethically responsible individuals, and on mutual respect,

- and, to add the notion of "good" governance to the definition of governance of higher education as such, serves to identify and to realise these objectives best and at least to an optimum of compromise between conflicting aims and devices and also between expense and outcome;

what does this mean in concrete terms, and how can answering this question and implementing the answer be put into operation? And while asking these questions, what are, and how do we define in due process, the aforementioned operational objectives of societal and individual benefit which should provide the qualitative yardstick for judging the "fitness for purpose" of good higher education governance set-ups and devices?

b. Itemising a few concrete questions

The full span of both basic and concrete issues unfolding from this summary view on higher education governance is impressive, and dealing with it certainly is unmanageable within the constraints of a single publication, thus leaving enough

---

13. The Council of Europe has repeatedly advocated the following itemisation of purposes of higher education, i.e. of higher education values and ulterior objectives, which are listed here without indicating any prioritisation: personal development (which relates, *inter alia*, to traditional concepts of *Bildung* and indicates the development of intellectual, emotional, interpersonal competences); maintenance and development of a broad, advanced knowledge base (which denotes research activities in order to widen knowledge as well as the preservation and promulgation of knowledge gained); preparation for the labour market (which stands, *pars pro toto*, for what could be understood in a wider sense as being relevant to societal needs); and preparation for life as active citizens in democratic societies (which denotes both preparedness to take on responsibilities and accepting principles of ethics and mutual respect). The Bergen Communiqué, in its final considerations, has now largely adopted these orientations.

to be done later. To name just the main items which appeared in the course of debate when preparing this publication:

- Locating and defining higher education governance as a term and as a substantive concept of culture, actors, institutions, structures, processes in relation to notions such as devising and implementing "policy", employing "strategy", making use of "management" and "administration", all these items both with regard to differences and to overlap. This task is particularly difficult but also necessary due to the fact that many European languages do not provide fitting parallels to the English words "governance" and "policy" and possibly even "management".

- Understanding the essence and notion of "good" governance by clarifying the purpose of higher education governance beyond maintaining social harmony and cohesion inside and outside the institution through identifying and matching the institution's mission, vision and role vis-à-vis educational, research, services, knowledge transfer or dissemination and other individual or social objectives of higher education in general, such as regional development, and the given institution in particular, doing all this effectively and efficiently. Exploring this encompasses taking into consideration that there are different aspects and value systems of various parties – stakeholders – concerned.

- Assessing, selecting, and developing the type(s) of structures, responsibilities, personal competencies, and processes which best contribute to identifying and achieving valid, mission-related objectives and opportunities, bearing in mind that there may be numerous answers due to, among others, mission, size, environment, cultures and funding structures of a given system and a given higher education institution.

  – In doing so, the point of view may need to be shifted from the rather traditional focus on institutional layout towards a "perspective of process and interaction" and proper definition and sharing of roles, both inside the institution and between governmental agents or representatives of civil society, which covers all aspects related to steering processes such as defining tasks and responsibilities, setting timetables and milestones, signalling a sense of direction, organising input of expertise, summarising and arriving at decisions.

- Following on from that and, in particular, addressing the issues which arise from the stratification of participants and institutional structures by ensuring not only proper sharing but also proper interface structures by optimal intertwining of legal, economic, and political tasks and responsibilities, which means striking a balance between "unitary", "federalist" and "individualist" approaches, including the aspects of institutional leadership and the principles of subsidiarity and collegiality.

  – This encompasses considering who the relevant units and stakeholders are or might preferably be, for example, institution and government, government and society, national and international level, "internal externals" such as boards or trustees, but also donors and contract partners in research projects or in teaching, vis-à-vis the university, in addition university and departments/faculties either in a traditional interpretation or seen as "cost centres", and finally institution, groups, and individuals of various kinds, what their roles, perspectives, interests and conflicts – as well as modes of solving these – are, and in what capacity and to what extent they are supposed to participate in higher education governance, and how perspectives, interests and functions of various units and stakeholders at different levels relate to each other.

– This analysis should contribute to solving conflicts between aspirations at overarching state and institutional and sub-institutional entity – namely faculty/department – levels, and aspirations of specific groups, namely students but also others, and of individual members, which are noticeable problems in a number of systems.

– This item also raises the question of due balance between democratic "lay" participation, weighing partisan interests, and developing and employing professionalism required to steer higher education systems and institutions; these questions can only be answered with respect to identifying choices between various modes of participation ranging from information via consultation to decision making in a fair and workable overall system.

• Also in particular: the place of the individual in a collective system which as such is bound to define and realise institutional mission, vision, and policies, needs to be identified with regard to individual academic freedom and to the protection of minorities, including non-mainstream thinking, in various circumstances. It must be borne in mind that protecting the individual's academic freedom is to be seen both as a value in its own right and a prerequisite for true creativity in the sense of "enabling the disclosure of the unexpected and unplanned", and that there may be clashes with institutional policy and the notion of "leadership" which should be resolved.

• Assessing governance matters from the viewpoint of ownership and inclusion, which pertains to questions such as the connection of different members and stakeholders at different levels, how coherent strategies, policies and convictions between top-down or bottom-up approaches and external influence are developed, and how transparency, communication and, if necessary, mediation are organised and safeguarded in at least both a bilateral bottom-up and top-down mode or preferably in a multilateral way.

• Contextualising higher education institution governance with external factors, namely regional, national, European, global policy issues in general and in education and research in particular, but also incentives or constraints caused by economic factors, by location, by size, and by elements of culture and prevalent value sets in general.

• Exploring and validating modern trends of multitier institutionalisation, either internally when considering substructures such as the position and role of spin-offs, clinics, technology parks, etc., or externally with a view to networking brought about by joint programmes in research and teaching which develops into institutional intertwining and formation of "partnerships", "trusts" or "concerns" as known from the world of business.

• Assessing tools useful for designing, validating and monitoring policies and their implementation as instrumental facets of effective governance in its overlap with management. Here the role of law – be it top-down regulative or based on the notion of contract management –, of economic devices – be it market-oriented and success-driven formulation of funding or input-based funding –, but also of cultures and in a wider and at the same time essential sense of trust and of ensuring conviction and a sense of ownership enter into the arena of governance considerations.

 – The question may be raised as to what extent there is a shift towards the "entrepreneurial university" as contrasted to a traditional collegial type, and what the reasons as well as the pros and cons of such a development may be.

• Finally, assessing the validity and success of governance objectives, strategies, and outcomes, thus including the role of quality assurance and quality enhancement for higher education governance.

II. The Council of Europe Forum on Higher Education Governance, September 2005

The wide array of purposes illustrated above made it imperative to be selective with regard to which aspects to address during the forum in September 2005. In no way could all aspects be covered, and any attempt would have been a futile overburdening of the conference and the scope that could possibly be covered within less than two full days.

1. Emphasis on workshops

It was, therefore, decided to follow a programmatic approach which centred the investigation on a pathway leading from the macrocosm of context and systems level to the microcosm of the institution and of the actors therein. Thus, as for the workshops the programme was structured as follows:

• the mission of higher education in the changed societal context and its implications for governance;

• the governance of higher education systems;

• the governance of higher education institutions;

• the actors in higher education governance.

These four items were to be reflected upon in the light of the substantive issues mentioned by the keynote speaker, as well as in the light of the literature survey provided. Another itemisation that proved to be useful was the following:

- mission and stakeholders: considering more and more diversified missions of higher education institutions, and how these reflect governance models and involvement of different stakeholders in the decision-making process;

- governance of higher education systems: looking into governance of "complete" systems of higher education, i.e. the national – or even European and global – level, including identification of current practices and best practices;

- autonomy and external participation: autonomy of an institution and the role of society, state, and other "external" stakeholders in governance;

- internal participation and levels of governance and management: concepts of governance within a higher education institution and practical implementation;

- interdependence between culture, management and governance: influence of the overall cultural setting on higher education governance, different notions of governance between the strategic policy level and the technocratic management approach, also related to the discussion on legitimacy of representatives in governing bodies and the call for professionalism;

- stimulating stakeholder participation: from making legal provisions for stakeholder – namely student – participation to ensuring widespread acceptance of opportunities to participate in democratic governance structures;

- collectivism in governance and safeguarding academic freedom in research, teaching, and learning: considering the limits of governance and institutional policies vis-à-vis the individual person;

- the role of higher education governance for fostering democratic culture of tolerance and inclusion: design and examples of positive influence of higher education governance on the wider community, especially in conflict areas;

The choice and structure of the four workshops, while admittedly not being extravagant, allowed a number of things to be achieved. First, the topics chosen evolved with a view to interpreting and solving their specific topical challenges in the light of all the concrete aspects of the governance issue mentioned above. Second, proceeding from the macro- to the microlevel helped to reflect and make use of the specific advantage of the set-up which characterises the Council of Europe higher education sector, i.e. to integrate both the governmental and the academic sides, but also stakeholders represented, such as students, in fruitful debate relevant to all concerned. Third, since the issue is rather complex it promised to be easiest for participants to address the debate from the angle of archetypal questions which as such are easily understood since they are basic in structure and in political debate.

The second guiding principle of conference programme design, apart from having to be selective and basically transparent in approach, was to try and give participants as much of a voice as possible. It is for this reason that the allotment of time for workshops had been extended to the utmost, bearing in mind the request to do so by those who attended the 2004 conference on higher education as a public good and a public responsibility. This lead organisational idea led the Council of Europe working party to integrate the subject-related input into the respective workshops rather than present the general substantive remarks in the plenary at the onset of the conference, which might have been too overburdening.

2. Input and winding up

However, in order to facilitate the debate in general the keynote presentation served as an overarching, possibly even provocative, introduction to the challenges of the higher education governance issues at all levels, i.e. at systems, at institutional, at group, and at individual levels. The exposition of political context and of concrete questions provided in the previous section of this introduction served the same purpose, especially in order to identify the catchwords and their correlations as challenges to higher education governance. The subsequent literary review eventually cast light on what has already been thought about and worked out in substance, showing the fields of research but also the white spots on the map, the unknown stretches of land waiting to be discovered – hopefully in part by the conference itself.

The panel debate on the second day helped integrate findings in the workshops and to bring about a coherent picture of the issue.

III. Expectations

What outcome then, by and large, can be expected from this undertaking?

1. The conference per se

Certainly the conference was expected to have results per se. It offered a forum for exploring the topic and for debate which helped to bring the issue forward by raising awareness of challenges, choices, and solutions. Of course, beyond the live experience which participants shared there is value in the survey and documentation of research material available on higher education governance. Finally, the present Council of Europe publication preserves and disseminates the presentations, the essence of debates in workshops and in the plenary, and the conclusions drawn from these. The Council of Europe would also like to take the matter further by means of adequate follow-ups, such as workshops on concrete issues.

2. Political programmes, namely of the Council of Europe

Recommendations formulated at the end of a conference hopefully influence real political decision making on governance issues at European, national, institutional, and stakeholder group levels. So there is the promise of an impact on the future work of the Council of Europe in its operations in the field of higher education. The conference certainly was of ad hoc significance to Council of Europe activities in a wider sense in as much as it contributed to the EYCE by advocating that higher education governance is required to ensure participation of stakeholders and partners adequately, i.e. namely of students but also of others such as young researchers aspiring to doctorates, and that higher education institutions should provide space for experiencing social inclusion and for learning democratic self-organisation.

3. The Bologna Process – the link to quality and quality assurance

Beyond reflecting on the Council of Europe's institutional and core missions as such, in the medium-term perspective the Bologna Process may also incorporate the issue of higher education governance more strongly and assimilate the findings outlined in this publication. This is to be expected since steering institutions properly with regard to defining and actually "living" educational and research missions, be it at systems or institutional level, has a profound impact on all issues of teaching and research quality and quality assurance. The very debate on addressing quality assurance matters either at the level of programmes or at the level of higher education institutions and their internal quality processes indicates the profound significance of the governance issue for matters of quality and its certification on the backdrop of the presence or absence of trust in the quality of proceedings in autonomous higher education institutions. Contributing to matters of the Bologna Process could therefore be another valuable outcome.

4. Outlook on follow-ups

There is an obvious warning of caution at the end of these introductory remarks. The topic is an enormously vast one. And since not only is *ars longa* a striking truth but also *vita brevis*, no miracles can be expected as to exhausting the topic. There are a few findings, hopefully, and in addition there are a number of open questions. Inasmuch as the publication succeeds in clearly formulating these questions, it will have fulfilled its purpose to initiate a political debate of which there is, and must be, more to come.

(In the) Context of change

Reconsidering higher education governance

Pavel Zgaga

Governance is an old term and at first sight it seems to be simple and clear. As a word with ancient roots it can be found in several modern languages, quite often with a variety of meanings. Nevertheless, in various languages we can say and understand that "a king governs (rules, controls) a kingdom well or poorly" or that "somebody's principles govern (influence, direct) their life" while we can also say that "people obey – or disobey – their king" or that "somebody complies – or does not comply – with their internalised principles", etc.

In general, governance is perceived as the exercise of authority, control or direction. We most often associate governance with political authority (government, but we should not confuse or equate them: governance is not government) and with broader issues in society and politics which demand institutions and control, yet we also associate it with the economy and organisations (for example, corporate governance). It is usually understood in relation to administrative and managerial issues; clearly governance comprises the processes and systems by which a society, an organisation, etc., operates although it cannot be reduced solely to this dimension. But how do we use this old term in the context of contemporary higher education? Before answering this question we will make a short detour into its history.

"The agents themselves must consider what is appropriate to the occasion"

As in so many other cases, the roots of this term go back to ancient times. The Latin '*gubernare*' still sounds quite familiar in various modern languages. Even its Greek background can produce a surprisingly contemporary linguistic association for modern ears: '*kybernaein*' – cybernetics? Not really; '*kybernaein*' means to steer (a vessel) while '*kybernetike* (*tekhne*)' is the art of steering (a vessel). Nevertheless, the two meanings – an old and a very recent one – call out to be compared: on the one hand 'navigation', the old art of ascertaining the position and directing the course of vessels at sea, and on the other hand, 'cybernetics', the modern theory of control and communication in machines and organisms.

With the ancient Greeks, when human conduct was being discussed by philosophers, the art of steering, navigation – or 'governance' in the sense of 'directing the course at sea' – was a frequently used metaphor, often paralleled to the art of medicine. Thus, in Aristotle's *Nicomachean Ethics* (1908) we find the following statement:

> But this must be agreed upon beforehand, that the whole account of matters of conduct must be given in outline and not precisely, as we said at the very beginning that the accounts we demand must be in accordance with the subject-matter; matters

concerned with conduct and questions of what is good for us have no fixity, any more than matters of health. The general account being of this nature, the account of particular cases is yet more lacking in exactness; for they do not fall under any art or precept but the agents themselves must in each case consider what is appropriate to the occasion, as happens also in the art of medicine or of navigation.

In this paragraph, Aristotle obviously dealt with ethical problems yet "matters concerned with conduct and questions of what is good for us" are seen as parallel to medicine and navigation. Let us pursue this example and say that matters concerned with navigation also "have no fixity"; "they do not fall under any art or precept" but sailors themselves "must in each case consider what is appropriate to the occasion". Like doctors in medicine: they do not study 'health itself', as Aristotle said, "but the health of man" (1908); doctors must also with every particular patient "consider what is appropriate to the occasion" – just like governors in governance?

Aristotle admonished about the uniqueness and singularity of 'the occasion' that we encounter again and again in our lives and always have to decide what is most appropriate in a particular case. He rejected 'precepts', that is, ready-made recipes. He relied on his idea of *phronesis*, 'practical wisdom' as a cultivated ability – the trained insight of man – which helps us make appropriate decisions in various unique human situations. When considering a decision, we have to "consider what is appropriate to the occasion": we have to take into account the always unique mixture of specific circumstances. Certainly, a sailor should be educated and trained for reading sea maps, understanding changing weather conditions and the nature of vessels, etc., but he has always to choose the appropriate decision in the given circumstances at sea, and not merely apply precepts learned on land. Therefore, nobody can learn how to navigate simply by consulting a set of prescriptions for the reason that they can never be detailed enough to be applied with accuracy to any case and because the selection of which prescription to apply is a matter of requiring a concrete insight, something that is not determined by an abstract rule. The stress is not on "precepts"; the stress is on "the agents themselves".

If we now change our focus from 'governance' as 'directing the course at sea' to governance in its modern sense at least two messages emerge from these considerations. Firstly, 'given circumstances' do not only apply to those 'objective factors' determined by nature: for example, buoyancy, the position of North, weather conditions, etc. They also apply to 'people on board': a reasonable captain would always take a decision after very carefully considering *who* he has on board – well-trained parachute troops or a group of tourists with small kids. The answer to this sensitive question can decisively influence the way of interpreting 'objective factors' and taking decisions. Furthermore, this is the point at which modern political philosophies and their popular applications in political culture generally established a new understanding of governance: people cannot be just an object of governing. Good and effective governance calls for 'ownership'; it is only achieved together with partners and stakeholders; it presupposes broader policy consultations and participatory processes. Here we are talking about democratic governance.

Secondly, for some – let us say relatively academic – purposes it might be absolutely legitimate to consider governance theoretically, that is, 'in general', as 'governance itself'; however, it is absolutely inappropriate to consider it in this way when we approach the singularity of a 'real life'. We reiterate: general precepts or ready-made recipes do not help at all when we find ourselves in the complex conditions of 'real life' and in a position to take decisions which could influence and/or direct other people (or ourselves alone). At this point, we should be particularly cautious today – especially within an academic context – when various governance issues are increasingly supported by 'theoretical counselling' from highly specialised science and research pools and when this kind of assistance has even become export merchandise. On one hand, it is sometimes argued that the real issue is just a matter of inventing, defining and applying 'the most efficient model of governance'. On the other hand, it is not difficult to agree that within this assistance as a rule "a very low value is placed on the cultural and historical skills" and that "the situation observed in recent years where social scientists offer advice to troubled countries while possessing minimal knowledge of local societies, combined with the frequently poor results" does not give a reason to be proud; on the contrary, it "provides encouragement to question the intellectual *status quo*" (Rosovsky, 2003).[14] We can also talk about 'fair governance' and the 'governance culture'.

A new concept with growing frequency

Now, how do we use this 'old' term in the context of contemporary higher education? In discussions on higher education, governance seems to be a relatively new concept and at least in some European languages there can also be certain problems of how to translate and use it in a context dominated by traditional terms. The term 'government' has been used, of course, very frequently in contemporary policy discussions relating to higher education although this has not been the case with higher education governance. For example, it has not been used in any well-known and influential international documents over the last fifteen or twenty years; nor in the *Magna Charta Universitatum* (1988), the Lisbon Convention (1997), nor in the Sorbonne and Bologna Declarations (1998, 1999), etc.

Modern electronic search tools allow us an excellent opportunity to check linguistic developments and changes. Searching for 'governance' within the so-called Bologna *Trends* reports can help us observe its coming into use: there are no hits at all in *Trends 1* (1999), two hits appear in *Trends 2* (2001), four hits in *Trends 3* (2003) and 8 hits in *Trends 4* (2005). Use of the term 'higher education governance' is obviously growing; however, the absolute figures do not seem to support the claim that it is really a frequently used expression today.

---

14. While discussing 'internal permeability' and disciplinary barriers within modern universities Rosovsky argues that "no one stands higher than theorists, today using almost exclusively the sophisticated language of mathematics. This methodology – this adoration of science – means that culture and history play almost no role in analysis. Business cycles are a worthy subject of study, but not Japanese or Argentinean business cycles. After all, one does not study Japanese or Argentinean physics; we simply study physics" he concludes cynically (Rosovsky, 2003: 20).

It is also interesting to see within which context the concept has been emerging. Surprisingly (or not), both references from *Trends 2* refer to higher education in south-east Europe: with regard to the Dayton Peace Accords the "unique problems of governance and co-ordination" in Bosnia and Herzegovina are mentioned on one hand and, on the other, "the Interim Statute" aiming "at restoring autonomous governance at the University of Pristina" (Haug, Kirstein & Knudsen, 1999: 47, 69). Already here it is impossible to overlook that the first reference refers to the governance of a higher education system while the second refers to the governance of a higher education institution. All four references from *Trends 3* stress institutional 'governance and management structures' (Reichert & Tauch, 2003: 24, 73) and the need to change or improve them (for example, in relation to quality assurance, supervisory councils, etc.). It is similar in *Trends 4*: internal 'governance structures' are most often used in relation to institutional leadership and internal management but also in relation to recent systemic reforms in various countries (Reichert & Tauch, 2005: 7, 32, 41, 42, 46, 62).

Thus, the concept of governance seems to be more frequently used within the institutional context than at the system level. In a compendium of basic documents in the Bologna Process, the earliest use of this term can be found in the EUA's Message from Salamanca (March 2001), this time in relation to quality issues: these issues encompass "teaching and research as well as governance and administration, responsiveness to students' needs and the provision of non-educational services" (EUA, 2003b: 64). The Message from Salamanca was addressed to the Prague ministerial meeting but the concept of governance as such did not find any echo in the Prague Communiqué. Nevertheless, an important change in accent did occur: the social dimension of higher education was recognised in Prague[15] and thus a new context was also provided for the emerging concept of 'higher education governance'.

As may already be seen from checking the *Trends* reports, the frequency of the concept's use increased during the period between the Prague and Berlin conferences (2001-03). Thus, in May 2003 the EUA Graz Convention put the topic of "improving institutional governance and management"[16] firmly among its five key themes and launched it in the middle of further discussions on the role of higher education institutions while, on the other hand, a special Bologna seminar was organised only a few days later in Oslo on "student participation in governance in higher education".[17] This seminar broadened the meaning of higher education governance to encompass an important dimension that was later confirmed by ministers in Berlin: "Students are full partners in higher education governance.

---

15. "Ministers affirmed that students should participate in and influence the organisation and content of education at universities and other higher education institutions. Ministers also reaffirmed the need, recalled by students, to take account of the social dimension in the Bologna Process" (Prague Communiqué, 2001).
16. See *Graz Reader* (2003b: 12-14). It contains 17 such references, equally as *Glasgow Reader* two years later; they are mostly related to governance structures and university management. Yet, the Glasgow Declaration contains only a vague reference to "governing structures and leadership competence".
17. This has so far been the only official Bologna event directly related to – a particular dimension of – higher education governance. See *Bologna follow-up seminar* on *Student participation in governance in higher education*, Oslo, 12-14 June 2003. Report from Council of Europe, Annika Persson. Article by Sjur Bergan, Council of Europe. Ministry of Education and Research, Oslo, 2003. Also see Bergan (ed.), 2004.

Ministers note that national legal measures for ensuring student participation are largely in place throughout the EHEA. They also call on institutions and student organisations to identify ways of increasing actual student involvement in higher education governance" (Berlin Communiqué, 2003). In fact, this was the first – and so far the last – time that an official Bologna document adopted by ministers used the term 'higher education governance'.

Higher education governance is obviously a *multidimensional concept*. On one hand, it can be connected directly to government(s): in modern times, governments 'govern' social subsystems like higher education, etc. It is important to note even here that this task has already exceeded the limited national scope. On the other hand, in its common use it is close to 'management' and/or 'administration', particularly with regard to institution(s) and/or organisations. Furthermore, it also provokes questions of participation in governance, etc. At this point, before examining any further details, we propose to roughly distinguish between the three structural dimensions of higher education governance (HEG):

    a. *internal or institutional HEG*: governance of higher education institution(s);

    b. *external or systemic HEG*: governance of higher education system(s); and

    c. *international or global HEG*: governance of higher education systems within an international (global) perspective, for example, the Bologna Process.

Structural dimensions of governance: an interdependent totality

The term 'higher education governance' as we use it today did not appear in traditional discussions on higher education; yet, this does not mean that traditional higher education institutions were not 'governed'. Since the origins of the European university, it has always been very important to steer the course of an institution and regulate its internal organisation as well as its relationships with both the environment and 'external authorities'. Therefore, for any period it is possible to distinguish between internal and external 'governance' or 'government'[18] in a certain way. However, higher education governance as today's concept radically differs in certain aspects from older traditions.

There is much evidence that the conceptual origins of the modern term 'higher education governance' are closely linked to the complexity of the societal context characterised by the transformation from elite to mass higher education which has occurred during the last few decades. The phenomenon of mass higher education involves a demarcation between traditional and modern higher education in several respects. A review of developments in the past two or three decades shows that the democratising and liberalising of access to higher education put the need for systemic reforms onto national and institutional agendas everywhere. Mass higher education challenged – and in its further course totally changed – the

---

18. In dealing with the management and resources of medieval and early modern European universities *A history of the university in Europe* contains detailed contributions on its 'internal' and 'external' government' (Rüegg, 1992: 1:119-133; 2:164-183).

traditional university as well as its complex relationships with the modern state. A few years ago, the Eurydice network produced a very instructive study covering twenty years of reforms in European higher education at the end of the 20th century and found that "the major focus of legislation and policy was the management and control of higher education institutions and in particular the financing of such institutions" (Eurydice, 2000: 33).

Since the 1960s higher education systems worldwide have been constantly expanding. At a certain level of their expansion and in combination with the broader economic and political agenda of the time – for example, the budget constraints of the 1970s and 1980s in the West or the 'transition' of the early 1990s in the East – these processes raised the question of the efficiency of both higher education institutions as well as systems. Country by country this issue was approached in discussions at the national level via thorough reforms of financing and management as well as the preparation of new qualifications structures. These reforms were underpinned by a radical conceptual shift in understanding of the relationship between institutions and the state; in the literature, it was remarkably described as a move away from the traditional *"interventionary"* towards the new *"facilitatory* state" (Neave & Van Vught, 1991).

It is widely recognised that throughout Europe the government's role in the governance of higher education institutions has been and remains very significant. However, since the 1980s governments have been gradually withdrawing – in various directions – from direct institutional governance. The state's influence was redirected to setting general higher education objectives, that is, to higher education *output* rather than the *process*. The circumstances of mass higher education in combination with the challenges of the emerging knowledge society demonstrated that effective governance in higher education requires much more decision-making freedom at the institutional level. The concept of the *autonomy of universities* moved to the centre of discussions. Consequently, legislative provisions were redirected from, for example, funds allocated to institutions strictly by budget lines (salaries, equipment, maintenance, etc.) to the allocation of block grants. This redirection aimed to increase university autonomy in terms of its 'financial dimension'; yet it included the need and opportunity to search for alternative financial resources. A well-known slogan often heard since the 1980s is that higher education institutions deserve *more autonomy* but they should become *more accountable*.[19]

After the unannounced and unexpected storms of the late 1960s and early 1970s, universities found themselves up until the 1980s – in some places a little earlier, in others a little later – in a totally new environment. As universities, they had to be able to reflect these changes and to understand that they should take them into account while reconsidering their mission. An important and today well-known

---

19. "The granting of greater autonomy to institutions, particularly in institutional governance, budget spending and course planning was intended to encourage an entrepreneurial spirit and thus promote efficiency, cost-effectiveness, flexibility and quality in educational provision. At the same time, institutions were encouraged to seek additional funding through bids for governmental contracts and the sale of their research and teaching services" (Eurydice, 2000: 177).

convention of European universities took place in 1988 – "four years before the definite abolition of boundaries between the countries of the European Community" and, we should add this from today's point of view, two years before the fall of the Berlin Wall – to stress the importance of being "aware of the part that universities will be called upon to play in a changing and increasingly international society". Its most remarkable message is that "the university is an autonomous institution at the heart of societies [...]. To meet the needs of the world around it, its research and teaching must be morally and intellectually independent of all political authority [...] and economic power" (*Magna Charta Universitatum*, 1991: 59).[20]

However, this is not the first time universities have found themselves in radically changed circumstances. The debate on autonomy goes back to the very beginning of universities. Yet, as the discussions on university relationships with the 'external world' in general and on university autonomy in particular can sometimes be treated as 'eternal issues', in reality these issues have been appearing each time as different: always in concrete ways and under a new light. If we compare the concept of autonomy as it appeared during previous centuries and in modern times then there are actually two concepts which differ substantially at least on one point. Universities of the 'old times' had to negotiate and articulate their relations with 'external' – either secular or church – authorities; at first sight similarly to today. Like today, they depended on them to grant them their particular power (autonomy) as well as for the more 'material' troubles of their survival. However, they were confronted by circumstances prior to the appearance of a modern nation state.

The birth of the industrial society in the 19th century marks a sharp turn in the development of higher education. The traditional mission expressed as the 'pursuit of truth' and 'disinterested research' was challenged in a radical way and for the first time it confronted the 'needs of the economy' very directly. Universities met a new, previously unknown agent; as a consequence, they also encountered competitors, other higher education institutions closely related to *professional training* aimed at the 'needs of the economy'. The challenge was even bigger: they faced a newborn *modern nation state* that understood the protection and acceleration of economic development in terms of the 'national market' as the most important issue on its political agenda. The dissemination of knowledge and skills and organisation of research as the means for strengthening 'productive powers' simply became an integral part of this agenda. "Until the nineteenth century one cannot observe any visible direct connection between the economic development of countries and their university systems" (in 't Veld, Füssel & Neave, 1996: 20-21); now, this question was raised loudly and it was necessary to respond to it – yet in circumstances that had radically changed.

---

20. In his speech on the occasion of the adoption of the *Magna Charta Universitatum*, the Rector of the University of Bologna, Fabio Roversi-Monaco, was even more direct about how "to take up the challenge of what is new". "The society into which this new University has to integrate itself is the advanced industrial society of our time [...]. It would be a serious mistake if the University, in this new society, decided to withdraw into itself, into its pride of academic corporation" (*Magna Charta Univsersitatum*, 1991: 13).

In practice, these circumstances differed from country to country; nevertheless they had a common denominator: the challenge to universities to become 'national' universities. This meant a huge challenge to their traditional, 'universal' role. There were no geographical, political and institutional delimitations for universities in the middle ages[21] but in the 20th century we experienced borders between various higher education systems. They grew up parallel to the industrialisation processes in modern nation states. Thus, as a sub-chapter to the protection of domestic markets protective measures in the field of higher education qualifications emerged and various national recognition procedures – predominantly for professional recognition – were also put in place. At the national level decisions were made to classify institutions, their qualifications, etc., on one hand and to establish selection procedures on the other. In these circumstances, it became necessary to not only regulate relationships between the state and an individual institution in a new way but to regulate the system, namely, to govern the national system of higher education.

From this angle, the 20th century was a period of growing regulation of national systems of education; the importance of systemic governance was continuously increasing. Specific features of particular countries and/or regions which developed originally as cultural traditions were gradually transformed into sophisticated legal systems and reinforced by political action. Europe developed strong public education systems but the management, control and financing of education institutions are simply not the only legislative issues. Knowledge and skills as defined in national frameworks of qualifications – usually based on a special legislative provision – had throughout the century their closest relation with the approval of curricula; exact procedures of selection and examination were developed (for example, the 'state examination') and the working conditions of teachers in public institutions were regulated by governments in detail. The practices of national regulations sometimes overlapped one another but were also separating. A serious problem was encountered when these 'extremely different' and in many respects 'incompatible' national systems started to emerge as a significant obstacle to the new political agenda encompassing mobility, employability, attractiveness and co-operation in society at large as well as in higher education.

Within the historical context we have just sketched we should also reconsider developments in higher education after new challenges appeared in the last quarter of the 20th century and which we briefly reflected on at the beginning of this paragraph. The importance of higher education for economic development has only increased to date; in fact, it has grown enormously and continues to rise. Under this 'new light' mass higher education and its rapid internationalisation require an even greater concern over governance. It seems that there are at least two new elements that can significantly influence further developments. As a result of processes in the last two decades, governments are increasingly occupied by systemic governance and institutions are recognised as being the most responsible

---

21. "Until the sixteenth century European universities were to a large extent all organized on the same line. They showed no national particularities or local focuses. [...] The picture changed with [...] the emergence of the European nation state" (Zonta, 2002: 25-37).

for their internal governance. On the other side, the globalisation of economies, the emerging knowledge society, integration processes and international co-oper-ation in the broadest sense also definitively bring a new challenge to higher edu-cation – the challenge of higher education governance in an international context. It is needless to argue here in detail that all three structural dimensions of gover-nance – institutional, systemic and international – construct a triangle: an inter-dependent totality.

Governance: between academic aspirations, market forces and demo-cratic culture

The concept of higher education governance is obviously multidimensional. However, only considering its structural dimensions or 'levels of governance' would leave further dimensions unexplored. Its multidimensional 'space' can be defined by another triangle delineated by academic aspirations, market forces and democratic culture. This scheme links three key factors together which influence higher education today but at a certain point it seems rigid and deficient. The rigidity can probably be softened if the three 'fixed' views – the academic view, the government's view (external itself) and the external view (non-governmental) – were to be established as opposed to a 'fluid' one, the students' view. In such a classification, the academic view exposes the institutional dimensions of gover-nance as collegiate governance (that is, epistemologically based self-governance), the government's view stresses the systemic dimensions of governance (legal framework, public financing), and the external view calls attention to the 'reality dimension' (efficiency in economic, cultural, etc., terms). The students' view is connected to all previous views and, thus, sets the concept in motion.

From certain points of view, the pressure of the economy towards the traditional role which universities have played in the societal environment may today seem inconvenient and even dangerous; however, even when criticisms of the commer-cialisation of higher education yield convincing arguments we cannot avoid the fact that neither institutions nor society at large can simply return to the middle ages. It is similar with governance at the system level: the legal regulations of national education systems may seem overstated – and they may indeed be over-regulated and may urgently need reforms leading towards deregulation – but their radical abolition would put both institutions and individuals into serious trouble as regards standards, financing, qualifications, transparency and compatibility, mobility and employability, etc. To summarise, from a 'pragmatic' point of view neither the influence of the economy nor the legislative burdens on higher educa-tion can be seen only as a *threat* to academic aspirations; they can also be seen as *supportive*, that is, as 'external' factors which make these aspirations feasible. It is very important to analyse this triangle precisely and thoroughly: as an interde-pendent totality which is a characteristic of modern times. The threat is not just an illusion – nor a support.

This is particularly important when considering the relationship between internal and external governance. If external factors were treated merely as threats, inter-nal aspirations should be closed within 'ivory towers'. The metaphor suggests a closed universe of scholars – probably not students – delineated from the 'external world' which hinders them in their pursuit of the truth and disinterested research. However, "the ivory tower is a myth, because in modern institutions of higher education[22] there has always existed tension between service to the public and more contemplative scholarship" (Rosovsky, 2003: 14). Why can these external factors not be treated as challenges, proactively, instead of threats from which academia has to withdraw behind their walls? In fact, who says that academia avoids contacts with the 'external world'? In modern academic practice disinterested research is being ever more 'challenged' by research that yields interest. The real question is not 'to close or not to close from the external world' nor 'to start or not to start commerce with the external world'. The real question is how to respond to the new challenges in a way we will not come to regret.

Probably the biggest challenge of the 'external world' to contemporary higher education institutions is commercialisation. Within our societal environments accustomed to well-developed public education systems, initiatives to reorient institutions towards alternative financial resources and entrepreneurship have not only met scepticism and restraint but also criticism and protest. Nevertheless, the proposed reorientation seems to be more and more firmly found on political agendas in all countries. Here, it can remain an open question of whether budget cuts pushed universities to search for alternative funds or universities' success in finding alternative funds influenced governmental budget cuts. In any case, since the 1980s it has become quite clear that the extraordinary expansion of the higher education sector for structural reasons cannot expect a proportional expansion in terms of national budgets – particularly if additional pressure from sectors like health care and social security as well as the fact of the ageing society is taken into account. These questions importantly influence governance issues and raise several new dilemmas. However, is commercialisation the only alternative? And what does it actually mean?

In this respect, Europe probably started to encounter similar questions which North America had experienced earlier; for that reason it is also useful to cite the American analyst, Derek Bok, formerly President of Harvard University:

> If there is an intellectual confusion in the academy that encourages commercialization, it is a confusion over means rather than ends. To keep profit-seeking within reasonable bounds, a university must have a clear sense of the values needed to pursue its goals with a high degree of quality and integrity. When the values become

---

22. Rosovsky argues that "the ivory tower does not describe the modern research university: learning and service are always present. External influences are becoming more powerful for many different reasons: the power of government, the search by commercial interests for knowledge within the university, and – not least – the opportunity for individual faculty members to make economic gains. […] Can universities preserve their objectivity as disinterested researchers and social critics if current trends persist?" (Rosovsky, 2003: 18). In contrast to the common comprehension that links the metaphor of the 'ivory tower' to centurial academic traditions, Rosovsky prescribes its first application to universities or scholars to H.G. Wells in *The New World Order* (1940).

> blurred and begin to lose their hold, the urge to make money quickly spreads throughout the institution. (Bok, 2003: 6)

It is obvious that we cannot only speak about 'external' threats to institutions but institutions themselves should also be scrutinised; it is important for them, for example, to avoid self-illusions. The almost proverbial truth says that academic institutions have not always been an example of a transparent and efficient organisation;[23] on the other hand, unfortunately, academic values could suffer from distortions within and not only from pressures stemming from outside institutions. Therefore, interference with the external world can be productive. "Left to itself, the contemporary research university does not contain sufficient incentives to elicit all of the behaviours that society has a right to expect" (Bok, 2003: 28).

As we mentioned above, *efficiency* is increasingly being demanded from higher education in contemporary systemic reforms. Institutional as well as systemic governance should be improved to bring better results: this claim seems to be undisputed. However, it would seem quite a joke if one were to propose the transplantation of an efficiency matrix from economic enterprises straight into academic institutions. The nature of teaching and research is 'strange' – as creative work they are characterised by 'soft' standards – and efficiency as expressed in exact, for example, quantitative, terms is not a helpful guide for them. 'Entrepreneurial' efficiency measures can help in administration and services but can easily damage the quality of education; the quality of education should be approached differently. The education process has certain features which distinguish it from ordinary profitable services competing in the marketplace: "a major reason why competition does not yield optimal results in higher education is that students cannot adequately evaluate the options available to them" (Bok, 2003: 179). Efficiency in research as valued in terms of commercially profitable results can only be trivial from a scientific point of view while, on the other hand, the fundamental inquiries in science – for example, the solar system, cell, the subconscious, etc., – have been always useless from a short-term enterprise's point of view.

For these and similar reasons the university cannot be governed as an enterprise. Service to the public and more contemplative scholarship have always co-existed at universities – together with the tensions between them – and the form of institutional governance has always had to bear their uneasy balance in mind. Ivory towers and knowledge enterprises can only be regarded as extremes. Today, searching for a balance requires a deliberate analysis of the costs and benefits of commercialisation; yet it puts modern universities into a Ulysses-like position

---

23. Bok argues that "universities have something to learn from the world of commercial enterprise. […] In the first place, university administrators do not have as strong an incentive as most business executives to lower costs and achieve greater efficiency. […] university officials will be less successful than business executives in operating efficiently. Presidents and deans lack the experience of most corporate managers in administering large organizations. […] A second important lesson universities can learn from business is the value of striving continuously to improve the quality of what they do. […] corporate executives have made major efforts to decentralize their organizations and give more discretion to semi-autonomous groups to experiment and to innovate" etc. (Bok, 2003: 24, 25)

between the prospects of bringing in substantial new revenues[24] and the risks to genuine academic values.[25] What should we do in this position? Bok calls for clear academic guidelines: "Setting clear guidelines is essential to protect academic values from excessive commercialization".[26] But guidelines alone will not be enough: "Unless the system of governance has safeguards and methods of accountability that encourage university officials to act appropriately, the lure of making money will gradually erode the institution's standards and draw it into more and more questionable practices." He is quite a pessimist: "Unfortunately, the structure of governance in most universities is not equal to the challenge of resisting the excesses of commercialization" (Bok, 2003: 185).

The university in the market place is a university under public scrutiny. Several authors, including Bok, have argued that universities are becoming more susceptible to public criticism because of their increased importance to the economy and society at large; similarly, the decline of confidence so far characteristic of governments and their agencies can now also be applied to academic institutions. Here comes an important warning signal:

> The university's reputation for scholarly integrity could well be the most costly casualty of all. A democratic society needs information about important questions that people can rely upon as reasonable, objective and impartial. Universities have long been one of the principal sources of expert knowledge and informed opinion on a wide array of subjects [...]. Once the public begins to lose confidence in the objectivity of professors, the consequences extend far beyond the academic community. [Namely, any damage to the reputation of universities] weakens not only the academy but the functioning of our democratic, self-governing society. (Bok, 2003: 117-118)

The problems which universities and higher education institutions generally encounter today would be trivial if academic institutions were not "at the heart of societies" (*Magna Charta Universitatum*, 1991: 59), that is, if they were not crowded with students and if they were not expected to contribute to dramatic environmental, energy, health, communication, etc., problems through their teaching and research. However, if this were the case they would not be 'modern' academic institutions. Modern institutions have to compete with problems that are not trivial at all.

The increasing external demands on modern universities require internal adjustments: universities must reorganise themselves, find new modes of operating and answer the challenges of how to carry out their new roles, yet without sacrificing

---

24. Bok admonishes that revenues are not as high as usually expected: "Despite their attractive features, commercial profits do not always live up to expectations. [...] Of an estimated 200 or more patent licensing offices on American campuses, only a small fraction received more than $10 million in 2000 and a large majority failed to earn any appreciable profit" (Bok, 2005: 100-101).
25. "Another educational cost that commercialization can incur has to do with the moral example such behavior gives to students and others in the academic community. Helping to develop virtue and build character have been central aims of education since the time of Plato and Aristotle. After years of neglect, universities everywhere have rediscovered the need to prepare their students to grapple with the moral dilemmas they will face in their personal and professional lives" (Bok, 2005: 109).
26. Similar statements can be found in other places: "What universities should do instead is to look at the process of commercialization whole, with all its benefits and risks, and then try to develop clear rules that are widely understood and conscientiously enforced" (Bok, 2003: 121). "When rules are unclear and always subject to negotiations, money will prevail over principle much of the time" (Bok, 2003: 156).

their basic values. Basic academic values – for example, "research and teaching [as] morally and intellectually independent of all political authority […] and economic power", "scholarly integrity", etc., – are not academic caprices at all. They are of vital importance for society at large: "strong universities" (EUA, 2005b) are today a well-recognised and important lever of democratic society and economic development. They must set clear academic guidelines, including in terms of governance. However, the increasing external demands require some 'external' adjustments as well: the governance of a higher education system should support universities in being successful in their endeavours. For (not only) this reason the public responsibility for higher education has been stressed several times in recent discussions and documents. Legislation should contain clear provisions not only about the relationship between higher education institutions and the (nation) state; the relationships between academic aspirations and market forces should also be specified in a similar way.[27]

In the last instance, the increasing external demands on modern universities have started to require *international* and *global* adjustments. These demands are largely accelerated by the globalisation of markets and growing internationalisation of higher education. This dimension is no less important when the interplay between academic aspirations and market forces and democratic culture is considered; yet it differs from the previous two. Responsibility for higher education remains with nation states but there are many problems which exceed the level of national higher education systems. When problems like the recognition of degrees and periods of study – particularly with regard to transnational higher education – come under discussion then the responsibility for higher education becomes international.

There is no supranational political authority in higher education today but there is growing co-operation as proved in Europe's Bologna Process. It is not only a forum in which authorities responsible for the governance of national systems can come together; it also challenges higher education institutions and their governance. As Rector Fabio Roversi-Monaco once said in Bologna: "In the name of the unity of culture the needs for supranationality of Universities could once more confront the difficulties ensuing from the birth of national States and nationalisms" (*Magna Charta Universitatum*, 1991: 11).

A conclusion: a concept open to further reconsideration

Here, at the conclusion we can return to the beginning of this paper and say that questions of what is supposed to be 'effective', 'fair', 'good', etc., governance also "have no fixity" and "they do not fall under any art or precept" but as sailors at sea we ourselves "must in each case consider what is appropriate to the occasion".

---

27. Bok argues that "the state must intervene to protect legitimate interests apart from the universities themselves" and stresses that "reasonable financial stability is the ultimate guarantee against irresponsible entrepreneurial behaviour". Within this context, in Europe we stress the responsibility *for* higher education; however, not forgetting the responsibility *of* higher education: "Unless universities create an environment in which the prevailing incentives and procedures reinforce intellectual standards instead of weakening them, commercial temptations are bound to take a continuing toll on essential academic values" (Bok, 2005: 196-198).

The analysis of 'the occasion' is therefore crucial. It can – and should – take place in institutional, national and international environments.

There is a certain difficulty in undertaking this analysis. At the institutional level broader dimensions are often invisible while at the international level the 'uniqueness and singularity of the occasion' could be ignored. There are several types of higher education institutions and several clusters of higher education systems; all of them are legitimate in so far as they all rest on pronounced philosophies and cultures. It is similar with governance: it is absolutely not a 'neutral technical matter' but is founded on types of institutions and/or systems, that is, on conceptual and cultural backgrounds. This is another argument why there is no 'best precept' for governance. Yet, there are basic principles and there can be no effective, fair, good or democratic governance without them: shared responsibilities and levels of governance, participation and partnership, etc., aiming at strengthening the basic roles of higher education.[28]

Therefore, the concept of higher education governance is not 'uniform', 'finished', 'unproblematic' nor 'indisputable'. Far from that! As we have seen, it is connected with several open questions, problems and dilemmas. It is welcomed and will surely bring about positive results in that this concept has finally found appropriate attention to be considered from various angles within a broad discussion. Asking these questions and disputing existing dilemmas enables us to identify potential collisions that could affect higher education, and to leave the concept open for further reconsideration by never treating it as a final one.

---

28. "Having considered the philosophical substance of [...] university styles that have had an influence in different parts of the world, we can say that the university differs in the priority that each places on scientific research, on the development of the human being, or on the various forms of service to society. It is a question of preference and practical emphasis, not exclusion so that a balance among all three objectives can be reached" (Borerro Cabal, 1993: 30-31).

Bibliography

Aristotle, *The Nicomachean Ethics*, translation by W. D. Ross, Clarendon Press, Oxford, 1908.

Bergan, S. (ed.), *The university as* res publica, *Higher education governance, student participation and the university as a site of citizenship*, Council of Europe Publishing, Strasbourg, 2004.

Bok, D., *Universities in the marketplace, The commercialization of higher education*, Princeton University Press, Princeton, 2003.

Borrero Cabal, A., *The university as an institution today – Topics for reflection*, UNESCO Publishing, Paris, 1993.

EUA (2003a), *Graz Declaration*, EUA, Brussels.

EUA (2003b), *Graz Reader*, EUA Convention of European Higher Education Institutions, Graz, 29-31 May 2003.

EUA (2005a), *Glasgow Declaration*, EUA, Brussels.

EUA (2005b), *Glasgow Reader*, EUA Convention of European Higher Education Institutions, Glasgow, 31 March – 2 April 2005.

The European Higher Education Area. Joint Declaration of the European Ministers of Education [Bologna Declaration]. Convened in Bologna on 19 June 1999 (4 p.).

The European Higher Education Area – achieving the goals. Communiqué of the Conference of European Ministers Responsible for Higher Education [Bergen Communiqué]. Bergen, 19-20 May 2005 (6 p.).

Eurydice, *Two decades of reform in higher education in Europe: 1980 onwards*, Eurydice, Brussels, 2000.

Haug, G., Kirstein, J., & Knudsen, I., *Trends in learning structures in higher education [Trends 1]*, *Project report for the Bologna Conference on 18-19 June 1999*, The Danish Rectors Conference, Copenhagen, 1999.

Haug, G. & Tauch, C., *Trends in learning structures in higher education [Trends 2]*, Follow-up report prepared for the Salamanca and Prague Conferences of March/May 2001, Finnish National Board of Education; European Commission; Association of European Universities (CRE), ETF, 2001.

in 't Veld, R., Füssel, H.-P. & Neave, G. (eds.), *Relations between state and higher education*, Kluwer Law International, The Hague/London/Boston, 1996.

Magna Charta Universitatum, Bologna, 18 September 1988, Segretariato Europeo per le Pubblicazioni Scientifiche, Rome, 1991.

Message from the Salamanca Convention on European Higher Education Institutions. Shaping the European Higher Education Area. Salamanca, 29-30 March 2001, (5 p.).

Neave, G., & van Vught, F. (eds.) *Prometheus bound. The changing relationship between government and higher education in western Europe*, Pergamon Press, Oxford, 1991.

Realising the European Higher Education Area. Communiqué of the Conference of Ministers Responsible for Higher Education [Berlin Communiqué]. Berlin, 19 September 2003 (8 p.).

Reichert, S. & Tauch, C., *Trends in learning structures in European higher education [Trends 3]*, *Bologna four years after: Steps towards sustainable reform of higher education in Europe*, EUA Graz Convention, 29-31 May 2003.

Reichert, S. & Tauch, C., *Trends 4: European universities implementing Bologna*, EUA, Brussels, 2005.

Rosovsky, H. "No ivory tower: University and society in the twenty-first century" in Werner Z.H. & Weber, L.E. (eds.), *As the walls of academia are tumbling down*, Economica, London, 2002: 13-30.

Rüegg, W. (ed.), *A history of the university in Europe*, Vols. 1, 2, Cambridge University Press, Cambridge, 1992.

Towards the European Higher Education Area. Communiqué of the meeting of European Ministers in Charge of Higher Education [Prague Communiqué], Prague, 19 May 2001 (4 p.).

Zonta, A.C., "The history of European universities: Overview and background" in Nuria, S. & Bergan, S. (eds.), *The heritage of European universities*, Council of Europe Publishing, Strasbourg, 2002: 25-37.

The objectives of and expectations towards higher education in the changed societal context – An overview

Virgílio Meira Soares

1. Introduction

I was asked to present an overview of the present situation and of the possible effects of the societal changes on the governance of higher education. The topic is too wide to be addressed in such a short time and, indeed, the personal position of the speaker should not be discarded even if s/he tries to maintain a neutral position. As a matter of fact different researchers in this field draw different conclusions, although some efforts to find common patterns can be found (see, for example, Amaral, Fulton & Larsen).[29] Therefore the views I am going to present will be personal, based on my readings and contacts (this is not a research paper) and will be, probably, a source for discussion.

2. Evolution during the last decades

It is widely accepted that the challenges universities are facing nowadays have their main roots in the developments of the last three to four decades. The so-called state control model gave place to the state supervisory model in the 1970s/80s.[30] This was mainly due to the 'massification' of higher education (HE) that led to increased difficulties in financing the HE systems. Governments were faced with competition for more funding from the different sectors of society (health, social security, etc.). This suggests that governments, pressed with the need to cut funding of HE institutions, had to introduce measures that, on the one hand, would safeguard them from accusations of decreasing the qua-lity of teaching and research in HE and, on the other hand, would also put the ne-cessary pressure on the institutions to demonstrate that they were doing their best to maintain quality while they were given more autonomy and, hence, more responsibility – accountability was one of the new words introduced in the vocabulary and was (reluctantly?) accepted by the universities, being also a means the governments used to steer the institutions.

These conditions paved the way for the introduction of forms of evaluation (quality assurance and quality evaluation are now widespread) that were viewed by the universities as a means to continuously improve their performance and by the governments as a means to introduce accountability, to steer the system and to justify the decreasing financing of the HE systems. Not surprisingly, the results of these "exercises" led to some obvious conclusions. Universities were not models of efficiency and the funding cuts would affect the quality of their performance.

29. Amaral, A., Fulton, O. & Larsen, I.M., "A managerial revolution?" in Amaral, A., Meek, V.L. & Larsen, I.M., *The higher education managerial revolution?*, Kluwer Academic Publishers, Dordrecht, 2003.
30. Neave, G. & van Vught, F. (eds.), *Government and higher education relationships across three continents: The winds of change*, Pergamon Press, London, 1994.

Therefore it was also not surprising that some (many?) governments started to encourage universities to diversify their funding base and launched campaigns to discredit their decision-making processes, calling for changes that would make them more efficient and responsive to the "needs of the society", by doing more with less, by changing their own internal structure and balance of power, in short, by changing their governance to meet those demands. And it seems that society at large has been supportive of these attitudes.

In addition, the rise of the private sector changed the paradigm in which the State, as the main employer until then, was responsible for the definition of what should be "useful knowledge".[31] The emerging ideas were that the private sector should from then on play a key role in the definition of what should be considered as "useful knowledge".

At this point one can easily accept that the states, incapable of "controlling" the institutions, but feeling also the impossibility of increasing funding, and knowing that HE institutions could not maintain the same quality without finding other sources, began to shed some of their responsibilities while, at the same time, creating conditions for the private sector to intervene in the *Academies.*

The first steps taken by public authorities in many European countries were well received by the institutions: accepting members of the private sector as advisers to their democratic decision-making bodies was indeed a way to meet one of their missions (to offer their potential for knowledge production to society) while, at the same time, the prospect of increasing their income was also a good perspective.

Despite these changes HE institutions were still considered a "model" of ineffi-ciency mainly attributed, among other factors, to their collegial decision-making organisation, to their "organised anarchy", to their difficulty in reaching conclu-sions quickly and to the idea that they were acting as organisations whose main interest was to defend the privileges of academics. As a result, according to the governments, their power structure and their decision-making bodies should change to meet the demands of society, as if their main mission was to "contribute to the development of the economy of the[ir] country[ies]". This would be the beginning of a new era and also of new fights, discussions, resistances, reorgan-isations, in short, of new forms to look at the governance of higher education.

Words like stakeholders, managerialism, entrepreneurialism, market, for-profit activities, competition, just to mention some of them, started to be part of the offi-cial discourse. The so-called New Public Management (NPM) started to emerge and to be applied to the public sector. Universities, like many other public services, were progressively pressed to act like private enterprises, public authorities trans-ferred part of their steering functions to "external stakeholders" or the "market", although not leaving their main control functions, whereas "internal stakeholders" (teachers, non-academic staff and students) were more and more regarded as con-sultative actors, while students were being regarded as "consumers" or "clients".

---

31. Neave, G., "The European dimension in higher education; an historical analysis" presented at the con-ference "The relationship between higher education and the nation state", Enschede, Netherlands, 1997.

As a result, in many European countries, the central administration of the institutions was strengthened,[32] in some cases "external stakeholders" were appointed to the directive boards as "representatives" of different sectors of the society and of the market, forcing the marketisation of universities (or shall we call it "privatisation"?) so that they could "contribute to the development of the economy of the country" and to obtain funding from market-oriented activities, instead of protecting them from that same market (one must not forget that until the 1980s the state used to protect them from external interferences! – the mythical Humboldtian model), the internal stakeholders were kept away from the decisions or saw their influence decreasing. This is not the practice in the US, where trustees are external people, "typically well-regarded business people or other professionals in the community", not representing any specific sector of the society, who "offer their services and advice in support of the institution's goals and may also be critical of the institution's activities and in many instances [they] make financial contributions to the institution",[33] acting as "board members in their capacity of individuals, not as official representatives of a specific 'stakeholder' group or organisation".[34]

Changes have taken place either by internal decisions of the institutions or due to external impositions. In any case external pressures seemed to have had an impact on the governance of the institutions. As we have already mentioned, universities, under pressure from the governments to become more managerial and more entrepreneurial, started to look for new management tools. According to Teichler:[35]

> On the one hand, there is [was] a wide criticism that the traditional managerial modes of a relatively weak rector, a limited number of administrative staff, and a strong academic staff in decision-making at universities is [was] no longer appropriate in times of increased importance of institutional policies. On the other hand, the US model of institutional management is [was] frequently criticised for subordinating academics and their rationale to a managerial class ...

Some results of these new changes are reported by Clark[36] in his work about the creation of entrepreneurial universities. It is interesting to note that in all the examples he describes, the changes took place internally and not as a result of external imposition. These findings, somehow, seem to be in contradiction to the tendency of the governments to impose new forms of institutional governance. Nevertheless it is happening, or it has already happened, in some countries, with results that are still to be seen.

---

32. It must be noticed that, even before the development of these new trends, some HE institutions might have decided to strengthen the central administration as a means to survive. The research by Clark (1998)[36] on entrepreneurial universities may lead us to that conclusion.

33. El-Khawas, E, "Governance in US Institutions", in *Governing higher education: National perspectives on institutional governance*, Kluwer Academic Publishers, Amsterdam, 2002: 263.

34. Fisher, 1991, cited in reference 32.

35. Teichler, U., "The challenge of lifelong learning for the university", *AUE: Informationsdienst, Hochschule, und Weiterbildung*, 2, 1990: 12.

36. Clark, B.R., *Creating entrepreneurial universities: Organisational pathways of transformation*, Pergamon Press, Oxford, 1998.

It is still early to draw conclusions from these latter changes and how universities are adapting or reacting (when and if they are!) to the new situation. There are reports suggesting that "internal stakeholders" are not very willing to co-operate with these new developments but, at the same time, others suggest that the strengthening of the central administration is providing good results in the performance of the institutions. In many cases there are reports of tensions between the central management and the faculties or the departments. New "alliances" are to be expected and this will also have an impact on governance. It is still too early to see how the paradigm of the "entrepreneurial university" as defined by Clark, together with the changes in governance, can be sustainable, especially concerning the "stimulation of the academic heartland" and the "integrated entrepreneurial culture", if the imposed government tools receive a lot of opposition from the *Academia*.

Maassen,[37] based on works of several authors, suggests that one can consider five strategies to deal with outside pressure: acquiescence, compromise, avoidance, defiance and manipulation. Every institution in each country will undoubtedly develop its own strategy. From our own personal experience we know examples of applying several of those strategies. However, all of them will have an impact on governance. And, notwithstanding the different reactions, one important aspect we should look at is how institutions have adapted (or are adapting) to the new circumstances and how successful they have been (or are being). Additionally, it is also important to address the (few?) cases where resistance is still prevailing and how, despite this resistance, some institutions are responding successfully to the societal changes. As regards this latter case, we have all heard of cases where the external actors simply do not have the time to spare for the activities they should perform, while "internal stakeholders" are resisting changes in every possible way in spite of their usual lack of participation (a very telling case is the University of Cambridge and the attitudes of its Regent House). However, these institutions not only do survive but are also very active in the new environment!

The resistance of academics to changes in organisation of higher education institutions should not be ignored or minimised. De Boer mentions that reforms intending to decrease the power of academics need to be based on trust and states that "if we want to have a better understanding of 'good governance', the concept of trust deserves more attention"[38] but also warns that externally enforced reforms "tend to increase resistance to change even further, especially when they go against the wishes of those undergoing the reform".[39] The introduction of NPM as an ideology to be followed by all HE institutions is inducing resistance among many academics and may prove not to be the right option. Moreover there are also good examples of institutions that deal with the challenges of the market and with low state funding successfully without accepting NPM, although some internal

---

37. Maassen, P., "Organisational strategies and governance structures" in *Governing higher education: National perspectives on institutional governance*, Kluwer Academic Publishers, Amsterdam, 2002: 26.
38. De Boer, H., "Trust, the essence of governance?" in *Governing higher education: National perspectives on institutional governance*, Kluwer Academic Publishers, Amsterdam, 2002: 43.
39. De Boer, H., "Who's afraid of red, yellow and blue?" in *The higher education managerial revolution?*, Kluwer Academic Publishers, Amsterdam, 2003: 89.

changes in the balance of power had to be introduced. Maassen[40] writes that "it is not assumed that all new governance models with respect to higher education are market models, nor that all management developments in higher education institutions concern variations on NPM or 'new managerialism' ".

More research in this field is necessary.

3. New challenges

The situation, as it is now, poses some questions resulting from the new attitudes of society and of public authorities towards universities.

The increasing importance of the market will have an impact on the traditional missions and values of higher education: creating knowledge (research) and transmitting it (teaching), being places of free debate and critical thinking, independence from outside interests, educating students to respect ideas and their free expression (Amaral and Magalhães).[41]

We need to ask ourselves what the place of those values will be in this new situation and how the internal organisation and the regulation of academic work will be affected.

3.1. Democratic citizenship

Universities have been, for centuries, places where staff and students not only interact in the processes of teaching and through research, but also where the free exchange of ideas is praised and put into practice. Moreover the traditional forms of decision making include the participation of the different members of the institutions in this process.

The fundamental challenges consist of balancing and promoting the different strands of the mission of higher education. In the executive summary of the final report of the project "Universities as sites of citizenship and civic responsibility"[42] launched by the Council of Europe, this is described in the following terms (p. 4):

> The challenge of advancing universities as sites of citizenship comes from the tension between the fundamental mission of developing expertise and human capital while attempting to devote time and resources to the development of attitudes, dispositions, and functionality of democratic citizenship. These educational aims are often treated as something mutually exclusive or conceived in zero-sum terms in decisions pertaining to the allocation of resources and in the reward structures of universities. Small wonder that students leave universities conditioned to treat their personal welfare, career endeavours and financial success as something apart from their perception of their place in society as a citizen. We can push universities to create new courses or to

40. Maassen, P., "Shifts in governance arrangements: An interpretation of the introduction of new management structures in higher education" in *The higher education managerial revolution?*, Kluwer Academic Publishers, Dordrecht, 2003: 31.
41. Amaral, A. & Magalhães, A., "The emergent role of external stakeholders in European higher education governance", in *Governing higher education: National perspectives on institutional governance*, Kluwer Academic Publishers, Amsterdam, 2002.
42. "Universities as sites of citizenship and civic responsibility – executive summary of the final report", CD-ESR, Council of Europe, Strasbourg, 2002: 7-9.

formalize democratic education, but such changes will remain nominal and in fact increase political cynicism and apathy if there are no changes in institutional and educational processes as well. A university that is a site of citizenship will be a place where all individuals that interact in the context of its environment will have their interactions structured by processes that are characterized by the democratic attributes of openness, accountability, transparency, communication and feedback, critique and debate, dispute resolution, and the absence of idiosyncrasy, arbitrariness, and privilege.

Later, in that same executive summary,[42] a number of conclusions are presented which express in some detail the conflicting elements present in the different views of higher education as well as in the day-to-day life of higher education institutions:

- civic engagement versus "useful" education;

- formal provisions versus actual practice;

- structures and arrangements versus generating motivation and facilitating participation;

- resistance to change and lack of resources.

Higher education governance needs to take all these into account, providing a structural framework for democratic processes to take place. However, the same document (p. 10) also reflects on the salience of the issue, on the perceived priorities of students leading to passivity or disinterest despite formal provisions for democratic participation.

We can see, there is a lot of work to be done in the institutions to strengthen their role of disseminating the values of democracy and democratic participation, be it connected to students' and teachers' behaviours or to their internal governance. Under the present conditions does it make sense to insist that universities continue to be sites where education for democratic citizenship is part of their mission? Is that compatible with a market-driven organisation? Should they give up these functions? Or will the new paradigm, despite its main basic, market-oriented assumptions, take democracy and democratic participation on board?

It is legitimate to have some doubts.

3.2. Research and academic freedom – the issue of intellectual property

Independent and free research has always been one of the main assets of the academic staff. Their work has been for a long time considered as disinterested, their mission being to produce knowledge to be used by society. The subordination of university research to the impositions of the market poses some questions deserving our special attention. I heard Giovanni Agnelli in 1988 during the celebrations of the 900th anniversary of the University of Bologna (two or three days before we signed the *Magna Charta Universitatum*). Although we must not forget that he was an invited speaker, who could be trying to be polite to his host, he was clear when he declared at a certain point:[43]

---

43. Agnelli, G., "Industry's expectations of the university", *CRE-Action* 3, 1988.

> ... from their very beginning universities were free institutions, even in societies ruled by despots; they were disinterested, for their task was not imposed on them from outside, but chosen by themselves, and that task was the pursuit of knowledge. And from the first they were international in spirit. Even in the most intolerant and difficult [of] times they held that knowledge should be free and universal.

At the time there had already been decisions in some countries that were not in conformity with these words. For instance, the government of Mrs Thatcher was already trying to change this tradition. Robert Cowen[44] has described the situation, taking account of the main "accusations" towards higher education: universities ought to contribute to the economy, students were merely looking for jobs at the end of their studies and the disciplinary basis of universities were increasingly irrelevant – by saying that:

> ... Government has taken direct policy action to alter the basis of university funding, in order to make universities more entrepreneurial. ... the social pressure that is currently developing is not merely that the university should try to link itself more tightly with industry and business. The central core of the present process is that the university itself should become a business, and it is in this sense that we now think of the English university as 'entrepreneurial'.

In spite of such reactions, the "example" of the UK was followed by several other countries.

The impositions of the market, with the approval of some governments, may change the attitude of academic staff not willing to give up their "academic freedom" or even to accept that their research should mainly be driven by market "needs". Above all, freedom of research has always been a source of progress for society. The newly imposed conditions are introducing constraints as to "what you should work for" and restricting one of the basic principles of university research: freedom of publication of the research results. As a matter of fact when research is controlled by industry some of the results may be, necessarily, withheld from public knowledge under certain circumstances. But how far can those restrictions go? Should academics abdicate their right to publish their research work? This may be a case of violation of the beliefs and rights of academics under any new terms of any new governance. It is a question of intellectual property and ownership. Who owns the rights of research results: the research group, the university or the contracting companies?

This raises another set of questions: how can "universities provide a research base vital for the solution of problems of public concern, even where markets for the solutions do not [yet] exist" and how can "Governments offer incentives to conduct free and fundamental research", as recommended by the Committee of Ministers of the Council of Europe recommendation (R (2000) 8)? Certainly the internal mechanisms of higher education institutions will have to deal with these contradictions. How? Will the "academic heartland" be willing to give up their traditional academic freedom to subordinate their actions to the "dictatorship" of the

---

44. Cowen, R., "The management and evaluation of the entrepreneurial university: the case of England", *Higher Education Policy* 4, 1995: 3.

"market regulation"? Are Reed et al.[45] right when they say that "universities may be regarded as the prototypical 'knowledge intensive organisations' and university academics may be likewise be treated as the prototypical 'knowledge workers'"?

3.3. Autonomy and the concept of higher education as a "public good"

The paradigms being imposed on universities may raise another question of utmost importance to the present discussion. Some governments have a strong belief in the virtues of the market. This "belief" may lead institutions to search for external funding mainly based on contracts with the private sector, leaving aside the main traditional missions of the universities. The "final product" may be rich institutions, with an important role in the so-called "development of the economy of the country", but without any clear mission regarding their role as "public good" or the production of "a good of public interest".[46] It is not at all obvious that a "market-driven" approach can fulfil a public service, since the private sector has, with legitimacy, the right to work for profit. If that same private sector has a decisive weight on the mission of universities, by having a decisive role in the important decisions, it is also legitimate to have doubts about the public usefulness of such higher education.

At this point it is worth mentioning an excellent paper by William Massy[47] in which, at a certain point, he states that:

> Internal subsidisation is what distinguishes non-profit from for-profit enterprises. Non-profits recycle surpluses to boost mission attainment, whereas for-profits distribute the money to shareholders. Most universities rely on positive margins from popular programmes to boost discretionary spending capacity, which in turn allows them to express their values through internal subsidies.

and later stresses that:

> Universities buck the market by injecting their own values into decision making. This means support of things the market does not care about, which requires discretionary spending. Institutions without spending discretion cannot assert their values. They must respond to supply and demand and only supply and demand. For example, the aforementioned literature programme[48] might well be downsized if the university suffered a major financial setback. For-profit universities do not emphasise literature programmes because of the subject's weak demand, just as they do not support much faculty scholarships.

The author also quotes his colleague Bob Zemsky: "Universities should be mission centered as well as market smart." How are these statements compatible with the present tendencies of relying entirely on the market? Although the author suggests some solutions like "performance-based steering", the answer should come

---

45. Reed, M.I., Meek, V.L. and Jones, G.A., "Introduction", in *Governing higher education: National perspectives on institutional governance*, Kluwer Academic Publishers, Amsterdam, 2002.
46. In our view even for-profit HE institutions should only be allowed to function if they pursue the goal of providing a "good of public interest".
47. Massy, W.F., "Markets in higher education: do they promote internal efficiency?" in *Markets in higher education*, Kluwer Academic Publishers, Amsterdam, 2004.
48. This is an example given earlier in the paper by the author referring to a specific programme "that a school would like to expand but cannot because of weak demand".

from public authorities in charge of higher education, taking into account the public interest of non-profit higher education institutions.

Being driven by the need to look for huge external funds, some of which are to be used only for specific objectives, how can universities be fully autonomous and free from external interference? Under these circumstances, is higher education still a public good (as the European ministers in charge of education stated in Prague)[49] to be protected and where society should invest for its own benefit, or is it a private good with all the consequences especially with regard to its social function?

Whatever the answers to the previous questions, there remains one more to be answered. Civil society, represented by the governments or by any other form of organisation (for example, NGOs), is also a stakeholder to be taken into account be it through contracts or funding arrangements. How does that civil society look at universities and their roles? Do they consider them as simple places of "knowledge production" or do they think of universities as places to turn to for their activities which can be of use to that same society? These attitudes may not be easy to distinguish, but they may make an important difference.

3.4. Transnational education and GATS

The "explosion" of new providers of higher education some years ago has created a new business branch. New ways to sell higher education degrees through what is now called "transnational education" have emerged and are in competition with traditional higher education institutions. This trade develops, in many cases, without the intervention of public authorities (neither in the countries of origin nor in the receiving countries) and, therefore, without any submission to the usual quality assurance procedures. Marchese,[50] following a study about American higher education, characterises the main trends as follows:

- many of the existing universities and colleges are developing remote-site strategies, provoking an explosion of branch campuses;

- a growing percentage of institutions are offering distance education courses;

- big conglomerates of universities are creating powerful virtual universities to act as brokers for their distance learning courses;

- for-profit networks, including universities, are attracting big investments from Wall Street for the provision of post-secondary education and training in a market considered to be "huge and ripe for the picking";

- for-profit universities, well capitalised and national/international in ambition, are rapidly expanding;

- a host of new providers "hope to be the brokers of choice for the flood of courseware hitting the Web";

---

49. "Towards the European Higher Education Area", Communiqué of the Meeting of European Ministers in Charge of Higher Education, Prague, 2001.
50. Marchese, T., "Not-so-distant competitors: How new providers are remaking the postsecondary marketplace", *American Association for Higher Education Bulletin*, May 1998.

• industry groups combine to produce their own education enterprises, with the aim to lessen their dependence on existing campuses due to dissatisfaction with traditional higher education.

All these trends of transnational higher education, and combinations thereof, can be found in many countries – in Europe and beyond. Santos[51] gives an overview of the situation in Europe, pointing to the very high number of students involved and of programmes delivered. It doesn't come as a surprise to learn that the number of non-recognised institutions offering programmes at transnational level is too high to be ignored.

One of the reasons for the existence of these new providers is the imbalance between supply and demand. Transnational higher education as such would not be a matter of concern if some important issues such as quality assurance and consumer protection were not at stake. We are facing a big problem if nothing is done to force these providers to submit to the quality assurance procedures of their own country or of the receiving country. The Lisbon Recognition Convention Committee, aware of this situation, issued a recommendation[52] on the rules to be applied to transnational higher education. If this recommendation were to be followed by all the countries we would have much less reason to be concerned.

The search for private funding is leading some universities to look for students elsewhere either by "importing them" or by creating branches abroad (the extreme case being, very likely, Australia) or even by launching distance learning programmes. Acting like private providers in other countries, these universities may be jeopardising their prestige by competing with non-scrupulous providers that do not care about any social function, do not see higher education as a "public good" or not even as a "good of public interest", and only care about profit regardless of the quality and validity of their services. Transnational education, especially in the context of GATS, following the trends imposed by the existing notion of globalisation, sees higher education as a "private good". How can these contradictions be addressed? There will indeed be necessary internal consequences and implications for the governance of higher education institutions. And we can already see some of those in some universities.

3.5. The Lisbon strategy

A lot has been said and written about the Lisbon strategy and this is not the place to discuss what has happened since 2000. Nevertheless one cannot ignore the effects of the Lisbon agenda and its consequences on the behaviour of the universities and it is particularly important to reflect on how this affects higher education governance.

---

51. Santos, S.M., "Introduction to the Theme of Transnational Education", communication to the meeting of Directors General and Presidents of the EU Rectors Conferences, Aveiro, Portugal, April 2000; Santos, S.M., "Regulation and Quality Assurance in Transnational Education", *Tertiary Education and Management*, 8, Kluwer Academic Publishers, Amsterdam, 2002: 97-112.
52. "Code of Good Practice in the Provision of Transnational Education", adopted by the Lisbon Recognition Convention Committee, Riga, 6 June 2001.

The European Council in Lisbon (2000) decided to set the aim of Europe becoming "the most dynamic knowledge-based economy in the world, capable of sustainable economic growth with more and better jobs and greater social cohesion". To reach these objectives universities are clearly needed. A number of issues, identified by the European Commission, such as continued democratisation of access to higher education, new access conditions, in particular the recognition of past professional experience, setting up of lifelong learning schemes, increase of funding diversification, co-operation with industry, EU research funding mainly directed to networks of excellence, increasing interdisciplinarity, intellectual property rights and many others are on the table of the decision makers of the EU as part of their duties to accomplish the aims of the agreed strategy.[53] Some of these issues will force *Academies* to think about their own organisation and decision-making processes. And, indeed, they will have to think how to restructure their own governance. But I underline again that they should not be forced to do so: they will meet the external demands in their own way. Europe is not going very fast. The recent "no" votes to the so-called European Constitution (and one's position is irrelevant to the debate here) show that universities cannot be blamed for the failures and delays of the EU and, therefore, should have the necessary time to adapt, although, we must recognise, that they could move faster.

It must be said that very recently the European Commission issued a paper[54] where it says that more funding is necessary, so that universities can fulfil their "mission" as defined by the European Council; it does this very "carefully" however, in that it states that this funding should be private!

The tasks universities have to perform under the Lisbon strategy are not new but it is important to take these concerns into account: the need to define long-term strategies seems to be a particularly important and useful one. New governance arrangements are expected to be one of the results, and, as already mentioned, such changes shall be at the initiative of the universities. However, what is disturbing is that the paper indicates how these changes should happen. Despite a very carefully chosen discourse, there may be no doubt that one particular approach is favoured: the participation of external stakeholders in the decision-making bodies of the institutions. As I mentioned before, this may not be a wise decision, although it should not be discarded either, but care must be exercised.[40] The necessary development of European higher education will certainly lead to changes in governance but, as the paper recognises, the differences between countries do not allow for advising institutions to follow a particular pattern.

The Bologna Process will have a more important role with regard to governance issues than universities expect. However, despite the efforts of the Commission to "harmonise" (introduce uniform methods of governance?), diversity will prevail and that is one of the strong points of European higher education. When trying to

---

53. "The role of the universities in the Europe of knowledge", *Communication from the Commission*, COM(2003)59 final, Brussels, 2003.
54. "Mobilising the brainpower of Europe: enabling universities to make their full contribution to the Lisbon strategy", *Communication from the Commission*, COM (2005) 152 final, Brussels, 2005.

"copy" the US system, the Commission should take into account the diversification of that same system.

The remaining question is: how will higher education institutions cope with the necessary transformations to meet the aims of the Lisbon strategy and of the Bologna Process? Something will have to change with regard to governance beyond the point of no return. Old methods of participation will have to change, somehow. How? Do we need a uniform pattern of what could be called "good governance" bearing in mind the different points of departure? We might, just for the sake of fairness, compare, for example, the UK system with the French system. Is one of them better than the other for the purposes of the Lisbon strategy? If the answer is "yes", which is the better and "why"? In spite of our personal conclusions we must not forget that, at least in this particular matter, the Commission does not take a side, although one can have a suspicion about its preferences.

Moreover, it would be important to discuss how far the Lisbon strategy has influenced, or is influencing, the Bologna Process. Is the latter autonomous and is it being considered as an independent process by the decision makers at the Commission level? Either way, the answer is of great importance and consequences. The Bologna Process and the Lisbon strategy, although necessarily linked, are supposed to be autonomous but to complement each other at a later stage. Is this still the case? Sometimes one has the feeling that the former is being subordinated to the latter. I wonder if we are faced with a de facto strategy to mix the two processes and "force" the Bologna Process to become a by-product of the Lisbon strategy, with some important negative consequences in terms of governance and other issues.

Such considerations deserve a thorough discussion from our side, from academics and non-academics.

4. No conclusion!

The questions raised above are only part of the changes in different paradigms that will have an effect on governance and on what one can expect from the higher education institutions in future, either as a reaction or as an adaptation to those changes. Will their mission and values change, or can they "circumvent the obstacles"? There is no doubt that the university, seen as an ivory tower, will have to change and that may not necessarily be a disaster. Perhaps it is a good development. But, as Amaral and Magalhães[41] justly write, this "ivory tower" model is now challenged by "the new 'Babel tower' model, in which national interest is supposed to be protected and enhanced by representatives of the outside world acting within the academic institutions themselves" and that may be, and already is, a matter of concern. As we have just seen there are challenges and threats. Will universities, as we understand them, survive? How, and at what cost?

European university governance in urgent need of change

Luc Weber

1. Preliminary remarks

In this contribution based on the opening address at the conference as vice-chair of the Steering Committee for Higher Education and Research (CDESR),[55] I want to focus upon what seems to me one, if not the, most important challenge for the future of European higher education and research, and hence for European universities: the urgent need for change in university governance. The topic of the conference "Higher education governance between democratic culture, academic aspirations and market forces" is obviously broader than that as it raises also important questions like the role of education in promoting a democratic culture or the choice of a decision mechanism putting the human being at the centre. However, these essential values, particularly cherished in Europe and in most universities all over the world, are powerful only if the system of higher education and research, as well as each institution, can keep up with the increasingly rapidly changing world so that knowledge creation and dissemination become the driving forces of the European economy and society.

I shall briefly:

- convey a few messages about the consequences of the rapidly changing world for the governance of higher education institutions, and

- suggest a few ways for institutions to meet the challenges.

Before, two preliminary remarks are necessary. First, to me, the term "governance", which has recently emerged as the buzzword *à la mode*, refers to the system by which decisions are taken (or not taken) at system and/or institutional levels, which covers the bodies concerned, their composition and competences, and the formal as well as actual decision-making processes. Secondly, I shall mainly refer in this chapter to higher education institutions, although the issue of governance applies to both the institutions and the system.

2. The rapidly changing world is challenging the universities and the system

Origins of the changing environment

The origins of the changing environment for European higher education institutions are threefold:

---

55. Elected chair by the steering committee on 29 September 2005.

- *Globalisation, as well as scientific and technological progress:* these phenomena which strongly impact on our society and economy have been widely described and analysed elsewhere (see Friedman, 2005);

- *The voluntary policies launched in Europe:* the initiative taken in 1998 at La Sorbonne by the ministers of education of France, Germany, Italy and the United Kingdom to create a European Higher Education Area (EHEA) without border, which was then confirmed a year later by 29 ministers meeting in Bologna, is without any doubt a massive shake-up of the higher education sector in Europe. Not only are 45 countries now participating in the process, but the initial objectives have been broadened to include crucial questions like doctorate studies, quality assurance and the social well-being of students. Even if the participating countries and their higher education institutions are implementing "Bologna" at unequal rhythms and with a rather high degree of interpretation of the agreed rules and principles, the whole process already appears to be a massive shake-up of the system, creating great opportunities for improvement, but also containing many unknowns.

The second set of deliberate policies is known under the heading "Lisbon agenda". The Lisbon agenda is a set of initiatives taken at the level of the European Union since 2000, aiming at reinforcing the European research place thanks to a better integration of national and European Union research efforts, to a higher priority given to research at EU level and to the creation of new instruments like the European Research Council, a funding body which should be set up at the European Union level to support research projects on a competitive basis, and to the idea, still to be developed, to create a European Institute of Science and Technology, on the model of MIT or another model to imagine (see Weber & Zgaga, 2004; Weber, 2006; Bologna and Council of Europe websites).

- *Challenges inherent to the development of the higher education and research sector:* the sector is facing many other challenges (see *The Economist*, 2005; Weber, 2006), in particular: (a) if many countries must still respond to an increasing participation rate, some will soon enter into a post-massification stage, due to the strong decrease of the fertility rate in Europe since the seventies; (b) institutions have a real challenge recruiting academic staff to replace the great number who were recruited in the 1970s and 1980s to respond to the need of the demographic baby boom of the 1960s and the simultaneous increased participation rate; (c) the variety and the pressure of demands addressed to higher education institutions is increasing with the need to develop continuous education, set up more specialised training and degrees and multiply research partnerships; (d) the cost of doing research is increasing rapidly due to the increasing sophistication of scientific equipment, the demand for equipment of scientists who traditionally were working with paper and pencil and the increasing cost of recruiting and installing new researchers; (e) the cost of teaching and learning is also increasing with the multiplication of master degrees, the increasing personalisation of the teaching-learning processes with tutorials and action-learning and the cost of developing e-courseware; (f) last but not least, public authorities – and this is particularly true for Europe with its rapidly ageing population –, are strongly under pressure to increase their budgetary appropriation to the sectors of health, assistance to the underprivileged and elderly, and security; (g) finally, even if Europe seems for the time being relatively preserved from the wave of new types of higher education providers which rolls over developing countries in Asia, Africa and Latin America, this commercialisation of the higher education sector is bound to also have an impact on European higher education.

3. The consequences for universities are real and serious

Peter Drucker, the well known author of numerous books on business issues, said in an interview given to the magazine *Forbes* in 1997: "Thirty years from now the big university campuses will be relics. Universities won't survive. It's as large a change as when we first got the printed book." Even if very few university leaders believe in such a gloomy statement, it is true that higher education institutions have to adapt faster. Better still, it has become an obligation for them to lead the change, and not simply undergo it as is presently the case in too many institutions. The two main trends are: the accommodation of increasing competition and the obligation to collaborate.

- The changing environment is disrupting the monopoly position that most higher education institutions were enjoying (*The Economist*, 2005), in particular in continental Europe, where they were merely attracting regional staff and students. The competition develops first within traditional institutions, which are competing more than ever for funding, faculty and even students. The increasing scarcity of public resources forces institutions to compete for other sources of funding, like students' fees, donations and contractual research. The necessity to be better than the others creates also a climate of increasing competition for higher education institutions which more than ever have to compete for the best professors-researchers, as it has become crucial for them to attract research funding and good students. Secondly, competition is arising from other types of higher education institutions (private universities, subsidiaries from off-shore well-known or less well-known institutions, corporate universities, media or publishers' universities, as well as degree mills) or new ways to transfer knowledge (open universities, distance learning, developers of e-courseware, like the open courseware initiative from MIT (Vest, 2006)). Even if it does not seem that these new developments are having a great impact in continental Europe yet, they are coming and will influence the scene.

- One of the paradoxes of the present developments is also that higher education institutions are, even if they are entering a highly competitive environment, obliged to collaborate with other higher education institutions, businesses and government. In particular, they have to network to reach a sufficient critical mass to develop specialised teaching programmes, to engage in important research projects and even in re-engineering themselves to focus on what they are best at, which means also closing departments or transferring them to other universities. Europe is characterised by too many too small institutions; universities will eventually have to merge to gain a critical mass and therefore gain in efficiency (Weber & Duderstadt, 2004).

4. The specific challenge for Europe

Europe is rightly proud of its democratic values, cultural diversity and high sense of social equity and should therefore do everything it can to maintain these or even improve on them. The sense of high accomplishment linked with it should not prevent European countries and governmental organisations from seeing that their world has entered into a fierce competition with countries like the USA, which have overtaken it in matters of science and innovation, or with the new developing countries, which can count on an unlimited reservoir of young people eager to learn and ready to work hard and also able to make and implement important political and business decisions. This is why, rightly, the European heads of state decided in 2000 in Lisbon that Europe should become the most competitive and dynamic world economy based on the knowledge society (Lisbon European Council, 2000). In other words, developing the knowledge society is the only chance for Europe to keep its envied standard of living and relatively good social cohesion. Although it took time for the fact that Europe needs strong universities to be recognised at the European Commission level, it is still not recognised by many governments. This is why "Strong Universities" was the topic of the convention organised by the European University Association in March 2005, which was honoured by a speech of the president of the European Commission (EUA, 2005, Barroso, 2005). Probably, higher education and research have never been so high in the agenda of the European Commission. Another proof is the recently published Communication on the role of universities (2005a). In analysing these positions, one has to keep in mind that the trend following Lisbon 2000 was not at all in conformity with the objectives for 2010; this is why the Commission is presently trying to give a new start to the Lisbon agenda (2005b). Europe seems to be trapped in a vicious circle: without a faster economic growth, it is impossible to invest sufficiently in higher education and research and without these investments, it will not be possible to stimulate the economic growth and thus secure the public and financial means to sustain the comfortable labour conditions and generous social security system. Europe is at a turning point.

5. The challenge of leading the change

Anyone who has been in discussion with university leaders or faculty members or has been advising universities knows perfectly well that most of the rhetoric turns around the question whether the glass is "half full" or "half empty"? Obviously every university continuously adapts to the changing teaching and research environment, in particular to the arrival of new knowledge, new research methodologies or approaches, thanks to the spontaneous capacity of adaptation of their academic staff (teachers and/or researchers) or on the occasion of the recruitment of new staff. The real question is how fast? If there are neither incentives nor sanctions, whatever the reason, weak leadership, organisational paralysis or lack of external competition, the effective adaptation process will obviously be slower than the changing environment requires. And more than that, initiatives taken at department or faculty level will depend on their own relative dynamism, but will not necessarily be in accordance with what seems to be best for the future of the institution.

In view of the deep transformation which is taking place, my sense is that universities – and this is also true for the university system – are not adapting fast enough and that it no longer suffices to count on individual departments or faculties to lead the change. Today, in order to become stronger and to improve, the whole institution needs to define and implement a long-term strategy on the basis of its strengths and weaknesses, as well as its opportunities and threats (SWOT analysis) (Weber & Duderstadt, 2004).

Moreover, my strong belief is that small- and medium-sized, as well as decentralised comprehensive research universities – typical for the European university of the previous centuries – are no longer a viable option. Obviously, any institution is bound to be good if the new entering students are well prepared, if the staff, the facilities and equipment are good and if funding is generous. However, today's challenges require that each institution becomes better; this holds true for good institutions as well as for mediocre ones. I bet that the types of university which will succeed in the future will be larger, in terms of academic staff, and more centralised, in terms of strategic decision making, comprehensive or specialised in a few interconnected disciplines; moreover, they will be strategically led at institutional level.

6. Ways to take up the challenge: strong universities

Now that some of the challenges have been described, I am proposing below five key conditions which should allow universities to address these challenges successfully. If four of them apply, to my mind, to all types of higher education institutions, I am aware that the first one related to university autonomy should probably be varied according to the type of institution.

a. Universities should be autonomous

Probably my strongest message is that universities, in particular research universities, should be very autonomous. To me a very autonomous university should in particular be free to organise itself as it sees fit (system of governance and selection of leaders, internal structure), to choose the disciplines taught and the degrees delivered, to choose its academic, technical and administrative staff and fix their remuneration and finally, to choose its students.

The reasons in favour of such a large autonomy are twofold:

- Firstly, history teaches us that each time the sovereign (church, emperor, dictator or political regime) restricted the autonomy or took control of universities there followed a period of intellectual and social stagnation or decadence. Society needs universities to research freely, with a high level of scholarship and the most appropriate scientific methods possible and to develop new knowledge. Any tentative to "regulate" this process of creative destruction is bound to fail or at least be reductive because the regulator does not benefit from the same space of freedom of inquiry and expression and will in most cases not have the same level of scholarship. Moreover, the politicians who fix the regulatory rules and control their implementation are condemned by the democratic system to have mainly short-term objectives, whereas universities best serve the community if they pursue mid- and long-term goals.

• Secondly, all the recent university ranking exercises show that, by far, those universities considered as the best are very autonomous institutions. Certainly, there also exist excellent universities with little autonomy in countries like Russia or China; there are two reasons for that: (i) they benefit from far more generous funding by the government than the other institutions in the country which are not considered to be flagship institutions; (ii) they have a strong top-down decision-making process which allows them to fix clear priorities, contrary to most universities in the western world.

Autonomous universities are better because they can be more proactive and entrepreneurial in positioning themselves in the competitive environment; in other words, they are in a better position to lead the change than simply adapt to it. It is extremely important here to understand that too much regulation, often bad regulation, as well as too many short-term and often cyclical outside pressures or incentives are hampering the willingness to take initiative and – and this is most preoccupying – invite more regulation and even political micromanagement because institutions are perceived as too passive. Too many and bad regulations or pressures contribute to weakening – instead of reinforcing – institutions. This is a clear case of a vicious circle!

Some will argue that if universities are largely independent from government, it should stop funding them. This is a very dangerous argument for a country as it derives from the wrong understanding that education expenses are consumption expenses. If one correctly understands that funding universities is a high return collective investment (which adds to the private return for the students), it is obvious that public authorities must financially support universities in a substantial way.

After this reminder, it is also obvious that a government should have a higher education and research policy, which implies the fixation of priorities and their concretisation through the grants appropriated for the different priorities. At the level of an institution, this can be done in different ways. Let me just mention two of them: (i) by a contractual agreement between the government and the institutions; (ii) by adapting the grants appropriated to groups of disciplines and/or to research versus teaching over time according to the priority attributed to them.

There is obviously a risk here that a government chooses to restrict the institutions' autonomy by way of financial instead of legal and administrative regulations. Therefore, it is also crucial that the implementation of a governmental policy based on financial incentives and disincentives should only be done with a high level of bundling the appropriations for different activities, and universities should have the possibility to fix their own priorities within the block grant they receive and in particular to finance by other means the activities which are not a governmental priority, but their own strategic priority. Obviously, the borderline is blurred and only a correct perception of the justification of university autonomy for the good of society will allow universities to pursue their own strategy.

In addition to fixing broad financial priorities, governments should make sure that each institution – public and private – has a sufficient level of quality. But this regulatory role of governments should respect the subsidiarity principle. This means that universities should spontaneously develop a rigorous quality culture. In other words, universities should be the key players and the owners of the system (Weber, 2005) and the public authorities should audit these practices to make sure that universities take it seriously and do it well.

Let me conclude by saying that if a very broad autonomy is essential for the performance of research universities, the situation is slightly different for other types of higher education institutions (professional colleges, teaching universities and community colleges), where a stronger public guidance and supervision is probably advisable.

b. Universities should be proactive, transparent and accountable

Securing the framework conditions for proactive universities should mainly be the concern of the public authorities (government, ministry and parliament), which are challenged to trust universities, as well as, but probably to a lesser degree, other higher education institutions, and to refrain from politically interfering and micromanaging the institutions. As we know by observation, most governments in Europe have a restrictive view of institutional autonomy and/or fall into the trap of believing – or behaving as if they believed – that they know better what should be done than their leaders at the different levels of their organisation. Obviously, granting a large autonomy to universities enters into conflict with the sovereignty of the state over public or publicly funded institutions. However, history as well as today's ranking of universities shows unambiguously that granting a real autonomy to universities is an essential step in higher education policy.

However, obviously, the trust which should be granted to universities is by no means a blank cheque given to them to do anything or nothing. It assumes that universities are proactive and "aggressively" make the necessary effort to improve and even search for excellence in teaching and research, as well as to take their great and numerous responsibilities towards society very seriously. This means among others that universities should not be satisfied with simply adapting to the changing environment, but should lead the change. This implies in particular the following for universities:

- *Good understanding of their environment:* universities should monitor and analyse the changing environment to be aware of the changes which are taking place and are about to come in order to perceive the consequences these will have on their activities and organisation.

- *Good knowledge of their portfolio:* the output of a European university is essentially the fruit of history, which is of a succession of microdecisions taken decade after decade. In a rapidly changing world, universities should analyse critically their portfolio of teaching and research programmes, as well as services to society, on the basis of a fair SWOT analysis. Too many activities are pursued simply because they have always been done and because no serious analyses have been made which would have shown they are less important than others which cannot be developed because of that. Moreover, too many opportunities are wasted because they have not been identified early enough or not at all and possible threats are generally recognised too late.

• *Fixing missions and elaborating the strategy accordingly:* the SWOT analysis should also help to refine or revise the institution's missions. Drafting a mission statement is more than an exercise in rhetoric and communication; the mission statement of an institution should reflect where the institution really wants to position itself and serves as the main foundation of its strategic plan.

• *Set up a system of governance favourable to decisions:* the immense majority of European universities are not able to take decisions other than with small incremental steps. The decision processes are too cumbersome and clearly biased in favour of the status quo. The only competence of the institution's leaders is to convince; leaders can rarely impose their views.

• *Being accountable and transparent:* the more universities are autonomous, the more they have to be accountable to their founders and stakeholders. This means first of all that institutions should be transparent, that is to say, give fair information about their activities, recruitment procedures and accounts, and secondly should be accountable, that is, able to justify to their stakeholders that their activities are in accordance with their missions, adequate and cost-efficient.

• *Develop a rigorous quality culture:* in addition to being transparent and accountable, institutions should be quality conscious, among others by setting up and developing a rigorous internal institutional quality enhancement system focused on the capacity of the institution to change. The system should be articulated around self-assessment, the visit of peers and a rigorous phase of follow-up. The ownership of the quality enhancement procedures is a necessary condition to guarantee that the institution looks at itself in a critical manner. The more the quality assurance process is external, the more it turns into a beauty contest.

c. Universities should have the right degree of (de)centralisation

Another delicate question is the structural organisation of an institution. Many university rectors or presidents are testifying that the biggest impediment to change comes from the too large autonomy of faculties and/or departments. This is certainly true. On the other hand, universities, more than any other institutions should secure a great degree of decentralisation. There exists no other institution with so much knowledge at the basis of the "virtual" hierarchical pyramid. Therefore, it is essential to guarantee that professors, researchers and advanced students can fully realise their potential and have the possibility to take initiatives.

I have argued elsewhere that universities should somehow be organised like a federal country (Weber, 2001).

Basically, the organisation should respect the subsidiarity principle, which signifies that decisions should be taken at the lowest level possible. In other words, decisions should be made at a high hierarchical level only if it is not adequate to make them at a lower hierarchical level. This principle prescribes that many decisions should be taken at department or faculty levels, as they are best placed to make informed decisions. However, there are three important limitations to that general rule:

- *Existence of good or bad externalities:* if for example a department or faculty is weak and has a bad reputation, the reputation of the whole institution is affected: the leadership of the institution should therefore be competent to take the necessary measures. The opposite case is also true: if a department is excellent, the leadership of the institution should be in a position to take the necessary measures to develop it even more. In a situation of rapid change, numerous opportunities and threats and scarce resources, it is crucial that the institution's leaders are in a position to modify the relative importance of a department or of faculties according to the strategic objectives of the whole institution. The specific units which would lose out in the change will obviously oppose the change with all the means at their disposal; however, the university authorities should have the power to take these decisions because an unsatisfactory situation at department or faculty level reflects badly on the entire institution. There are many other situations where it would be advisable to reallocate resources according to priorities and posteriorities.

- *Search for economies of scale:* in a time of scarce resources and increasing costs, it has become more important to recognise that the unit cost of an activity depends on its size, which depends generally on the level at which the activity is done. As an example, let us just consider the management of libraries: it is obvious that the implementation of a comprehensive electronic cataloguing and management system should be done at the highest level possible. Today's tendency is clearly to run many activities at a higher level in order to gain in efficiency.

- *High preference for equal treatment of equals:* the level of centralisation or decentralisation depends finally on the degree of preference for equal treatment of equals. An institution which is not very sensitive to that aspect can make most decisions at department or faculty levels whereas an institution which is very sensitive to it has no other way than taking decisions at the top of the institution to ensure that the same rules and interpretation apply to all. This is, for example, the case regarding the admission of students.

d. University decision making should be improved

In order to improve the governance of higher education institutions, it is also necessary to improve decision making. I shall raise here only two aspects of the problem:

- *Increase the decision power of the leaders:* even if the formal decision structures and processes may give a different impression, most university leaders (rectors, presidents) are hardly in a position to make repeated important decisions. Compared with private firms, this situation certainly reflects the special nature of universities as described above. However, in a rapidly changing world, it is problematic if university leaders are not in a position to make the necessary decisions to better adapt their institutions to the new environment. This situation contributes to the widely spread image in public opinion and political spheres that universities are unable to change, which explains public interference. The difficulty is that the solution to that problem lies more in the decision process than in the decision-making competences given to the leader.

- *Simplify the decision process:* one of the main weaknesses is that there are too many bodies, some being redundant, and that the exact role and competences of each of them are not clearly defined. The effort should go towards a decrease of the number of bodies, a clarification of their competences and an increase in the decision power of the leaders. It is also necessary to choose a mode of selection of the leaders, at university as well as faculty and/or department levels, which is favourable to decisions. However, with regard to the very nature of a university (high competence at the base of the hierarchy and many stakeholders), it is also very important to guarantee an extensive and true consultation of all those concerned by a decision (including students for issues which concern them).

e. Professionalise the decision mechanisms and the administration

Too many universities have an "amateurish" system of management with regard to strategy setting, decision making and management. It is particularly desirable that:

- the leaders have management skills in addition to academic ones. This implies that they should at least have the opportunity to get serious training in university management and possibly also that they benefit from some coaching during their first years in office;

- the decisions are based on evidence in particular due to a rigorous accounting and controlling system, to an extensive statistical database and adequate performance indicators and, finally, to the systematic analysis of important questions.

7. By way of conclusion

The purpose of this introductory chapter drawn from my introductory statement at the forum was mainly to send a message of warning. Without a significant change in the governance system and leadership of its higher education institutions, Europe will not succeed in increasing the number of strong universities or network of universities (*The Economist*, 2005; Weber, 2006).

Hopefully, I have identified where – and somehow also how – action should take place. I am very well aware that this contribution raises many questions and does not solve them all, or even that some of the ways proposed are controversial.

Hopefully, the forum organised by the Steering Committee for Higher Education and Research of the Council of Europe and this publication will not only initiate a broader awareness of the urgency of the question, but will identify some common views on how to make universities capable of faster change.

References

Barroso, J.M., *Strong universities for Europe*, speech at the Convention of the European University Association, Glasgow, 2 April 2005.

Bologna Process website: http://www.dfes.gov.uk/bologna/

Commission of the European Communities, (2000), Communication from the Commission to the Council, the European Parliament, the Economic and Social Committee and the Committee of the Regions, *Toward a European research area* (COM(2000) 6 final:
http://europa.eu.int/eur-lex/lex/LexUriServ/site/en/com/2000/com2000_0006en01.pdf

Commission of the European Communities (2005a), Communication from the commission, *Mobilising the brainpower of Europe: enabling universities to make their full contribution to the Lisbon strategy*, (COM(2005) 152 final.

Commission of the European Communities, (2005b), Communication to the spring European Council, *Working together for growth and jobs, a new start for the Lisbon strategy*, COM(2005) 24, Brussels.

Council of Europe Steering Committee for Higher Education and Research website: http://www.coe.int/T/DG4/HigherEducation/Default_EN.asp

Drucker, P.F., Interview: "Seeing things as they really are." *Forbes*, 159, 1997: 122-28.

European University Association, *Glasgow Declaration: Strong universities for a strong Europe*, EUA, Brussels, 2005.

Friedman, T.L., *The world is flat, A brief history of the twenty-first century*, Farrar, Straus and Giroux, New York, 2005.

Lisbon European Council, *Presidency conclusions*, 23-24 March, 2000:
http://ue.eu.int/ueDocs/cms_Data/docs/pressData/en/ec/00100-r1.en0.htm

The Economist, "The brain business, A survey of higher education", 10 September 2005.

Vest, C.M., "Best practice in knowledge transfer", in Weber L.E. & Duderstadt J.J. (eds.) *Universities and business: Partnering for the knowledge society*, Economica, Paris, 2006, Chapter 23.

Weber, L., "Critical university decisions and their appropriate makers: Some lessons from the economic theory of federalism" in Hirsch L.E. & Weber L.E. (eds.), *Governance in higher education; The university in a state of flux*, Economica, Paris, 2001, Chapter 6.

Weber L.E., "European strategy to promote the knowledge society as a source of renewed economic dynamism and social cohesion", in Weber L.E. & Duderstadt J.J. (eds.), *Universities and business: Partnering for the knowledge society*, Economica, Paris, 2006, Chapter 1.

Weber, L.E., "Nature and scope of the public responsibility for higher education and research" in Weber L.E. & Bergan S. (eds.), *The public responsibility for higher education and research*, Council of Europe higher education series, No. 2, Council of Europe Publishing, Strasbourg, 2005, Chapter 2.

Weber L.E. & Duderstadt, J.J., "Challenges and possible strategies for research universities in Europe and the United States", in Weber L.E. & Duderstadt J.J. (eds.), *Reinventing the research university*, Economica, Paris, 2004, Chapter 17, 237-254.

Weber, L.E. & Zgaga, P., "Reinventing the European higher education and research sector: The challenge for research universities", in Weber L.E. & Dudestadt J.J. (eds.), *Reinventing the research university*, Economica, Paris, 2004, Chapter 3.

Concepts

Higher education governance in Europe: autonomy, ownership and accountability – A review of the literature

Jochen Fried

1. Introduction

For a long time, the discussion about higher education governance issues has been confined to the circles of policy makers and reseachers. The term itself was not much used, let alone well understood outside of the English-speaking countries, in part perhaps because most languages seem to lack a straightforward equivalent and are thus importing the word 'governance' into local parlance, often with a certain sense of uneasiness. This has changed quite radically during the past decade or so following the sweeping transformation of higher education systems in many European countries in the post-1989 period as well as far-reaching revisions and adjustments regarding the structure of university organisation in numerous other countries. Governance has not always been the label under which the discussions about these changes have been taking place, but it has been at the heart of most of these debates.

With the proliferation of governance literature in more recent years, the meaning of the term has become more expansive and, unavoidably so, more diffuse. Even a passing glance at the literature on this topic reveals that governance is a trendy subject among scholars of a surprisingly broad scope of subjects which range from political philosophy to organisational psychology. There is a general consensus among researchers that governance is a relatively recently coined term for an age-old phenomenon. Conceptually, governance exists for as long as ships are crossing the sea which created the need for 'steering'. The anglophone word 'governance' can be traced to the classical Latin and ancient Greek words for 'steering the boats' (Jessop 1998: 30). This observation is not entirely trivial because in the literature about 'governance' it is often noted that metaphors and especially the connotations of words such as 'steering', 'leadership', 'stakeholder', 'ownership', etc. play a certain role in the governance debate.

Another common denominator in the literature that is of some significance is the widespread complaint about the indistinctness of the concept of 'governance' due to overuse, as the following quote indicates: "The general debate on governance takes place in a very large and creative research field – to put it in an optimistic way. The apparent disadvantage of this 'fruitfulness' is that many different uses and analyses of governance have emerged. It has thus become almost a tradition for researchers in the field to start an article or a book by deploring the many uses of the word governance, saying for example 'that there are perhaps as many different views about governance as there are scholars interested in the subject' (Pierre & Peters, 2000: 28)" (Lond, 2003: 3). This uncertainty is not a result of sloppy thinking, on the contrary, it reflects the ambiguity of a situation in which some of the stable distinctions of the past (in the case of higher education, for instance, between public and private, autonomy and interdependence, power and legitimacy) have become blurred and the concept of governance steps in to reassert coherence where it is in question. It is one of the underlying premises of this review that the emergence of the governance discourse is a symptom of the search for a new balance of societal forces, actors and structures which no longer follow the given rules and patterns. Therefore, governance is seen as a dynamic concept.

The following text is intended to provide a common framework for a more in-depth discussion, initiated by the Council of Europe, of the evolution of governance modes and models in European higher education over the past couple of decades or so. This discussion is, at least in part, motivated by the conviction that a stronger emphasis on good governance could help foster a more holistic approach to the various reform agendas that the higher education sector is undergoing, notably those reforms that are induced by the Bologna Process. Whether spelled with a capital or a small letter, this is by no means a uniform process, and also not a process aiming at uniformity. It should thus be stated at the outset of this review that a single European model of higher education governance does not (yet?) exist. Instead, there is a broad variety of governance regimes in the different European countries, reflecting the specific histories and socio-economic as well as political forces that have shaped their respective higher education systems. All attempts to provide a broad transnational overview are, therefore, inevitably liable to a certain degree of generalisation and approximation.

Accordingly, the present report does not attempt to offer an encyclopedic survey of governance schemes and arrangements in Europe; instead the discussion focuses on patterns and actors, thus trying to identify a certain convergence or common trends that characterise the evolution of governance structures in European higher education. In the interest of providing a broad supranational framework for this discussion, some of the more specific thematic areas and aspects that would deserve a more thorough consideration are deliberately de-emphasised. In particular, the report does not explicitly address the question of various types of institutions which contribute to the diversity and complexity of higher education in Europe. It assumes a relatively coherent tertiary sector with the traditional university as its lead institution, obviously at the price of paying only passing attention to the non-university segment (for example, polytechnics in their different national manifestations, institutions of further education and other types of institutions) but also private or non-governmental universities. However, by analysing the scope and the configuration of governance structures of the former, it is hoped that this will also shed some light on the relevant developments of the latter.

The review focuses on some of the typical fault lines in the governance debate, for example, the one that runs between governance on the one hand, and autonomy and academic freedom on the other; another fault line lies between the university understood as a loosely coupled system and a streamlined approach to forcing all units under the same 'new public management' rules; yet another one demarcates the time-honoured principles and procedures of academic self-government vis-à-vis a stakeholder model of university governance. There are many more contentious issues that are discussed in the literature under the general heading of 'governance', though the one that perhaps is stirring up the most vehement reactions is the thorny question of how governance and management are related to one another. Not surprisingly, there is no authoritative answer to this question based on the literature. According to one's own viewpoint, persuasive arguments can be extracted for either of the competing positions: that governance and management are opposed to each other, implying different understandings of purposes of higher education; or, on the contrary, that they are of a complementary nature and that it is in fact the interlinkage of governance and management which enables a given institution to pursue its own goals and be self-reliant.

However, regardless of one's own position in these sometimes heated debates, the review of the relevant literature also strongly suggests that governance is not just a detached set of formulas and rules which define the process and mechanism of collective decision making; instead, it is always situated and contingent upon context and environment. Ulrike Felt, in her essay on University autonomy in Europe: Changing paradigms in higher education policy (Bologna, 2003), convincingly argues that the advent of the knowledge society makes it imperative to renegotiate the social contract under which universities were operating since the 1970s (14, see also Chapter 2.1). It seems important to underline the term 'negotiation' in this statement since it evokes an active role and participation of the citizens of the university in the shaping of this new contract – whereas the critics of the 'managerial revolution' in higher education in the 1990s depict the academic community as the more or less passive object and victim of what they see as a top-down and unfriendly takeover of the university by its own senior management. It would be healthy for the debate about governance issues if there was less institutional navel-gazing and more context awareness guiding the discussions.

The concept of governance emerged within the context of the more recent devolution of state authority, decentralisation and non-intervention as a result of the growing complexity of the sociopolitical and economic environment which requires new approaches to the steering of the public sector. Governance in its contemporary understanding implies a re-orientation of the universities away from an inward-looking perspective of a self-contained autonomous space to emphasise the 'embeddedness' of higher education and research.

Good governance strives to preserve the integrity of the academic value system while at the same time it positions the university vis-à-vis the larger environment to make it receptive and answerable to external messages, demands and expectations. In this respect, governance becomes the conduit for expanding the mission of the university by including a dimension which is captured in the notion of service as the third key component of academic work next to teaching and research. It therefore seems expedient to combine the discussion about good governance with the question: Who are we serving as higher education institutions? Governance itself is only a means to an end, and unless we have a clear understanding of the purpose of higher education, we lack the criteria to distinguish between good and bad governance. In other words: the purpose of higher education must precede the decisions about the means to pursue these.

It is precisely for this reason that governance is the "juncture where the distinctive social and cultural identity of each institution is formed" (Marginson & Considine, 2000: 8).

2. Governance: concept, dimensions, procedures and functions

2.1. The emergence of a concept

In the past two decades or so, the term 'governance' has had a remarkable career within higher education (HE) circles (and beyond) throughout Europe. The following study, while primarily providing an overview of some of the most essential literature on this topic, can also be read as an attempt to uncover the reasons for the appreciation and recognition which this term now enjoys and which is by no means self-explanatory. On the contrary, it is in some respects a difficult and even an awkward term that defies a straightforward understanding as numerous authors confirm. Peter Scott writes that 'governance' is "a relatively novel derivation from the root word 'govern' – or, more precisely, it has acquired a new currency and meaning... to denote a much broader account of the governing process going beyond the actions of 'governors' and 'governments'. 'Governance' embraces a wider set of actors, it ranges beyond the territory of state institutions into the private and voluntary sectors; and, consequently, it is a more ambiguous and volatile process" (Scott, 2001: 125).

Accordingly, 'governance' encompasses many areas and is used in a broad variety of contexts, for example, as corporate governance, governance as New Public Management, good governance, global governance, economic governance, participatory governance, governance as "institutional management/steering", etc. Equally diverse are the definitions of this notion though they all emphasise three main characteristics:

a. governance means regulation, steerage and control (*Steuerung* or *Regelung* in German) within the context of a given (social, political, economic, institutional) order;

b. it can be described and analysed as "a set of practices whereby independent political and/or economic actors coordinate and/or hierarchically control their activities and interactions... Governance structures are therefore formal and informal institutional devices through which political and economic actors organize and manage their interdependencies" (Hirst & Thompson, 1997: 362);

c. these structures ultimately serve to enhance or promote the legitimacy and efficiency of the social system by way of organising negotiation processes, setting standards, performing allocation functions, monitoring compliance, reducing conflict, and resolving disputes (ibid.).

A useful example to illustrate this complex concept is the emergence of the term 'good governance' in the public domain: "Since the early 1990s, the notion of 'good governance' as a necessary prerequisite for sustainable development and poverty reduction has gained widespread currency, especially among international organisations. ... The World Bank was the first major donor institution to adopt the concept of good governance as a condition for lending to developing countries" (Simonis, 2004; 2f). In this case the "set of practices" that this concept refers to is of course the interaction and interdependence between donors and recipients. It indicates certain expectations and stipulates a more or less clearly defined code of conduct: good governance relates to democracy, the rule of law, human rights, decentralisation, transparency, accountability, and reducing corruption to ensure maximum effectiveness of international development programmes. It is also obvious that in this example the term 'governance' carries a *normative* connotation by making universalistic assumptions regarding the applicability of the principles of what merits being called 'good governance'. (This is further confirmed by the fact that 'good governance' has been included as one of the targets of the Millennium Development Goals (MDGs) of the UN which are normative by nature.)

These assumptions concerning shared values, however, are first of all postulated by those who have the defining power; they are the values within a predominantly donor-driven discourse about suitable policies to manage and implement development projects according to acceptable rules. No doubt that apart from the donors there are other stakeholders that also subscribe to those values (for example, NGOs in the given recipient countries that might blame their governments for certain 'leakages' in processing donor funds). But for the broader purposes of this study it is important to keep in mind that along with its descriptive and analytical meaning 'governance' has an implicit or explicit normative dimension which is not always acknowledged.

The example also provides a hint to one of the principal influences and underlying rationales that gave rise to the prominence of the notion of governance. In the international donor discourse, insisting on good *governance* is a consequence of the experience of dealing with bad (inept, incompetent, incapable or immoral) or weak *governments*. But also in the industrialised countries, the changing role of the state from the early 1980s onwards instigated a search for an enhanced understanding and new models of how public affairs can be run more effectively and efficiently. Prompted by the general waning of trust in the state as the curator and executor of the *volonté générale* as well as the provider and/or guarantor of public welfare, the governance approach presented itself as a remedy both to reconceptualise and to overhaul those tasks that had traditionally fallen under the authority of the state. In other words: it is the classic government function in public affairs that is challenged by the more recent concept of governance. This juxtaposition is very clearly being expressed in the title of a seminal book called *Governance without government: Order and change in world politics* edited by James Rosenau and Ernst-Otto Czempiel (1992).

Whether it is being seen as a sign of an unfortunate atrophy of the state or as a deliberate devolution of governmental authority, the growing importance of governance is in many aspects closely linked to the neo-liberal reshaping of the public sphere in economy, society and politics. "(...) classic forms of welfare state have been superseded by neo-liberal and entrepreneurial forms, which have required a shift from straightforward notions of democratic 'government' to more sinuous notions of stakeholder 'governance'" (Scott, 2001: 126). New networks, forms of co-operation and partnerships are developing at different political levels between the three sectors: state, business and civil society. Traditional forms of (hierarchical) "government" are losing significance; new forms of (horizontal) political regulation are emerging.

The notion of governance refers precisely to a decentralised constitution of the social order with an emphasis on the way in which power and authority relations are structured in different institutions and contexts. As far as public institutions are concerned, governance focuses on the rules and mechanisms by which various stakeholders can influence decisions and hold those in power accountable. In the private sector, the concept of corporate governance is challenging non-transparency and non-accountability not only towards shareholders but the wider public. As for multilateral organisations such as the IMF, the World Bank or the United Nations, they are deeply involved in discussions about global governance prompted, among other reasons, by the demand of greater responsiveness of these organisations towards civil society in its broadest sense.

Universities everywhere have not been exempt from this development. At the heart of the governance debate "are the notions of autonomy and academic freedom, i.e., the new forms of responsibility towards society and of accountability towards stakeholders. (...) In a way, the contract negotiated between universities and society, under particular conditions in the 1970s and based on a certain set of values, is now being renegotiated in the context of wider societal changes" (Felt, 2003: 14). The dominant characteristics of these changes is the well-known combination of the increased student demand for higher education, the relative decrease of public expenditure for higher education institutions, diversification of financial resources, a growing national and international competitiveness among universities, the introduction of quality assurance regimes and performance-based allocation of funds, new demands of employers and students towards university education (caused, for example, by the advent of the 'knowledge economy') or the shortened cycles of innovation in science and technology, to name just the most prominent factors. These changes are affecting universities throughout Europe and beyond in similar ways though the manner in which individual countries are reacting to them can be rather diverse reflecting different and deeply-rooted histories, political cultures and state/university relationships.

Against this background of rapid changes both in terms of internal demands and external expectations, the increased emphasis on the concept of governance must be seen as an indication of a broader need to rethink and redesign the way universities go about doing their business. As a response to a crisis of legitimacy and capacity to (re)act which is similar to that of the nation-state governments, the wider idea of university governance "has begun not only to embrace but also to replace the traditional notions of academic self-government" (Scott, 2001: 126).

2.2. Governance dimensions

In the most elementary sense, governance is "the formal and informal exercise of authority under laws, policies and rules that articulate the rights and responsibilities of various actors, including the rules by which they interact, so as to help achieve the institution's academic objectives" (Hirsch & Weber, 2001: viii). In other words, governance is stating the answers to the fundamental question: who is in charge, how are the rules applied, and what are the sources of legitimacy for executive decision making by different actors?

The current changes in governance regimes of higher education systems and institutions (the 'renegotiation of the contract between university and society') are often described as a shift from the traditional mode of academic self-government to a new model of managerial self-governance that attempts to re-arrange the internal organisation of the university around the idea of a modern service enterprise with its emphasis on more accountability towards stakeholders, flexibility and responsiveness to market needs and a capacity for developing strategic goals that are attuned to the people that universities are serving. Much of the literature on this topic focuses on the consequences of the introduction of managerial self-governance for teaching and research, often by comparing countries which have already made more progress on the way from an over-regulated central administration to a performance-driven and externally guided model of university governance. What emerges from these analyses are five principal mechanisms of co-ordination or collective control relevant for the steering of the university sector (cf. Clark, 1979; Braun & Merrien, 1999; Schimank, Kehm & Enders, 1999):

- *External regulation* refers to the authority of the state to lay down the rules under which universities are allowed to operate. It typically consists of a set of strict and binding orders prescribing the institutional behaviour and course of action under given circumstances. There are certain mechanisms of control which monitor adherence to these rules (inspectorates, a bureaucratic apparatus, certification procedures, conditional approval for certain activities and, last but not least, financial incentives or disincentives). Thus, this governance dimension is characterised by the traditional top-down approach of governing public institutions through a formalised set of legal rules and specific regulations.

- *External guidance* can be given by the relevant state authorities (ministry) or be delegated by the state to other actors/stakeholder representatives, for example to members of the university boards. The mode of exercising steering power and co-ordinated action is not by formal determination but by negotiation and goal-setting (performance contracts are an example of specifying the goals to be reached without prescribing the ways and means of achieving these goals).

- *Academic self-governance* relates to the processes and procedures of building consensus within and among the 'academic tribes' as to the course of action to be taken. The steering, co-ordination and control of university agendas is largely left to the collegial decision making in committees or peer groups which subscribe to the values of egalitarianism and academic meritocracy as their operating principles.

- *Managerial self-governance* emphasises the hierarchical position of the senior leadership and management of an institution (rector/president, deans) in terms of goal-setting and executive decision making. Their authority is controlled by a system of intra-institutional checks and balances both in the form of written regulations (for example, the statute of the university) or of publicly stated strategic goals which serve as a yardstick of success, or lack thereo.

- *Competition* has become a governance dimension as the underlying rationale for the co-ordination of priorities and decision making in higher education on institutional as well as system level. It is the logic of the market which determines action and thereby establishes order. The allocation of scarce resources (financial, staff, infrastructure) is nowadays mostly done on the basis of some form of competitive mechanism which introduces a strong layer of managerialism into the governance discourse.

Obviously, these different governance dimensions are abstractions which do not exist in an undiluted or pure manifestation. They are analytical categories to describe what is basically a 'fuzzy' reality of different and overlapping governance dimensions that have emerged under specific local and historical conditions. But as analytical tools these dimensions can be helpful to cut through the maze and identify trends and developments concerning the evolution of governance patterns from a national and transnational perspective. In a recent (and yet unpublished) article[56] de Boer, Enders and Schimank presented what they call "the governance equalizer" as "a heuristic tool for the international comparison of highly ambiguous concepts" (the latter referring to their contention that the concepts of governance, New Public Management and managerialism "have no clear or agreed definition of what they are or should be"). The five dimensions described above represent the different 'frequencies' that are being internally adjusted by the equalizer, a device to reduce distortion in a (sound) system. The model implies that the input into the system, i.e., the different governance dimensions, can be scaled along the levels of low and high and that governance regimes in general are always mixtures or specific combinations of all five principal mechanisms of co-ordination and collective control. "All five dimensions co-exist, though in a certain period one or more dimensions may predominate, or may be seen as the striking feature of an epoch. Thus, we assume that a mode of governance is made up of several dimensions that are combined in empirical situations."

To illustrate this tool, here is the example of the traditional modes of governance as depicted by the governance equalizer as well as the 'entrepreneurial' type:

---

56. De Boer, Enders & Schimank, "Orchestrating creative minds. The governance of higher education and research in four countries compared, 2005, 5 (unpublished).

Figure 1: Example of the governance equalizer

TRADITIONAL   ENTREPRENEURIAL

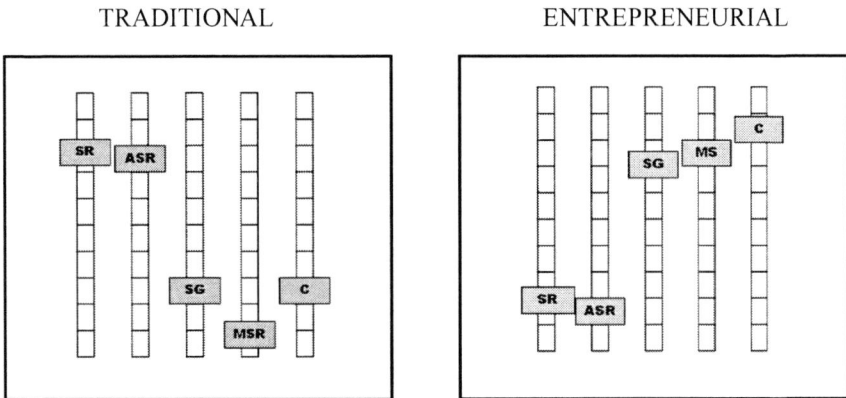

SR = State regulation, ASR = Academic self-governance, SG = Stakeholder guidance, MSR = Managerial self-governance, C = Competition

From: de Boer, Enders and Schimank (2005), Orchestrating creative minds

The discernible advantage of this model is that it avoids simplification by presenting governance arrangements as multi-dimensional configurations of contributing voices, tones and reverberations (and maybe sometimes also chatter and burbles) rather than a one-dimensional 'either/or'. For example, the much debated shift from a state control system to a state supervised system of higher education in most west European countries during the past two decades or so (in the terminology of the equalizer model: from "state regulation" to "stakeholder guidance") is not necessarily equivalent to a 'withdrawal of the state' but can also be read and described as a change of emphasis in the way that an actor pursues the goal of optimising the governance provisions (of exercising authority); in this case by attenuating the power of command from the top (because increasingly complex systems such as universities cannot efficiently be ruled top-down) and amplifying the forces of co-ordination, negotiation and ruling from a distance.

This also responds to an obvious objection against the equalizer model, namely that it suggests an 'invisible hand' which operates/manipulates this device to produce a sound governance system. The authors of the model avow themselves to a "state-centric approach" in the sense "that the composition of the dimensions of the equalizer always reflect a substantial contribution of the state" (p. 7). They exemplify their view by pointing to the 'audit culture' which has entered the scene of higher education governance concurrently with the new and supposedly deregulated mode of operation. The rhetoric is one of greater efficiency, increased autonomy, ownership and accountability. However, the execution of the audit and evaluation systems is more often than not meticulously prescribed by national governments or their subsidiary agencies which in the equalizer model would count as 'state regulation' under the guise of external guidance.

The discussion of this model will be taken up later again when we will be reviewing different modes and patterns of higher education governance (Section 3). For now, the exploration of the constituting elements of governance systems will turn to the various actors and their structural roles in ensuring co-ordination and participation in the steering of a university.

2.3. Actors in the context of governance

On the one hand, the actors could be seen as a factor of contingency in the governance equation. It is a matter of personality and attitude how they interpret and play their role in the handling of institutional affairs. But the notion of actors as it is referred to here highlights the more objectified or typified understanding of the different functions that are involved in the co-ordination of action within a university. It is, of course, conceded that this is only possible by passing over many of the particular features that characterise these actors in different countries under vastly diverse historical and legal circumstances. But in so far as there is a common structure that lies beneath the university systems at least in Europe this generalisation may be admissible. Thus, the framework structure that shapes, opens and limits the actors' radius of operation are: a. the universities as organisational units and their intra-organisational relations; b. the academic disciplines as professional communities; c. in the case of public institutions (on which we will confine ourselves in this review), the state authority to set the formal rules for governing and managing the higher education sector.

The key players portrayed here are:

- government;
- governing boards (board of trustees);
- the rector (or vice-chancellor/president);
- academic staff;
- central administration;
- students;
- stakeholder representation.

Consonant with its self-image as a (academic) community, these different constituencies come together in a co-operative effort to govern the given higher education institution (HEI). Based on this assertion, we will in the following try to summarise very briefly some of the structural characteristics that specify the role of the key actors in institutional governance without even attempting to go into details concerning national specificities.

2.3.1. Government

In the early 1990s, the authors of a comprehensive multi-country study on governmental policies in higher education (Goedegebuure et al., 1993) came to the conclusion that in continental European systems the reforms of the past two decades have led to a gradual replacement of the earlier *state control* model (with tight regulations and almost all-inclusive public/federal alimentation) by a *state supervising* model which gives more room for manoeuvre to the individual institutions in terms of decision making in academic, financial, entrepreneurial, personnel and other matters while the relevant government actors steer the system 'from a distance' (cf. Sporn, 1999). This finding corresponds to the overall pattern of a devolution of state authority, decentralisation and non-intervention as a result of a growing complexity and dynamics of the sociopolitical and economic environment which requires new approaches to the steering of the public sector (the concept, or ideology, of New Public Management (NPM) which will be discussed later, came out to be seen as a kind of panacea to the ills and problems of this sector). It does not, however, necessarily mean that the government is disappearing from the stage of higher education governance. Instead, it reflects an increasing awareness of the limitations of the traditional public command-and-control as a governing mechanism and an openness on behalf of governments to different and more adequate approaches in response to societal developments which call for new solutions (Kooiman, 2004).

It is, therefore, not contradictory that in the public perception (and in the eyes of HEIs) the government still seems to play a dominant role in the higher education arena: "In continental Europe, it is a generally held view that it is the core responsibility of governments to ensure the availability and adequate supply, as well as the quality of and access to higher education. (…) Whatever has changed in the financial levels and the governance systems, there is no indication whatsoever that this conviction has changed in recent years" (van Ginkel, 2001: 158).

The (d)evolution of state authority with respect to higher education institutions since the late 1960s has been of a typical dual nature reflecting the "fundamental changes in the constitution of public (and private) authority" (Scott, 2001) during this period. On the one hand, it gave way to the general move of societies in western Europe, and since 1989 also in the rest of Europe, towards more democracy and autonomy, and an emphasis on the politics of self-responsibility; on the other hand, in exchange for more independence, it brought about new laws and/or funding arrangements which aim at improving the transparency of university policies and the accountability of university management vis-à-vis the government and the public (steering by economy/finances instead of steering by law). The 'audit culture' – some prefer to call it an audit menace – which has already been alluded to and which has assumed such a prominent place in higher education, has its rationale exactly in this dual tendency: the abandoning of micromanagement and interference in academic policies by governmental actors in favour of new mechanisms, tools and incentives to ensure macro-efficiency. This formula was further 'enhanced' by the well-known factors of transformation that are external to the university, most prominently the relative decrease of public expenditure for higher education; the stress on economic rationality in the planning and delivery of public services, including higher education; the growing influence/interventions of stakeholders in matters that traditionally were regarded as internal to universities; the proliferation of expectations and demands mounted on universities to be the universal problem-solvers for the various troubles and concerns that have befallen society (as, for example, described by Clark, 1998). To put it pointedly, the meaning of decentralisation of responsibilities to the universities, then, is to do more with less (more independence, flexibility, responsiveness, demands, expectations or universities; less direct intervention, bureaucracy, restrictions, routine workload on the part of the government). Obviously, all of this combined necessitates an overhaul of governing activities and structures on all levels.

2.3.2. Governing board (board of trustees)

Different from the Anglo-Saxon tradition, continental European higher education systems had until recently not much experience with lay participation in governance matters. The institution of lay trusteeship is in particular characteristic of private universities and colleges in the United States which are genuine products of the civil society rather than entities of the state (Scott, 2001) which accounts for a more communitarian notion of higher education governance in the US compared to the predominantly state-centric understanding in Europe where universities were one of the key pillars in the process of nation/state building. The main purpose of these trustees is to preserve and protect the institutional integrity against undue outside interference, be it political, sectarian or otherwise, and to serve as the top decision-making body within the governance chain of the institution. With regard to internal governance, the tasks and responsibilities of the board of trustees are to a large degree of fiduciary nature: approving (or disapproving) annual budgets and financial reports, endorsing the strategic plan, deliberating major capital investments, etc. It is not considered to be the business of board members to meddle with internal affairs like admissions, curriculum or academic appointments with one notable exception: it is the sole prerogative of the board to appoint the president of the college or university. In other words, "(t)he job is to conserve, not to innovate (...) institutional development is regarded as the responsibility of the president and administration. The successful president who enjoys the confidence of his/her trustees is in a powerful position" (ibid., 136).

A variation of the above in the US is the board of regents (or similar bodies) of state-wide public university systems (for example, the University of California system consisting of ten campuses with more than 200 000 students, 160 000 faculty and staff and an annual budget of close to $12 billion). The modes of becoming member of these control bodies vary. In some cases the governor appoints the members, in other cases the candidates get elected by the general public or are being nominated by the legislature. This system obviously introduces a certain degree of politisation (or, more precarious still, an ideological bias) into the governance of American public higher education. But in general, it is fair to say that politics is kept out of the board room.

In Europe, more recent legislative changes in a number of countries led to the creation of boards of trustees. In the public discussions accompanying the introduction of these new governance actors, the advocates mainly quoted two sources as the models: the US higher education system and the boards of directors of big corporations; the first paying tribute to what is more or less undisputedly (though not always uncritically) being seen as the world's most successful higher education system; the second as a clear rejection of the 'old' civil service mentality at HEIs as an obstacle of reform and innovation within the inherited system of the given country.

The formal rights and responsibilities of these boards of trustees, while they may slightly differ in emphasis according to national legislations, are very much like their US counterparts. In terms of *internal* governance, they perform a supervisory function over the top executive management of the university. In this role, they act as an "intermediate layer between the government and the individual institution (…) and create the adequate distance between the ministry and the university" (van Ginkel, 2001), thus strengthening the notion of institutional autonomy and reducing direct (governmental) interference. With regard to the *external* environment, the boards are intended to link the university better to 'the outside world' in a non-political, broad sense by involving suitably qualified and dedicated representatives of society in the process of defining and refining the institution's present and future goals and objectives. It almost goes without saying that apart from other, more task-related qualifications and a genuine interest in the advancement of higher education, board members should not otherwise be linked to or personally have a stake in particular activities of the institution in any way (for example, by profiting from research results) and it is often stipulated that they should not hold a position in government or parliament.

The introduction of board of trustees into the governance structures of HEIs in several European countries is certainly not an uncontested change and has been met with some scepticism from the 'academic heartland' which sees it as a further move towards a 'corporatisation' of the university and a threat to the notion and the practice of academic self-government. Given that in most of these countries the boards of trustees have been established relatively recently, the jury is still out as to how they will amalgamate with the traditional modes of governance.

2.3.3. Rector (or vice-chancellor/president)

The place of the rector within the formal governance structure of a typical (continental?) European HEI is in many aspects a highly demarcated and circumscribed place, moulded by centuries of traditions and (institutional, social) expectations. For the longest time, he (and in very rare cases, "she") was seen as the *primus inter pares* of the scholarly oligarchy, the latest incarnation in a long succession of bearers and keepers of the insignia of academic self-rule and sovereignty. The fact that until quite recently the role of the rector was in some sense a matter of emulation and repertoire may be the reason for the somewhat surprising observation that there is actually not too much literature on the topic of the rectorial position on the market that goes beyond the personal memoirs and reflections which is in stark contrast to the US with its burgeoning publications on the nature, joys and perils of effective "presidential leadership". The standard requirements for a rector at a European university were: seniority, reputation, sometimes political patronage, and the ability to rally support on election day. Accordingly, the criteria specifying the professional qualifications for the position were not very well defined, and there was the prevailing assumption that 'learning by doing' is all that counts for the job (though there have been training seminars for aspiring or newly appointed rectors for quite some time offered by university associations on a national as well as a European level).

These traditions and assumptions may not hold much longer. For it is one of the central elements of the ongoing reforms in higher education systems in many European countries, and of the accompanying changes at institutional level regardless under which label they are being proposed (for example, entrepreneurial, responsive, adaptive, Mode 2, etc., university) to re-assess and upgrade the university leadership and role of the "chief executive", also known as the rector (Bargh, Bocock, Scott & Smith, 2000; see also Hanft, 2001).

Basically, the rectorate is the epicentre of both the hopes and the discontent concerning these governance reforms – an ambivalence which appropriately reflects their contrapuntal nature. For those applauding the changes, a 'strong centre' is the only way to sustain and develop institutional identity in an increasingly dispersed and volatile political, social and economic environment which has long entered the HEIs and which, unless it is being acknowledged, embraced and managed, will seriously hamper the universities as the foremost locus for knowledge production, distribution and preservation. Those, on the other hand, who raise a warning voice see at risk the very foundation on which the success and the resilience of the university is being built, namely "… the principle of academic collegiality that appears increasingly at odds with the drive towards the concentration of executive responsibilities around key individuals and key posts which is the essence of contemporary reform in the governance of Europe's universities" (Neave, 2001: 64). Looking back to the struggles of the late 1960s and 1970s when the reformers were revolutionaries who wanted to stage an institutional insurrection to abolish the old *"Ordinarienuniversität"* (the University of the Senior Professors), Neave comments: "It is from such a context that the thesis of a 'confiscated revolution' has drawn inspiration. Simply stated, this view interprets enhanced institutional autonomy as advancing less the autonomy of the academic estate so much as the power of its administrative counterpart", resulting in an uneasy "de facto co-existence of two conflicting interpretations of self-regulation, one operating in the institution at central level based on executive authority, backed by the weight of law, the other, collegial and representative, based on established practice" (ibid.).

In other words, legislative enactment to strengthen the senior management's decision-making power is one thing; dealing with the different "tribes and territories" (Becher & Trowler, 2001) on campus to move "from collegial academy to academic enterprise" (McNay, 1995) might be an entirely different matter. Universities are not known to be places where the mere insistence of acting on one's own executive authority conferred by the law would go down well with staff or students. On the contrary, universities are by definition, principle, intellectual passion and history an exemplary locus for deliberation, communication, interaction and searching for truth or intersubjective consensus. In theory, a CEO-like position for the rector is designed so as to streamline the governance *structure* and facilitate more time-efficient and cost-effective procedures of establishing and implementing common policies and objectives. However, executive power per se does not constitute legitimacy. The challenge for a strengthened senior management lies in the task to convert structure into process, i.e., to mobilise the best resources of a university for co-ordinated and consistent action that is consonant with the institution's mission and potential.

2.3.4. Academic staff

It would be wrong to assume that higher education governance at the institutional level is merely the enactment of legal rules and formal regulations. The more one follows the pathways of decision making into the thickets of an institution, the more it becomes obvious that the formal dimensions of the governance chain are intimately intertwined with, and sometimes redirected by, informal mechanisms of influence, arbitration and agreement. The internal governance of a university is to a large measure subject to the micropolitics of protecting spheres of self-interest, searching for consensus or negotiating compromises. Here, we are moving into a territory which is the genuine domain of the academic staff and its handling of institutional matters. From the perspective of the faculty, the meaning of self-governance in higher education very much rests on the possibility to exercise its power on the day-to-day level of articulating its concerns and brokering arrangements as a way of balancing out individual purposes and institution-wide goals.

In other words: "(G)overnance in universities is a highly distributed function. (...) In universities, to a greater extent perhaps than in any other type of institution, real authority is exercised at the grass roots – by individual faculty and (in a more limited fashion) administrative staff members. Faculties, Schools and Departments are intermediate arenas in which the formal authority of the governing body, senior management, administration and academic governance must be reconciled with the informal influence of academic guilds" (Scott, 2001: 127).

For the general understanding of higher education governance this observation points to an important aspect which is often neglected in the literature: governance is the product of a *social* relationship among the actors involved and as such a formation based on discourse. The laws, rules and regulations provide the formal framework and define the structural positions for these actors to engage in an ongoing discussion about institutional policies and priorities. They are the grammar of a governance discourse but they are not giving any answers to the practical issues a university is facing. It is only in the articulation and interaction of the different parties that governance becomes a means to an end, a consistent way of collective decision making combining multifarious voices and interests.

In the 1960s and 1970s, following the call for more democracy in society generally, faculty enjoyed a comparatively large influence in institutional governance at west European universities. The emerging 'mass university' which no longer served the (self-)reproduction of a small societal elite called for a different constitution that reflected its new role as "*Hochschule in der Demokratie*" ("University within democracy", by Nitsch et al. the title of an influential essay by the Socialist German

Student Union in 1965). The immediate and obvious response to this quest for a stronger impact of universities in raising democratic awareness in society at large (often with an emphasis on radical change of the capitalist order) was to push for a sweeping democratisation of university governance at all levels, thus making higher education institutions an 'avant-garde' of social transformation. Having abolished the dominance of the senior professorate in favour of the 'group university', the power gravitated towards a complex arrangement of committees and working parties which mostly relied on the commitment of academic staff to invest time and effort in matters of self-administration. Questions pertaining to governance became the litmus test for reasserting a strong notion of university autonomy understood as a safeguard to protect higher education institutions from unwanted external influence, especially from interventions by state authorities and from corporate interests. Large segments of the academic staff saw the university as a place of social experimentation at which an ideal of self-governance through an open discourse without hierarchical domination could be observed and operationalised.

The heydays of the group university were soon followed by the sobering realisation that the translation of democracy as an overarching political concept into the organisational structure of an institution is a thorny and often imperfect one. The three major stumbling blocks were: (i) a diffusion of responsibility due to the anonymity of decision making in committees whose members often represent group interests at the expense of overall institutional concerns; (ii) an inward-looking perspective when it comes to defining the goals and objectives of the institution's core activities (teaching, learning and research); (iii) a lack of organisational efficiency in arriving at executive decisions as a result of an unwieldly complex system of self-management. To a certain extent, the burden on academic staff to manage the group university outweighed the gains in terms of self-determination which has its clear limits considering the (legal, economic, political) changes of the external conditions that affect the development and sustainability of an institution.

The changes in governance regimes that have occurred more recently did not so much come from inside the universities and were certainly not pushed by the academic staff. They are by and large the result of external imperatives challenging the universities' capacity to adapt to a new environment of heightened competition for scarce resources. The faculty for the most part reacted defensively to these changes seeing them as a potential threat to the identities of their institutions and a weakening of the autonomous space that universities have carved out for themselves (but also a threat to the traditional role of professional guilds as the legitimating factor in academic self-governance). For academic staff, the main arena of exercising influence on institutional policies has shifted to the crucial intersection between central level strategic management (rectorate, governing boards where they exist) and the decentralised units (faculties, departments) where policies must be put into operation.

The role of deans and heads of departments under governance conditions which strengthen the central steering power of the university leadership deserves special attention (and will be discussed in more detail later in Section 3.2). Traditionally,

faculties have always aspired to the greatest possible degree of autonomous decision making, so much so that from a certain standpoint it seems questionable
whether 'the' university can indeed be called upon as an organisation in an
emphatic sense of the word or whether it is more of a loose association of individual units that still have to learn to behave and act as an organisation (Pellert,
1999). In this situation, the deans are placed at the precarious interface between
centralised and decentralised modes of steering and co-ordination. The current
discussions in many countries as to whether deans ought to be managers appointed
by the top leadership of the institution (like in the US), or whether they should
continue to be "equals among equals", i.e., elected speakers of their particular
communities, reflect the dilemma. But this question cannot be answered in a
vacuum; it takes the whole picture of the arrangements and the interplay between
the state, the universities and their subunits to come to a sensitive conclusion. The
dynamics of this interaction will be reviewed later in this report.

2.3.5. Central administration

Historically, the central administration at public universities in Europe played an
important role in that it constituted the link to the state bureaucracy and thus to
the centre of power and control. For a long time, there was a co-existence and
division of labour between the top administrative positions and the academic
leadership of the university with the former being responsible for the stable and
steady long-term order of operations according to the given rules whereas the latter provided the academic legitimation and credibility of the institution though the
term of office was usually short and the level of managerial proficiency therefore
limited. Governance (in the emphatic meaning of the word) at the institutional
level played a minor role because the key decision-making powers stayed within
the competence of the state.

This situation changed quite radically with the reconceptualisation of universities
as integral parts of an emerging knowledge economy. The proliferation of new
demands and expectations posed upon HEIs with the focus on efficiency, effectiveness and quality of service as well as the introduction of more performance-
based indicators and output control to measure success instigated the emergence
of a new layer within the central administration of the university, a group of highly skilled and specialised professionals who brought with them a different
approach to managerial issues which can broadly be subsumed under the heading
of NPM. We will come back to the impact of NPM on the overall management
style of universities. For now, there is only the general observation that the position of this group within the governance structure of the university was often not
very well defined which caused at least initially some discomfort and concerns
on the part of the academic staff warning against "the increased conflict and
alienation amongst rank and file staff as institutions become more corporate-like
and managerial in orientation. The executive appears to be in danger of increasingly distancing itself from the collegial needs and philosophical outlook of most
academic staff while itself lacking confidence in the institution's peak governing
body" (Wood & Meek, 1998).

2.3.6. Students

In 2002, the Council of Europe (on behalf of the Norwegian Ministry of Education and Research) undertook a major survey on the issue of student participation in the governance of higher education. The survey was intended to provide an input to the discussions surrounding this issue within the framework of the Bologna Process which at the ministerial meeting in Prague in May 2001 had recognised students as "competent, active and constructive partners" in the establishment and shaping of the EHEA affirming that "students are full members of the higher education community" and thus "should participate in and influence the organisation and content of education at universities and other higher education institutions".

The findings of this survey revealed that in the vast majority of countries "the formal provision of student participation (...) is largely settled" (Bergan, 2004) in the sense that student representation on the governing bodies of institutions is legally guaranteed although more so on the institutional level of governance whereas such representation on the department, faculty as well as at the national level, varies considerably among the different countries. Also, the student representatives in some countries do not enjoy full voting rights as members of these bodies but are restricted to only those issues which are considered to be of immediate concern to the students. In these cases, they are excluded from voting power on issues concerning staff appointments, administrative and budgetary decisions, the granting of doctoral degrees and sometimes even from matters pertaining to curricula.

Another bone of contention is the question of political student organisations (understood as 'affiliated with a political party'). There are countries that ban such organisations from campus. Not surprisingly, these countries can mainly be found in central and eastern Europe where not so long ago "the party" and their watchmen kept tight reigns on student life. However, sanitising student involvement in university governance from student politics might in the longer term not be a feasible, or in fact a desirable answer to the question of how higher education institutions can best prepare their students for a life as active citizens in a democratic society. For one thing, political practices look for other channels through which they enter the stage of decision making at a university. But more importantly, despite the crisis of legitimacy that political parties are facing in many parts of the world, they are still one of the main instruments of active involvement in matters related to the polity. Banishing them from the university does not bode well for a future commitment of students to public affairs and in fact reinforces the perception of politics as a somewhat shady business (as well as the image of the university as a place of seclusion and retreat) (see Bergan, 2004: 25f).

The survey also showed the deplorable lack of interest that most students have with regard to participation in university governance. The low voter turnout at student elections – on average no more than one third of the student population – speaks volumes in this respect. There have been many attempts to explain this apathy, but at least in the European context there still seems to be the prevailing perception amongst students that universities are not 'their' institutions but 'belong' to the state and are ruled by the professors. "Ownership", if it exists, focuses on the immediate environment (department) and on issues of direct concern. In a 2004 survey amongst German students only 19% confirmed that they had heard about the Bologna Declaration whereas 59% saw the pending introduction of tuition fees as the most serious topic of higher education reform. (Admittedly, the results would probably not be much different if one would ask the general voting population about the relative relevance of the EU Constitution compared to the next tax increase.) There is still a long way to go from the rhetorical affirmation that students are the most important stakeholders in higher education to the reality of a broad and active participation of students on all levels of governance (department, faculty, institution and national).

There are hopeful signs that the optimistic observer would interpret as a growing empowerment of students. In the larger political arena, we have witnessed the remarkably courageous role that students played in the toppling of undemocratic regimes in Serbia, Georgia and the Ukraine. On the level of current developments in European higher education, ESIB (the National Unions of Students in Europe) has established itself as a respected partner in the discussions and a strong voice of students across Europe. Within the institutions, students sit at the table when governing bodies discuss policies and strategies (in some instances, like in Serbia, the leadership of a university even has the right to appoint a student vice-rector). The areas in which students seem to feel least listened to are the departmental and the national end of the governance chain, i.e. the domains of professorial authority and political power. This may serve as an indication as to where governance reforms which aim at a more participatory approach ought to concentrate if student involvement is the goal that it should be.

2.3.7. Stakeholder representation

More recently, the concept of "stakeholders" has entered the discussion to describe the relationship between universities and the surrounding society. Stakeholders are individuals or groups with a direct interest, involvement, or investment in the given cause, for example, the employees, customers and shareholders of a company. In the case of universities, the groups included in this notion are rather numerous and diverse, as it befits an institution with multiple goals and purposes. Apart from the students and staff as the direct stakeholders, it comprises the state (government, ministries), business, the local/regional community, private individuals, the churches, media, etc. Basically the term is used to break down the broad and indistinct notion of "the society" into more definite and clearly defined areas (following the original meaning of the word 'stake', i.e. posts or other devices that mark out, confine or fence off a piece of land around the boundary). In its current usage in the higher education policy discourse it is taken over from the business world and conveys the idea of a targeted, organised and competent approach in dealing with the various internal and external interest groups which are affected by the activities of the university.

The stakeholder concept is closely associated with the current changes in the governance structures. A lot of the accountability measures that used to be part of the state control over universities has in one way or the other devolved to stakeholders, partly in a formal sense by including stakeholder representatives in the governance of the institution (board of trustees), partly in a more indirect sense by requiring universities to demonstrate their usefulness to different types of stakeholders. In general, this concept induced higher education institutions to develop a broader understanding of the demands and expectation that various, present or potential, 'beneficiaries' might have with regard to the services that the university can provide to them, and it also introduced new points of reference in terms of external guidance and strategic objectives that the institution wants to achieve.

Given the scarcity of financial resources, it is not surprising that universities more and more define and prioritise stakeholders in economic terms which can be at odds with the public mission of the university. Providing research and development capacity to a corporate stakeholder can be a profitable undertaking for a university and it can also help to improve technological innovation or even the employment rate. But can it be justified that a private company reserves certain rights for the exploitation of research results (for example, patents) for itself in return for supporting a research laboratory at a university? The new knowledge economy poses many questions of this kind and it is through the prudent use of the available governance instruments that universities must protect their integrity while at the same time pursue their legitimate self-interests.

3. Modes and patterns of governance

University governance is commonly understood as a set of laws, regulations, structures, norms and practices that constitute the framework for an institution to pursue its goals, objectives and policies in a coherent and co-ordinated manner. As the previous chapter has shown, today, under conditions of increased complexity and uncertainty, governance is not so much a static formula which could be applied regardless of context and circumstances, but the product of an interrelation among different actors who occupy certain (more or less distinctly defined) structural positions that allow them to influence decision making according to their notion of what serves best their legitimate self-interest as well as the broader institutional purposes. In other words: governance, as opposed to mere (self-) administration, nowadays implies a dynamic concept of university autonomy – a concept that sees the meaning of autonomy in a state of flux and as constantly being shaped and reshaped by adopting or declining the various options for institutional development put forward by different constituencies and stakeholders.

The following section reviews the main (economic, ideological, pragmatic) motives underlying the changes in governance provisions in recent years from the traditional state-centered arrangements to a more decentralised and self-managed mode of planning and decision making. The focus is on the main interfaces of governance interaction where university autonomy is being articulated (verbalised/asserted and jointed/fitted together).

3.1. Government – University: ensuring legitimacy

In continental Europe, the state traditionally has a strong influence on matters related to education including higher education. The central authority of the state was manifested in the existence of rather extensive laws regulating and controlling vital aspects of university management like personnel, budget and finances, organisational structure, access to higher education or number of students per unit (department, faculty, individual universities), and leaving little room for manoeuvre in terms of specific governance arrangements and independent decision making. The extent of this regulation was reflecting both the legal status of universities as a statutory body subject to public law and their almost complete dependence on state financing.

More recently, there have been substantial changes in the way governments are discharging their public sector services to the general population prompted by the need for more efficiency and effectiveness in service provisions. In higher education, the shift from state control to state supervision which has been described earlier resulted in the devolution of authority into the hands of the top leadership of the university which was given enhanced responsibilities in particular regarding budget and personnel matters, for example, by the introduction of global or lump-sum budgets and the delegation of supervisory authority over university employees. However, the state is not simply 'giving up' its privilege of controlling the sector – in legal terms universities in most cases remained a subordinate part of the state administration – but rather is replacing the old centralised and input-oriented steering mechanisms by new modes of regulating and monitoring the sector with an emphasis on evaluation, accountability and indicator-based performance 'contracts' (*ex-post* instead of *ex-ante* control) while leaving it to the university and its subunits how to accomplish these stated objectives (Appendix 1 shows an example of a performance agreement between ministry and university).

Despite the rhetoric or reality of NPM and other approaches to enhance the organisational effectiveness (and the undeniable advantages in terms of less bureaucratic rule and a more distributed decision-making structure), this arrangement does not solve, but rather re-articulates the principal governance dilemma between the prerogative of the state to define the general goals and policy frameworks of higher education and the special institutional character of universities as autonomous actors. Governments can legitimately expect from universities to live up to certain political objectives, for example, to increase the output of graduates and ensure their employability, to contribute to the growth of the national economy or to compete on an international scale for the best students and scholars. Conversely, universities are equally right to emphasise that they are neither following political orders, nor can they readily adopt the general principles of the business sector (market, competition, profit orientation) because of the special nature of academic work with its multiplicity of purposes (education, knowledge production, dissemination and preservation, service orientation) and a certain "open-endedness" which is not compatible with the standard criteria of efficiency in the business world.

This dilemma at the interface between governments and universities is a functional one which must be addressed as a political challenge in order to stimulate the search for solutions and thus effect changes in the governance system of higher education. The example of Austria provides a suitable illustration which attracts attention beyond the national boundaries and especially in the neighbouring countries of east and south-east Europe where the process of university reform has slowed down and in some instances even has halted because the next step in the relations between state and university has been deferred.[57]

In 1993, a new University Organisation Act was passed in Austria replacing its predecessor of 1975 which was a model case of the "group university" type of governance. The new Act introduced elements of autonomy in matters of organisation and finance and laid the groundworks for the development of universities from tightly reigned state institutions to independently managed public entities. It followed the familiar reform discourse at the time pointing out that the expansion of the sector as a whole and the growing complexity of the universities made an overhaul necessary by which the individual institutions take more responsibility for their performance while in exchange the cumbersome decision-making structures of the group university were curtailed in favour of a more professional approach to strategic management involving all relevant constituencies of the university.

About half-way into the ten year implementation period for this Act, in 1998, the ministry in charge of higher education presented a discussion paper on a new law that would grant "full legal capacity" to universities. The initiative for this paper came mainly from the offices of rectors who thought that the 1993 Act fell short on a crucial element of full autonomy: the right of a university to act entirely on its own account and to allocate its budget without the existing legal and cameralistic constraints imposed by the ministry (while observing the customary procedures for public entities ensuring transparency and accountability in all financial matters). This initiative was taken up by the new centre-right government which came into office in 2000 and which, at least verbally, was intent on a far-reaching reform of the public sector by privatising state-owned enterprises, reducing state bureaucracy, downsizing the number of civil servants, abolishing obsolete regulations – in short, the standard formula of reforming the state apparatus inspired by the recipes and ideologies of the "New Economy". All the well-known catchwords of the latest reforms in public sector governance – increased efficiency, effectiveness and quality of service; decentralised management; the creation of competitive environments and the use of market instruments within the public sector organisations; flexibility and accountability for results – can also be found in the statements of the Austrian government explaining why it is necessary to initiate another reform process while the previous one has not yet been completed.

---

57. The following is in part based on an unpublished draft paper by Ute Lanzendorf and Michael Dellwing (University of Kassel, Germany) on *Changes in public research governance in Austria* (2004) written within the framework of a larger research project on "International competitiveness and innovation capacity of universities and research organisations: New forms of governance; Sub-project: Management and self-management of universities – comparison of decision-making processes and consequences for research".

Interestingly, a special emphasis was put on the aspect of international competitiveness. The new government took pride to stress whenever possible that it is (or strives to be) a 'model disciple' (*Musterschüler*) within Europe (maybe as an overcompensation after the sanctions of the EU countries against the new government), and the University Organisation and Studies Act which was passed by the education and science minister in 2002 was proclaimed to do just this: to advance Austria to the top of governance reforms in higher education in Europe.

The changes that this Act introduced merit indeed the term 'radical': Apart from (and complementary to) full legal capacity universities were granted global budgets, organisational autonomy, new employment regulations for academic staff (no civil service status any more for newly employed staff) and clearance for a debureaucratisation of the university administration. In exchange for endowing the university leadership with a whole set of new governance tools and with the executive power to use them, universities were expected to agree to a corresponding set of accountability measures, namely performance contracts over several years, regular evaluations, the definition of a distinct profile by each university, more competition among universities for public funds, and the introduction of boards of trustees (University Council/*Universitätsrat*). In order to underscore its stern determination to open an entirely new chapter in the history of Austrian higher education, and to fill the strapped coffer of the education ministry with money to finance the reform, tuition fees of about €725 annually were introduced virtually overnight in late 2001.

The transformation of Austrian higher education which was heralded by the 2002 University Act seems like taken from a textbook of the NPM persuasion. Its two corner pillars are: on the one hand, decentralisation of tasks, decision-making power and responsibilities up to the point where administrative units are being outsourced and given an independent legal status; on the other hand, retaining of steering capacity over the sector in the hands of those who are politically in charge by means of agreed-upon performance indicators and output contracts. After all, even after the transformation it is still meant to be a *public* management and not a sellout of the state (cf. Zechlin, 2002).

With regard to the government/university interface it is almost ironic that in the case of Austria, a country with a tradition of strong external regulation and state intervention into university governance, the deregulation is imposed 'from above', almost like a *coup d'état*, through strict state regulations (cf. de Boer, Enders & Schimank: 13). This is another indication for the ambiguity that was described earlier: in higher education systems that undergo similar changes like in Austria after they have been moulded for generations by governmental control (which is true for most continental European systems including the countries that liberated themselves from communism only some fifteen years ago) the meanings of autonomy are relative and multifarious and it is often difficult to draw a clear line of distinction between political intervention, strategic steering and operative management (see Felt, 2003: 38ff). It would be a gross simplification to understand governments only as the external force of coercion whereas the universities are populated by the champions of autonomy. One is tempted to quote Foucault:

> The contact point, where the individuals are driven by others is tied to the way they conduct themselves, and this is what we can call, I think, government. Governing people, in the broad meaning of the word, is not a way to force people to do what the governor wants; it is always a versatile equilibrium, with complementarity and conflicts between techniques which assure coercion and process through which the self is constructed or modified by himself (Foucault, 2004).

For very good reasons, universities have been described as slowly developing systems (see Daxner, 1999). Rapid changes in the exterior environment can take long before they become part of the fabric of an institution which is not always a sign for a lack of adaptability but can also reflect "how the different political traditions and histories have an impact on the way university-State relations are shaped" (Felt, 2003: 38).

In the case of Austria, the history and tradition is characterised by a very strong, even a dominant role of the state administration on the one hand, and a certain laissez-faire (sometimes also referred to as "organised anarchy") in terms of the internal governance process on the other hand. The "contact point" where, according to Foucault, government manifests itself (and where also system-level governance and institutional-level governance intersect) was thus fairly loose because the organisational goals were often ambiguous or uncertain. This created the impression of the university as an autonomous space almost regardless of the very real dependences in terms of the legal status of the institution (which in effect were departments of the ministry), the strict appointment and employment regulations, let alone the complete economic reliance on state support. For academic staff, the meaning of autonomy was almost synonymous with "a high degree of discretion over the tasks they perform" (Scott, 2001: 132) and the possibility to pursue their individual aspirations. The consequence for governance (not only in Austria) was the "legitimization of a division of labor" (ibid.) whereby state regulation and micromanagement in administrative matters was taken for granted and the organisation of academic affairs became the subject of negotiation and bargaining in committee or senate meetings. The understanding of autonomy and governance on which this system was built was largely inward-looking, apolitical and insular which is probably why it enjoyed popularity under the most dissimilar political regimes including undemocratic ones.

Therefore, the extent of the transformation that the Austrian higher education system experienced within a short time span of only a bit more than one decade cannot be underestimated. On a formal level, this is evidenced by the fact that all Austrian universities were required to undergo a process of legal reconstitution in order to start the implementation of the 2002 University Act (i.e., the regulations to deregulate the sector). Apart from an abundance of changes and adjustments in the internal organisation of the university at all levels which came along with the new legal status as a public (quasi-)corporation, the key transaction that took place at the state/university interface was the introduction of a new 'currency' to ensure the legitimacy of university operations. Whereas in the past the state as a sovereign power and legal 'owner' of the institution guaranteed due process and quality, this responsibility has now been delegated to a variety of actors, notably to the board of trustees, the top leadership of the institution, but also to agencies and processes that serve as independent supervisory sources of accountability and thus legitimacy like national accreditation agencies, quality assurance mechanisms, performance contracts, funding councils, intermediary bodies (the newly established Austrian Science Council). In other words: parallel to the diversification of revenue sources as a means to ensure financial viability, universities now also have to master the diversification of sources of legitimacy which becomes a main management task and requires a cadre of highly skilled specialists within the institutional administration as well as the investment of a not inconsiderable amount of resources (time, money). A new governance equilibrium is on the horizon, certainly a new way of establishing "legitimacy through process" (Luhmann, 2001), though not necessarily a less intricate and bureaucratic one compared to the past, as is shown by the example in some countries like the UK which started this process earlier.

Considering these far-reaching changes in Austria, one of the interesting questions is: what happens to the state as the former prime source of legitimacy? In an article by Lothar Zechlin (2002) provocatively titled "No public management. Austrian politics bows out of strategic steering of its universities" the author contends that the political and administrative ranks are utterly unprepared to assume their new role of providing sound and consistent guidance and strategic orientation regarding the longer-term goals and directions in national higher education and science policies. Instead, they seem to concentrate their expectations regarding the positive impact of the reform on the "How" (the enhancement of efficiency and effectiveness by virtue of applying an NPM approach) while leaving it to the newly established university councils to voice the demands and viewpoints of the external environment as far as the "What" is concerned, i.e. the definition of the goals and objectives of a given institution. This, however, shifts the responsibility for the public policy dimension of governance away from the respective government branches which are accountable to the parliament, into the hands of the 'external experts' in the university councils who perform the controlling and steering function and are not accountable to anybody except their own best judgment (in Austria, half of the founding members of the councils were nominated by the senate, the other half by the federal ministry).

For Zechlin, this withdrawal of the state from the strategic steering of universities creates a dangerous void which is filled by private – in the sense of not publicly answerable – interests. If one looks at the composition of the university councils his criticism seems warranted: from a total of roughly 140 members of Austrian university councils close to 40 % were recruited from the business sector and about 30% from the broader university sector; the rest mainly have a civil service background whereas there is only very scarce representation of social interest groups, cultural or religious areas (see Laske & Meister-Scheytt, 2004). There was also some debate about political clientelism and patronage during the first round of appointments adding to the concerns of those who worry about a 'creeping privatisation' of Austrian universities.

Only time will tell whether these concerns are justified. Countries which have more experience in involving lay participation in the governance of an institution can perhaps offer advice how to meet such uneasiness. The UK may again serve as an example where recently a comprehensive compendium for governors was published by the Committee of University Chairmen (*Guide for Members of Higher Education Governing Bodies in the UK. Governance Code of Practice and General Principles*, 2004) spelling out in unambiguous terms what are the written and unwritten rules of conduct for members of such bodies.

The case of Austria shows that the interface between government and universities remains a contested territory of higher education governance, especially in those countries where a tradition of strong state control intersects with the latest adoption of private sector management concepts to public sector institutions. It would be too easy to accuse universities of inertia in emulating these concepts more readily and in a proactive manner. Unlike other public institutions it is an inherent characteristic of universities that they govern themselves for a very urgent purpose which is directly related to the fundamental mission of the institution: allowing the mind to explore its limits, examining and critiquing the common wisdom and the inherited truths, accepting no other authority than the power of reasoning. The conditions under which universities carry out their mission have changed quite dramatically in recent times. But governments would be well advised not to question the value of strong and inclusive self-governance at public universities by pushing them to adopt means that are unfitting for their purpose.

3.2. Management – academic self-governance: negotiating effectiveness

In many countries, legislative changes during the past decade or so have led to a reorganisation of universities which by and large follows the rhetoric and the prescription of the new European paradigm of the 'entrepreneurial university' (Clark, 1998) which includes: diversified funding base; strengthened steering core; expanded developmental periphery; stimulated academic heartland; and integrated entrepreneurial culture. The first wave of these changes mainly affected the central level of the institution and focused on the broadening and strengthening of the power and authority of top management. Within certain parameters, it was then left to the institutions themselves how to adapt their internal academic structure and governance to live up to this entrepreneurial spirit. Thus, the interface between the central node of steering and the decentralised units has become the scene of lively encounter between different interpretations of the new governance model.

In Sweden, for example, a comprehensive deregulation was introduced some time ago and many tasks and responsibilities were turned over from the government to the universities (Nickel, 2004). Within the institution, this brought about a significant shift in the relation between central level administration (rectorate, board of trustees) and the decentral units (faculties, institutes, schools). "The spontaneous interpretation among the majority of academic staff members to the decentralisation was that the devolution of authority to the institutions was to be followed by a similar devolution within the institutions" (Askling, 2003: 166). As a consequence, the faculties acquired more independence. Each unit got its own administration and deans occasionally took over tasks that traditionally fell under the authority of the rectorate. Parallel to the strengthening of the decentral level, however, the power of the rectorate and the board of trustees was also expanded. The result was "a federal model of institutional governance" (Askling, 2003: 167), though the balance of power was very unstable and frictions in the relation between deans and rectorates grew: Who actually has a say about what, and who is to listen?

Another sticking point is the question of which size and composition of the subunits is befitting to an entrepreneurial type of university. Some universities have drastically reduced the number of faculties and established larger conglomerates of departments arguing that this kind of pooling facilitates interdisciplinary or even transdisciplinary co-operation and creates synergies which will stimulate both the production of new knowledge and the adaptation of existing knowledge to solving practical problems. Other universities took the opposite view and expanded the number of units considerably explaining that smaller groups are more nimble and flexible, easier to manage and control, and therefore more likely to maximise their performance.

Equally inconclusive is the current debate about the adequate role of the deans. Should they be elected or appointed 'from above' (by the rector as the CEO of the university)? Do they act as a temporary 'first among equals' or are they faculty managers endowed with executive power in the allocation of resources or in personnel matters? Traditionally the dean has been in a co-ordinating role representing the specific interests of the faculty vis-à-vis the university community as a whole, a role which offers only limited room for manoeuvre of his/her own because all decisions require consensual agreement by the faculty peers. New steering tools like performance agreements between the rectorate and the faculties now enable the university centre to directly influence the work programme and the resource base of the organisational units and hold the deans accountable to the rector's office which potentially erodes the collegial style of self-governance at faculty level.

Another example of a difficult relationship between centre and constituent units: in some countries in south-east Europe academic faculties are still enjoying legal independence as an inheritance of an older and in many respects outdated governance system. The universities are literally a confederation of sovereign entities governed by the principle of non-interference in internal affairs, not unlike most international organisations and alliances among nation states. Faculties have their own budget, income and bank account, enroll their own students, employ their own staff, design their own study programmes and curricula, and manage their own matters. In the countries that belonged to the former Yugoslavia, this arrangement was introduced as part of the general political and constitutional system of worker self-administration in all spheres of social and economic life which some observers interpreted as a deliberate weakening of central control in favour of more democracy from below, whereas others saw it as a strategy of *divide et impera* from above.

The legal independence of faculties was also a transitory, though very indicative phenomenon in other countries of central and eastern Europe, like in the Czech Republic and in Slovakia, right after the collapse of communism when new higher education laws were passed that sought to foster academic freedom by freeing faculties from direct university control which in the past was synonymous with the firm grip of state centralisation. But it soon became apparent that the division of faculty and management had a dysfunctional effect on the development of the universities as a whole and caused serious disparities among the faculties. Needless to say that the power vacuum in the centre limited the possibilities of rectors and their teams to influence, let alone steer the comprehensive reforms that were needed to adapt their institutions to the rapidly changing external environment. Their only tool was the power of words and of the better argument which more often than not was met with scepticism and refusal by the group of sovereign deans protecting what they saw as being in the best interest of their faculties. It was the pressure from the outside that helped change the legal framework in some countries – governments keen to improve the effectiveness of their higher education system, but also the Bologna Process which requires a more integral approach to institutional governance; other countries, however, are still struggling with the anomaly of the legal independence of faculties.[58]

The examples show that the nexus between central level and subunits is crucial to the larger question of where the university is heading as an institution. It is here where governance as a set of formal rules and procedures encounters the different "governmentalities" which are ingrained in the academic cultures and which go together with certain characteristic habits, attitudes and behaviours. The following diagram gives a schematic overview of the most common (historical, systematic) approaches to academic staff participation in the governance process as they are described in the relevant literature. They are, of course, an abstraction – university governance is always multidimensional and never just a monoculture.

---

58. More as a side remark it should be mentioned that the two leading universities in Europe, Oxford and Cambridge, also adhere to a highly decentralised governance model which is rooted in the old college system. Most observers think that these universities are able to preserve their world-class status not so much because, but despite this traditional model of institutional governance. As a recent article in *The Economist* shows, this model is currently being challenged: "If YOU were starting to build a world-class university from scratch, you probably would not choose Oxford as your model. The university is essentially a collection of medieval monasteries run like a workers' co-operative. It includes 39 colleges of wildly different size, wealth and quality. Each operates independently, sometimes extravagantly so. Most dons, as Oxford and Cambridge academics are called, are paid partly by colleges and partly by the university. Colleges and academic departments work in parallel. Management is by committee. Ultimate power rests with a dons' parliament, the 3 552-member Congregation. Picturesque relics of English history are more fun to observe than to run, as John Hood, who took over in October as Oxford's vice-chancellor, has discovered. Decision-making at Oxford is piecemeal and takes ages. Although some teaching and research is awesomely good, quite a lot isn't. Some of the colleges are massively rich, some virtually bankrupt. Oxford is still the fifth-best university in the world, according to one recent study, and the eighth according to another, but Mr Hood believes that unless the way it is managed changes, it will slide down the rankings. The government has also been urging Oxford (and Cambridge, which has a similar structure) to modernise. Mr Hood's two big proposals have each sparked big rows. The first is to centralise decision making. A board of external trustees would set the university's overall budget; under them would be a single management body in which the heads of colleges would be in a minority. The second is to change the way in which dons' work is managed. The colleges, which do most of the teaching, assess their dons one way. Departments, where most of the research happens, have another. Both systems are informal and patchy. Good results rarely mean higher pay, nor do bad ones tend to hurt. Mr Hood wants to link pay and performance. Outside Oxford, these changes might seem mild and sensible, but things look different from inside the university. Opposition to Mr Hood's first proposal has been huge." ("Britain's oldest university wrestles with modernization", *The Economist*, 19 May 2005.)

```
                    High    Academic staff
                     |      participation
                     |      in management
                     |
         Collegial   |   Entrepreneurial
                     |
 Low ————————————————+———————————————————— High
                     |
         Bureaucratic|   Managerial
                     |
Professional         |
autonomy             |
of academics         |
                    Low
```

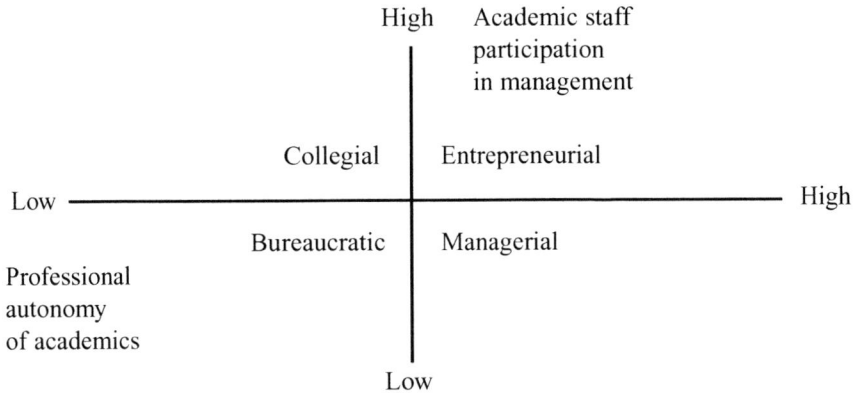

Models of university management (Farnham, 1999: 18)

As the literature also shows, the managerial/entrepreneurial turn in higher education has divided the academic community in two camps whereby not surprisingly the advocates often hold positions within the central unit of the university and the critics raise their concerns from the vantage point of the subunits. Both sides argue about the desirable or undesirable impact that this turn has on the organisational structure of the institution. But as an astute analyst of these structures remarks: "It is indeed difficult to address the university as an organisation because strictly speaking the university does not exist; it rather is a loose association of individual institutes and still has to learn to recognise itself as an organisation" (Pellert, 1999: 71 – my translation, J.F.).

Against the background of the time-honoured relative autonomy of the decentralised units, the shift towards a central steering authority at the top in the interest of the university as a whole (or "as an organisation") is prompting counterreactions as one would expect in other types of organisations as well. However, in universities these reactions are of a more fundamental nature since they raise the question as to what degree, if at all, scholarly production can be subject to steering, or whether it is, as has often been said, something that defies planning and calculation. While this may be a merely philosophical question, it is true that at least as far as research and development are concerned, increases in productivity cannot simply be ordered from above. The new steering instruments can help to create favourable conditions but it is ultimately the individual scholar or the team of scholars who succeed or fail. And not only this: professors and other staff are also protected against 'outside interference' in the content aspects of their teaching and research by the legal guarantee of academic freedom. All of this relativises the notion of a central steering authority.

This may sound trivial but it has implications for the new kind of executive power of the top university leadership and its 'will to manage'. Since it is responsible for the overall performance of the institution, it must strive to extend its influence into the subunits. The leverage of doing so, however, is limited because the character and the quality of work in knowledge and expert organisations is to a large degree a matter of personal commitment and self-interest on the part of the staff involved which is why universities traditionally are characterised by flat hierarchies, strong decentralised units (disciplines, departments and faculties) and a comparatively weak tip of the organisation (Nickel, 2004: 95). In an environment like this, it would be illusionary to assume that top-down management models from the business sector can be simply replicated. The formal decision-making power of the university leadership will effect to little or nothing unless the faculties and departments 'buy in' and are won over by the strategies and policies that are put forward from the top and that hold some realistic promise for a positive development of the institution or for financial incentives to the subunit.

Knowledge-based and knowledge-producing companies are a popular object of study in organisation theory. They show some interesting characteristics with regard to their most productive and valuable employees which distinguish them from conventional enterprises. These employees are what could be called 'Mode 2' knowledge workers who are highly self-motivated, allergic to formal hierarchies and control, independent thinkers, versatile team workers and adaptable to changing tasks and work pressures entailing flexible work time arrangements. Because of their hybrid profile as employees with an entrepreneurial mind-set and attitude they have been dubbed "intrapreneur". As Sigrun Nickel (2004) aptly observes, this new type of knowledge worker is a familiar presence among academic staff – individuals who have chosen to work in academia because it not only suits their drive for knowledge and their desire for intellectual independence, but who also are attracted to the institutional and organisational environment which at least in principle is conducive to knowledge intrapreneurship for the public good.

Through the centuries, universities developed an organisational matrix which shows many features of what is today known as network organisation: semi-autonomous and loosely coupled units with permeable borders to allow for inter-action, exchange and cross-fertilisation, and with lateral links and connections like a rhizome. The growth and reconfiguration of these units is a result of the functional differentiation of knowledge areas which in turn reflects the enormous proliferation of knowledge itself that we experience as a defining quality of our societies. Network organisations provide space for complexity, i.e. for growth by way of differentiation, without the need to restructure the entire architecture of the system in order to create this space. The integration into the system follows the horizontal lines of interlinking through discourse, shared professional interests and mutually beneficial co-operation, and not through vertical (hierarchical) addition to a predetermined order. The key advantage of loosely coupled systems (Weick, 1976) for an organisation such as the university lies in its fault tolerance. The lack of adequate performance or the failure of one semi-independent unit does not debilitate the entire system. For the survival of an institution whose inner logic of knowledge expansion is built on the criterion of falsifiability, and which constantly must adapt its operations to changing external environments, fault tolerance and the provision of space for independent work is absolutely vital.

Accordingly, governance structures at the interface between university centre and subunits must be supportive of the self-steering capacity of faculties, departments, schools, research groups and projects. The challenges to network governance are considerable, perhaps comparable to the art of conducting an orchestra playing a symphony *in status nascendi*. The new executive power that is put into the hands of the top management of an entrepreneurial university must be prudently used to create the conditions and to define the rules under which network units and intrapreneurs can excel, and unproductive or non-adaptable units can fail. Lateral steering which supports the evolution of transparent mechanisms of self-control and accountability is consistent with the dynamics of knowledge expansion whereas a top-down governance approach will inevitably increase the tension between centralisation and decentralisation.

3.3. University – civil society: demonstrating relevance and responsiveness

In Europe, the relationship between universities and the surrounding society has never been a smooth and easy one. In part, this has to do with the fact that for the longest time universities have been instruments for the self-reproduction of social elites and were thus somewhat distant to the broader concerns of society. Another reason is the traditional dominance of the state as the custodian, sponsor and legal 'owner' of higher education institutions including the power to make use of universities as vehicles of government determined priorities which are not necessarily congruent with those of society. Two forces had a counterbalancing effect: the advent of mass democracy and of steadily growing access to higher education of less privileged segments of the population ('massification') on the one hand, and the more recent retreat of the state from direct control and intervention resulting in more freedom for universities to determine their future and to establish their own priorities on the other hand. Have these developments opened the door for universities in a way that they are now more susceptible and responsive to engage with society instead of serving state or class interest?

Questions like this one have fueled many ideological debates in past years and decades. They are, by and large, of a theoretical or normative nature for as long as they refer to an abstract model of the purpose of higher education rather than to the policies and practices which are guiding the actual activities of universities with regard to teaching, research and service to the community. If universities are to foster the values of democratic citizenship and the commitment to social development and justice, their first measure of achievement must be how they incorporate these goals into the fabric of the institution.

In Europe, the most common way of articulating engagement including active involvement in larger societal concerns is through the participation of the various constituencies in university governance (which is different from the USA where the notion and the practice of democratic citizenship on campus and outside is more based on a communitarian tradition – see the Council of Europe's pilot project on "The university as site of citizenship" and especially the articles by Plantan 2004 and Daxner 2005). The main focus here is on participative management (*Mitbestimmung*) and on internal democratisation. The university is seen as belonging to the public sphere and its 'inhabitants' are asserting their rights as citizens by claiming their voices to be heard in collective decision making. The modes and modalities by which the principle of participative management is employed differ considerably from country to country.

Germany, for example, has a highly formalised system of involvement in decision making which still bears the marks of the group university and its rather intricate structures and procedures of shared governance. In this particular case the group university can be historically interpreted as a reaction against the anti-democratic stance of the old oligarchic *Ordinarienuniversität* ('university of the full-professors') which claimed a Humboldtian type of institutional autonomy for itself showing no intention of protecting the democracy of the Weimar Republic of the 1920s, or at least of mobilising more resistance, against the assault on political and academic freedoms by the totalitarian Nazi regime. The lessons that were drawn from this experience in the late 1960s indicate a deeply sceptical position towards formal autonomy as an excuse for political inactivity guised as 'neutrality', academic 'impartiality' or intellectual superiority over those who blindly follow deceitful ideologies. Therefore, the impetus for demanding participatory management in German universities was to a high degree politically motivated as a means of controlling institutional power and strengthening the democratic foundations and vibrancy of the institution. This concern articulated itself in three major objectives (Daxner, 2005): the demand to grant a "political mandate" to the university, i.e. to those involved in university governance and representing the various groups within the institution (meaning that self-governance is not strictly limited to self-management but implies a fundamental responsibility to promote civic engagement at all levels of society); the legal and statutory inclusion of the student group in university governance; and the hope and expectation to contribute to the democratic advancement of society by taking the criterion of 'soci(et)al relevance' as the ultimate measure of accountability for what is taught and researched at universities (and what professors have to substantiate).

The fate of the emphatically democratic reform movement of the late 1960s is well known: it got more or less bogged down in the day-to-day routine of university administration and in struggling to solve the equation between constantly growing student numbers, and the relative decline of financial resources to address this growth, i.e. the efficiency equation which led to the more market-driven approach to higher education including its definition of socio-economic relevance and responsiveness.

But the German experience offers some interesting analogies to the post-1989 situation in the countries of eastern Europe after the fall of communism. On the whole, universities did not play a very prominent role in the toppling of the old political system although many of the activists of the peaceful revolutions belonged to the academia and the first democratically elected governments included an extraordinary high proportion of scholars. It also seems fair to say that during the first fifteen years of transformation the universities in east and south-east Europe were not seen as a driving force of democratisation, or only in an indirect sense in that they educate the future generation of managers, politicians or civil servants who will be in positions of responsibility. Beyond their immediate concerns – teaching and research – universities were generally reluctant to adopt a more proactive role in the public arena[59] and preferred a position of 'neutrality' (for example, by barring political student organisations from campus, see Section 2.3.6). This is not to deny that these universities have undergone extensive reforms and demonstrated a remarkable degree of adaptability to the changing external (political, economic, social) conditions. But what seems missing, at least to the outside observer, is a more fundamental consideration of the social and civic responsibilities of the university including a discussion of the role that universities have played in the past as an integral part of an undemocratic system – not so much as a way of reckoning with individual misconduct or misuse of power but as a reaffirmation of academic integrity after decades of ideological heteronomy. Failing to do so can give rise to the suspicion that universities are willing to serve many masters – a suspicion that in fact was one of the factors that prompted the student movement of the mid- to late 1960s and that could at some point provoke a similar reaction in eastern and south-eastern Europe. The developments in Serbia, Georgia and the Ukraine where students were in the frontline of the successful removal of oppressive political regimes are a promising sign that universities are fertile grounds for strong and spirited democratic forces and for active citizenship, even if as institutions they have remained under strict government control.

Today, the debate about the contribution of higher education and research to "society at large", not only in Europe, focuses mainly on the stakeholder concept with a strong emphasis on the economy and industry. There are a number of forceful steering devices that are pushing universities in this direction: collaboration between university and industry researchers is a precondition for many of the EU-funded programmes, and the same is true on the national level; governments use the degree and the intensity of co-operation with industry as an indicator for the evaluation of university activities (and as a criterion for the allocation of financial resources); private companies are encouraged, for example, through tax incentives, to invest in partnerships with higher education institutions by setting up joint units or institutes; along the same lines, university researchers can get special funds to establish start-up companies or to have patents registered that promise profit both for the researcher and the university; close ties to the business sector also serve as a motivation to attract the best or the most solvent students to a university.

The economic paradigm combined with the forces of competition play an increasingly dominant part in the steering of universities and in the way they are accounting for their contribution to the advancement of the larger society. Since knowledge and knowledge-related technologies are an essential asset in almost every area of working-life, universities have become universally important and a "much larger group of users is now making claims on them" (Marginson & Considine, 2000: 8). For many, the "enterprise university" (ibid.) represents the future, whereas others perceive the 'corporatisation' and the commodification of knowledge

---

59. With some notable exceptions like the Babes-Bolyai University in Cluj-Napoca, Romania, with its study programmes in three languages which serves as a place of integration of the three main ethnic groups in the region.

as a serious narrowing of the scope of interaction between the university and society and thus of the identity of the university. It is a genuine task for the governance of an institution to address these concerns because governance mediates the expanding relationships between the 'internal' and the 'external' dimensions including those with business and industry. By doing so, it also shapes and re-shapes the values that an institution is adhering to or that it chooses to embrace. These values have been put to the test by the stakeholder concept.

Michael Daxner (2005) compares what he calls the "stakeholder ideology" with the broader and more comprehensive notion of "ownership" which has wide currency especially in the United States to characterise the interrelation between universities or colleges and the public. Ownership as a general principle in public policy matters has its roots in liberal and communitarian thoughts and theories and has a definite devolutionary and state-sceptical stance. An ownership society values responsibility, liberty, and property instead of dependence from government handouts and tutelage by state authorities. Thus, making individuals 'owners' means empowering them to be in control of their own lives and destinies. In the ownership society, patients control their own health care, parents control their own children's education, and workers control their retirement savings. It is obvious that these ideas have far-reaching implications for the governance of public institutions including those in higher education.

According to Daxner, ownership is based on a reciprocal understanding of belonging: 'something belongs to me' and 'I belong to something' are closely interwoven. The participatory ownership rights that are granted to me by belonging to a community (for example, a university) and sharing its values and assets correspond to my responsibilities to sustain and nourish this community or institution through commitment and active involvement. The reciprocity creates a social bond which connects those involved and constitutes a public space. In the case of universities and colleges, this implies a strong osmosis and permeability of the institution and its environment as it is confirmed by the influence of lay boards of trustees, the vigour of alumni organisations and the lifelong commitment of alumni to 'their' Alma Mater, but also by the emphasis on community service and service learning as an integral and central part of the mission of the institution and the curricula.

Ownership is thus closely related to the desire to belong to something that is seen as undeniably important and has a broad public appeal. But it also entails the intention of being actively involved in the shaping of the institution like an 'owner', instead of being just a passive part of it. Universities are thus public institutions in the sense that they are *res publica* – a matter that citizens take care of in their own capacity: a domain of republican rights and responsibilities (and this notion of 'public' of course also applies to private higher education institutions).

With regard to governance issues, ownership stresses more the communal aspects (to be part of a whole) and the character of the institution as a free association of equal-minded individuals who share similar values. In contrast, the stakeholder concept that is so prevalent in European higher education, emphasises the functional dimension: stakeholders are linked to a university in so far as it serves their specific interests whereby this link is not necessarily seen as a commitment to the values and the integrity of the institution but as an entitlement based on one's own status as citizen and/or taxpayer of the respective country. Under conditions of increased complexity and proliferation of tasks and demands, a functional approach to governance and the 'management of interests' which are often competing, or even conflicting, seems unavoidable. However, universities also occupy a very distinct place in society by providing a public space for free inquiry and the development of minds not only within their community of students and professors, but also beyond the campus. For a mass democracy in which the participation in public affairs is a critical issue and the feeling of alienation from power is widely spread, the cultivation of a republican spirit of governance, of being a *citoyen(ne)* and 'belonging to' a community that shares equal values is of vital importance. Governance is the core aspect in the way universities relate to their environment and whether they want to have a stake in democracy, or rather be efficient suppliers for the global knowledge economy. Both objectives are not mutually exclusive. But they also are not easy to combine.

4. Good governance in higher education

One of the difficulties of writing about higher education governance that many authors attest lies in a tendency to take it as an all-encompassing notion, a kind of master code that manifests itself in every aspect of university life. The following longer quote may serve as an example:

> Governance occupies the pivotal position between the inner world (or worlds) of the university, and its larger environment. Not everything in higher education can be explained by governance, or is contained in its practices, but when we are talking about *institutions* of higher education, then governance is always present. Governance is concerned with the determination of value inside universities, their systems of decision-making and resource allocation, their mission and purposes, the patterns of authority and hierarchy, and the relationships of universities as institutions to the different academic worlds within and the worlds of government, business and community without. It embraces "leadership", "management" and "strategy". Governance affects specialized administrative activities such as fund-raising, financial planning or industrial relations (…). Governance does not contain in itself the sum of teaching and research, but it affects them. It provides the conditions which enable teaching and research to take place. (Marginson & Considine, 2000: 7)

Not surprisingly, the authors reach the apex of their pan-institutional governance perspective by locating the concept at the very heart of what defines a given university: "Governance is where the identity of each university as a distinctive social and cultural institution is shaped" (ibid., 8f).

Such an all-pervasive notion of governance makes it difficult to break it down and examine the workings of the system in order to understand, re-arrange or fix it. If governance is (the condition for or impacting) everything, how can something be said or done about it without taking an external point of reference? In other words: from a purely functionalist point of view all governance provisions make sense or can be justified for as long as they establish a consistent (regulatory, administrative, managerial, strategic) context of steering an institution. Thus, the same governance model can serve different purposes, norms and values, just like the same economic model can either be said to promote more welfare for as many as possible, or more profit for a small minority. This does not deny that there are certain governance principles and arrangements which lean towards a more participatory culture and a bottom-up approach in decision making within the individual institution or the higher education system as a whole, whereas other organisational arrangements may reinforce a more heavy-handed executive approach or an autocratic leadership style. But it is the primacy of values over procedures that allows us to distinguish between "good governance" and its opposite.

Our understanding of good governance can therefore not be limited to the merely functional aspects of ensuring the adequate institutional conditions for efficient and effective decision making and problem solving. The qualitative or normative dimension of governance links it to the values which are the underpinning for higher education and research, as it has evolved historically, and which the actors are subscribing to as the defining characteristics of their work. Good governance translates these values into a set of cohesive institutional structures and practices.

These values are first and foremost related to the integrity of the university as a place of disinterested scholarship, learning and intellectual instruction, as they are embodied in the principles of academic freedom and institutional autonomy. They were traditionally conceived as the pillars supporting the academic system as "a discrete sub-system of society, which in important respects could be distinguished (and, therefore, was insulated) from other sub-systems, notably the market and politics. In this general sense, the university was regarded as an autonomous space, regardless of detailed constitutional, legal and administrative arrangements" (Scott, 2001: 130). As has been discussed earlier, governance in its contemporary understanding is synonymous with a re-orientation of universities away from an inward-looking perspective of a self-contained autonomous system to emphasise the 'embeddedness' of higher education and research into its environments (social, political, economic, cultural). It thus becomes "the key brokerage mechanism between the university and its stake-holder, partners and rivals" (ibid.). Good governance strives to preserve the integrity of the academic value system while at the same time it 'positions' the university vis-à-vis these competing spheres of interest to make it receptive, and answerable, to external messages, demands and expectations.

Accountability towards broader societal needs and concerns which is a major issue in the present governance debate underscores the growing importance of engaging with the public rather than defining university autonomy negatively as the absence from 'outside interference'. In this respect governance becomes the conduit for expanding the mission of the university by including more intentionally a dimension which ranges prominently in US higher education and which is captured in the notion of service as the third key component of academic work next to teaching and research.

In the European context, the term 'service' may not be as popular as in the United States to describe the contribution of higher education institutions to further larger concerns of the society (perhaps because for many academics it sounds somewhat demeaning of the independent value of scholarly work). But the pressure on universities to demonstrate their utility with regard to such concerns has of course been in existence for many years, and the changes in governance structures were largely driven precisely by the aspiration to make higher education more responsive and adaptable to external needs and demands. In Europe, the predominant rhetoric refers to the economic aspects of knowledge production (job creation, employability, industrial innovation, strengthening competitiveness of the local economy on the global marketplace, Lisbon Agenda, etc., to name but a few of the standard catchwords) whereas in American higher education the term 'service' is more often connected to 'softer' issues, especially to participation in community life and reaching out to diverse communities that form the social environment of the institution.

In what way do these political agendas influence questions of governance and, more pointedly, of "good" governance? In reviewing the pertinent literature on this topic, the answer becomes obvious: even when there is almost unanimous agreement regarding the need for ongoing higher education reform both at institutional and system level, views differ greatly when it comes to governance issues (irrespective of whether the term is used or not). There is a growing disenchantment with what is seen as the self-referential discourse of managerialism advocating efficiency, excellence, cost reduction, output indicators, performance/quality control, etc., but being unable to explain the rationale for streamlining the organisation in other than crude economic terms. These managers are (mis?)perceived as having forgotten the fundamental truth that governance is a means to an end and that the discussion about the end(s), i.e. the purpose of higher education, must precede the decisions about the means to pursue these.

Considering the multiplicity of conflicting objectives and the very real dilemmas that university leaderships are facing in aiming at moving targets, such misgivings might be undeserved. But they point to a shortcoming that apparently has its roots in an overemphasis on the management of change in universities during the past ten to fifteen years at the expense of a more consequential discussion about different governance cultures and what it is that defines the quality of governance relative to the purpose(s) of higher education. In the light of this, the scepticism (and occasionally even resentment) that the more outspoken supporters of NPM are facing at their campuses, might in fact not be a bad thing. It could serve as a catalyst for a very timely and relevant discussion on the topic of new public governance that takes account of the more fundamental political questions of what (higher) education in the public domain should be standing for (and what are the appropriate instruments for converting value-based policies into coherent institutional operations).

This discussion has in fact already started as the Council of Europe's programmatic focus on the "European Year of Citizenship through Education" (EYCE) in 2005 shows. Much of the literature on this approach to higher education governance still needs to be written. In doing so, it will be important to combine the lessons learnt in being more professional and proactive in terms of institutional self-management with the emphasis on the qualitative notion of (good) governance. In this way, university governance would indeed be the juncture where the distinctive social and cultural identity of each institution is shaped (Marginson & Considine, 2000: 8f) as a result of the complex interconnectedness with the communities that make up the university both within and beyond the boundaries of the institution.

References

Altbach, P.G., Gumport, P.J. & Johnstone, D.B. (eds.), *In defense of higher education*, The Johns Hopkins University Press, Baltimore, 2001.

Amaral, A., Jones, G.A. & Karseth, B. (eds.), *Governing higher education: National perspectives on institutional governance*, Kluwer Academic Publishers, Dortrecht/Boston/London, 2002.

Askling, B., "Deanship in transition. Amateurism and professionalism, collegiality and managerialism, empowerment and marginalisation" in Mayer, E., Daniel, H.-D. & Teichler, U. (eds.), *Die neue Verantwortung der Hochschulen*, Bonn, 2003: 166-168.

Association of Governing Boards of Universities and Colleges, "Renewing the academic presidency: Stronger leadership for tougher times", Commission on the Academic Presidency, Association of governing boards of universities and colleges, Washington, DC, 1996.

Baldridge, J.V., "Introduction: Models of university governance – bureaucratic, collegial, and political" in Baldridge, J.V. (ed.), *Academic governance: Research on institutional politics and decision making*, McCutchan Publishing, Berkeley, CA, 1971.

Baldwin, R. & Leslie, D., "Rethinking the structure of shared governance", *Peer Review*, 3(3), 2001.

Bargh, C., Bocock, J., Scott, P. & Smith, D., *University leadership: The role of the chief executive*, SRHE/Open University Press, Buckingham, 2000.

Bargh, C., Scott, P. & Smith, D. *Governing universities*, SRHE/Open University Press, 1996.

Barnett, R., *Recovering an academic community*, Jessica Kingsley Publishers, London, 1994.

Bauer, M., Marton, S., Askling, B. & Marton, F., *Transforming universities: Changing patterns of governance, structure and learning in Swedish higher education*, Jessica Kingsley Publishers, London, 1999.

Becher, A. & Trowler, P.R., *Academic tribes and territories*, SRHE/Open University Press, Buckingham, 2001.

Bergan, S. (ed.), *Universities as res publica. Higher education governance, student participation and the university as a site of citizenship*, Council of Europe higher education series No. 1, Council of Europe Publishing, Strasbourg, 2004.

Birnbaum, R., *How colleges work: the cybernetics of academic organization and leadership*, Jossey-Bass, San Francisco, 1988.

Birnbaum, R., "Faculty in governance: The role of senates and joint committees in academic decision making" in *New Directions for Higher Education*, 18(3), Jossey-Bass, San Franciso, 1991.

Birnbaum, R., *Management fads in higher education: Where they come from, What they do, Why they fail*, Jossey-Bass, San Francisco, 2000.

Boyer, E., *Scholarship reconsidered: Priorities of the professorate*, Carnegie Foundation for the Advancement of Teaching, Princeton, NJ, 1990.

Braun, D. & Merrien, F.-X. (eds.), *Towards a new model of governance for universities? A comparative view*, Jessica Kingsley Publishers, London/Philadelphia, 1999.

Braun, D. & Schimank, U., "Organisatorische Koexistenzen des Forschungssystems mit anderen gesellschaftlichen Teilsystemen: Die prekäre Autonomie wissenschaftlicher Forschung" in *Journal für Sozialforschung* 32, 1992: 319-336.

Campbell, C. & Rosznyai, C., "Quality Assurance and the Development of Course Programmes", UNESCO-CEPES Papers on Higher Education, Bucharest, 2002.

Cave, M., Hanney, S., Henkel, M. & Kogan, M., *The use of performance indicators in higher education: The challenge of the quality movement*, Jessica Kingsley Publishers, London, 1996.

Christensen, T. & Lægreid, P. (eds.), New public management. The transformation of ideas and practice, Ashgate, Aldershot, 2001.

Clark, B.R., "The many pathways of academic coordination" in *Higher Education* 8, Elsevier Scientific Publishing Company, 1979: 251-267.

Clark, B.R., *The higher education system. Academic organization in cross-national perspective*, University of California Press, Berkeley, 1983.

Clark, B.R., *Creating entrepreneurial universities: Organizational pathways for transformation*, Pergamon for IAU Press, Oxford, 1998.

Clark, B.R., *Sustaining change in universities: Continuities in case studies and concepts*, Open University Press, 2004.

Cloete, N. & Maassen, P., "The Limits of Policy" in Cloete, N. et al. (eds.), *Transformation in higher education. Global pressures and local realities in South Africa*, Juta & Co., Landsowne, SA, 2002: 447-491

Committee of University Chairmen (CUC), *Guide for Members of Higher Education Governing Boards in the UK. Governance Code of Practice and General Principles*, 2004 (http://www.shef.ac.uk/cuc/pubs.html).

Currie, J., De Angelis, R., de Boer, H., Huisman, J. & Lacotte, C., *Globalizing practices and university responses. European and Anglo-American differences*, Praeger Publishers, Westport, CT, 2003.

Davies, J.L., "The entrepreneurial and adaptive university", *International Journal of Institutional Management in Higher Education*, 2(1), 1984.

Davies, J.L., *The dialogue of universities with their stakeholders: Comparisons between different regions of Europe*, CRE (Association of European Universities), 1998.

Davies, J.L., "The emergence of entrepreneurial cultures in European universities", *Higher Education Management*, 13(2), 2001: 25-43.

Davies, J.L., "Cultural change in universities in the context of strategic and quality initiatives" (unpublished manuscript), 2004.

Daxner, M., "Entstaatlichung und Veroeffentlichung. Die Hochschule als republikanischer Ort", in Daxner, M., *Entstaatlichung und Veroeffentlichung?*/Luethje, J. & Schrimpf, H., *Eine neue Hochschulpolitik*, Cologne, 1991.

Daxner, M., *Die blockierte Universität. Warum die Wissensgesellschaft eine andere Hochschule braucht*, Campus Verlag, Frankfurt a.M/New York, 1999.

Daxner, M., "Hochschulpolitik" in Hanft, A. (ed.), *Grundbegriffe des Hochschulmanagements*, Luchterhand, Neuwied, 2001: 166-171.

Daxner, M., "Democratic citizenship – Bürgerschaftlichkeit, Bürgergesellschaftliche Kompetenz als Ziel und Qualitätskriterium von Studiengängen" in Benz, W., Kohler, J. & Landfried, K. (eds.), *Handbuch Qualität in Studium und Lehre*, Raabe Verlag, Berlin, 2004.

Deem, R., "New managerialism in higher education: The management of performances and cultures in universities", *International Studies in the Sociology of Education*, 8(1), 1998: 47-70.

Delanty, G.D., *Challenging knowledge. The university in the knowledge society*, SRHE/Open University Press, Buckingham, 2001.

Dinci, G., "Financial Management and Institutional Relationships with Civil Society", (Papers on Higher Education), UNESCO-CEPES, Bucharest, 2002.

Drummond, M. & Reitsch, A., "The relationship between shared academic governance models and faculty and administrator attitudes" in *Journal for Higher Education Management*, 11(1), 1995.

Duderstadt, J.J., *A university for the 21st century*, The University of Michigan Press, Ann Arbor, 2001.

Duke, C., *The learning university: Towards a paradigm*, SRHE/Open University Press, Buckingham, 1992.

Duryea, E.D. & Williams, D. (eds.), *The academic corporation: A history of college and university governing boards*, Falmer Press, New York, 2000.

Eckel, P.D., "The role of shared governance in institutional hard decisions: Enabler or antagonist?", *The Review of Higher Education*, 24(1), 2000.

Eckel, P., Green, M. & Hill, B., *On change V: Riding the waves of change: Insights from transforming institutions*, American Council on Education, 2001.

Ehrlich, T. (ed.), *Civic responsibility and higher education*, American Council on Education and Oryx Press, Phoenix, 2000.

Farrington, D., "Governance in higher education: Issues arising from the work of the legislative reform programme for higher education and research of the

Council of Europe, Strasbourg" (DECS/LRP (98) 28), reproduced as Appendix 1 to the Final report of the LRP (CC-HER (2000) 40).

Felt, U., "University autonomy in Europe: A background study" in *Observatory for fundamental university values and rights, managing university autonomy. Collective decision making and human resource policy*, Bononia University Press, Bologna, 2003: 7-104.

File, J. & Goedegebuure, L. (eds.), *Real-time systems. Reflections on higher education in the Czech Republic, Hungary, Poland and Slovenia*, CHEPS/VUTIUM, Twente/Brno, 2002.

Flecker, J., "Intrapreneure, Arbeitskraftunternehmer und andere Zwitterwesen" in *Kurswechsel* 2, Sonderzahl-Verlag, 2000: 28-36.

Foucault, M., *Geschichte der Gouvernementalitaet I: Sicherheit, Territorium, Bevoelkerung*, Frankfurt a.M., Suhrkamp Verlag, 2004.

Gibbons, M. et al., *The new production of knowledge. The dynamics of science and research*, Sage Publications, London, 1994.

Goedegebuure, L., Kaiser, F., Maassen, P., Meek, L., van Vught, F. & De Weert, E. (eds.), *Hochschulpolitik im internationalen Vergleich*, Bertelsmann Stiftung, Gütersloh, 1993.

Gornitzka, A. & Maassen, P., "Hybrid steering approaches with respect to European higher education" in *Higher Education Policy*, 13, 2000: 267-285.

Green, M.F., *Transforming higher education: Views from leaders around the world*, Oryx Press, Phoenix, 1997.

Gumport, P.J., "Academic governance: New light on old issues", Occasional Paper No. 42, Association of Governing Boards of Universities and Colleges, September 2000.

Gumport, P.J., "Academic restructuring: Organizational change and institutional imperatives" in *Higher Education*, 39(1), 2000: 67-91.

Hanft, A. (ed.), *Grundbegriffe des Hochschulmanagements*, Luchterhand, Neuwied, 2001.

Hecht, Irene W.D., Higgerson, M., Gmelch, W.H. & Ticker, A., *The department chair as academic leader*, American Council on Education and Oryx Press, Phoenix, 1999.

Henkel, M., *Academic identities and policy changes in higher education*, Jessica Kingsley Publishers, London, 2000.

Henkel, M. & Little, B., *Changing relationships between higher education and the state*, Jessica Kingsley Publishers, London, 1998.

Hines, C., "The Governance of Higher Education" in *Higher education: Handbook of theory and research*, 4, Agathon Press, 1990.

Hirsch, W.Z. & Weber, L. (eds.), *Governance in higher education. The university in a state of flux*, Economica, London, 2001.

Hirst, P. & Thompson, G., "Globalization in question: International economic relations and forms of public governance" in Hollingsworth, J. Rogers & Boyer, Robert (eds.), *Contemporary capitalism. The embeddedness of institutions*, Springer, Cambridge, 1997: 337-360.

Huefner, K., "Governance and funding of higher education in Germany", in *Higher education in Europe*, 28(20), Routhledge Journals, Taylor & Francis, 2003: 145-163.

Huisman, J., Maassen, P. & Neave, G. (eds.) *Higher education and the nation state. The international dimension of higher education*, Pergamon Press, Oxford, 2001.

Jackson, R., "The universities, government and society", in Smith, D. & Langslow, A.K. (eds.), *The idea of a university*, Jessica Kingsley Publishers, London, 1999.

Jessop, B., "The rise of governance and the risks of failure: The case of economic development", *International Social Science Journal*, 155, Blackwell Publishing, 1998: 29-46.

Jongbloed, B., Maassen, P. & Neave, G. (eds.), *From the eye of the storm. Higher education's changing institution*, Kluwer Academic Publishers, Dordrecht, 1999.

Kehm, B., "Higher education in Germany – developments, problems, and perspectives", *Monographs on Higher Education*, Institute for Higher Education Research and UNESCO European Centre for Higher Education, Wittenberg and Bucharest, 1999.

Knight, P.T. & Trowler, P.R., *Departmental leadership in higher education*, Open University Press, Milton Keynes, 2001.

Köhler, J., "Ethical frameworks of governance for higher education and science", paper presented at the conference on "Ethical and moral dimensions for higher education and science in Europe", UNESCO-CEPES, Bucharest, 2004.

Kogan, M. & Hanney, S., *Reforming higher education*, Jessica Kingsley Publishers, London, 1999.

Kogan, M., "Academic and administrative interface" in Henkel, M. & Little, B., *Changing relationships between higher education and the state*, Jessica Kingsley Publishers, London, 1998.

Kooiman, J., "Governance: A social-political perspective" in Grote, J.R. & Gbikpi, B. (eds.), *Participatory governance. Political and societal implications*, Opladen, 2002: 71-96.

Kooiman, J., "Governing as governance", paper presented at the conference "Governance-Forschung", Wissenschaftszentrum, Berlin, 2004.

Lanzendorf, U. & Dellwing, M., "Changes in public research governance in Austria (preliminary draft)", Centre for Research on Higher Education and Work (WZI), (unpublished manuscript), University of Kassel, Kassel, 2004.

Laske, S. & Meister-Scheytt, C., "Wer glaubt, dass Universitätsmanager Universitäten managen, der glaubt auch, dass Zitronenfalter Zitronen falten", in Luethje, J. & Nickel, S. (eds.), *Universitätsentwicklung. Strategien, Erfahrungen, Reflexionen*, Frankfurt a.M., 2003.

Lockwood, G., Davies, J. & Nelson, L., *Policy formation in universities: The management challenge*, SRHE/NFER-Nelson, Windsor, 1985.

Lond, R.M., "Governmentality, the Problem of 'Steering' and Public Administration", Copenhagen Business School, Department of Management, Politics and Philosophy, LPF Working Papers, 2003.

Luethje, J. & Nickel, S. (eds.), *Universitätsentwicklung. Strategien, Erfahrungen, Reflexionen*, Peter Lang Verlag, Frankfurt a.M, 2003.

Maassen, P. & van Vught, F., "Alternative models of governmental steering in higher education. An analysis of steering models and policy-instruments in five countries" in Goedegebuure, L. & van Vught, F. (eds.) *Comparative policy studies in higher education*, LEMMA, Utrecht, 1994: 35-65.

Maassen, P., *Government steering and the academic culture: The intangibility of the human factor in Durch and German universities*, De Tijdstroom, Maarsen, 1996.

Maassen, P. (ed.), "Higher education and the stakeholder society" in *European Journal of Education* (Special Issue), 35(4), Blackwell Publishing, 2000: 377-475.

Marga, A., *Education in transition*, Paideia, Bucharest, 2000.

Marginson, S. & Considine, M., *The enterprise university. Power, governance and reinvention in Australia*, CUP, Cambridge, 2000.

Marginson, S. & Rhoades, G. "Beyond national states, markets, and systems of higher education: A global agency heuristic" in *Higher Education*, 43:3, 2002.

McDaniel, C., "The Paradigms of Governance in Higher Education Systems" in *Higher Education Policy*, 9(2), Olof, 1998.

McNay, I., "From collegial academy to academic enterprise: The changing cultures of university" in Schuller, T. (ed.), *The Changing University*, SRHE/Open University Press, Buckingham, 1995.

Meek, V.L., "Changing patterns in modes of co-ordination in higher education" in Enders, J. & Fulton, O. (eds.) *Higher Education in a Globalising World. International Trends and Mutual Observations*, Kluwer Academic Publishers, Dordrecht, 2002: 53-73.

Meckling, J., "Netzwerkgovernance. Corporate Citizenship und Global Governance", WZB Discussion Papers, Berlin, 2003.

Metzger, W.P., "Academic governance: An evolutionary perspective" in Schulster, J. (ed.), *Governing tomorrow's campus: Perspectives and agendas*, MacMillan Press, New York, 1989.

Miller, M.T. (ed.), *Responsive academic decision-making: Involving faculty in higher education governance*, New Forums Press, Stillwater, UK, 1999.

Ministry of Education, Finland, *Management and steering of higher education in Finland*, Publications of the Ministry of Education, Helsinki, Finland, 2004.

Neave, G. & van Vught, F.A. (eds.), *Prometheus bound: The changing relationship between government and higher education in western Europe*, Pergamon Press, Oxford, 1991.

Neave, G., "The European dimension in higher education: An excursion into the modern use of historical analogues" in Huisman, J., Maassen, P. & Neave, G. (eds.), *Higher education and the nation state*, Pergamon Press, Oxford, 2001: 13-75.

Neave, G., "The stakeholder perspective historically explored" in Enders, J. & Fulton, O. (eds.), *Higher education in a globalising world. International trends and mutual observations*, Kluwer Academic Publishers, Dordrecht, 2002: 17-39.

Nickel, S., "Dezentralisierte Zentralisierung. Die Suche nach neuen Organisations – und Leitungsstrukturen fuer Fakultaeten und Fachbereiche", in *Die Hochschule* 1, 2004.

Nitsch, W., Gerhardt, U., Offe, C. & Preuss, U.K., *Hochschule in der Demokratie*, Luchterhand Verlag, Neuwied, 1965.

OECD (Organisation for Economic Co-operation and Development), *Governance in transition: Public management reforms in OECD countries*, OECD, Paris, 1995.

Pandza, D. & Kotlo, R. (eds.), *Student rights in SEE. Regional research work / Studenttska Prava. Regionalni Istrazivacki Projekat*, Human Rights Center in Mostar, Mostar, 2003.

Pechar, H., "In search of a new profession: Transformation of academic management in Austrian universities" in Amaral, A., Meek, L.V. & Larsen, I.M. (eds.), *The Higher Education Managerial Revolution?* (Higher Education Dynamics, 3), Kluwer Academic Publishers, Dordrecht/Boston/London, 2003: 109-130.

Pellert, A. & Welan, M. (eds.), *Die formierte Anarchie. Die Herausforderung der Universitätsorganisation*, WUV Universitätsverlag, Wien, 1995.

Pellert, A., *Die Universität als Organisation*, Vienna, Cologne, Graz (Böhlau), 1999.

Peterson, M.W., Chaffee, E.E. & White, T.H. (eds.), *Organization and academic governance in higher education*, (4th ed.), Ginn Press, Needham Heights, MA, 1991.

Peterson, M.W., Dill, D. & Mets, L., *Planning and management for a changing environment*, Jossey-Bass, San Francisco, 1997.

Plantan, F., "The university as site of citizenship" in Bergan, S. (ed.), *Universities as res publica. Higher education governance, student participation and the university as site of citizenship*, Council of Europe higher education series No.1, Council of Europe Publishing, Strasbourg, 2004: 83-128.

Pollitt, C. & Bouckaert, G., *Public management reform: A comparative analysis*, Oxford University Press, Oxford/New York, 2000.

Pollitt, C., *Managerialism and the public services. Cuts or cultural change in the 1990s?* (2nd ed.), Blackwell Publishing, Oxford, 1993.

Pusser, B. & Ordorika, I., "Bringing political theory to university governance" in *Higher education: Handbook of theory and research*, Springer, 2001: 16.

Readings, B., *The university in ruins*, Harvard University Press, Cambridge, Mass./London 1996.

Rhoades, G., "Rethinking and restructuring universities", *Journal of Higher Education Management*, 10(2), 1995.

Rosenau, J.N. & Czempiel, E.-O., *Governance without government: Order and change in world politics*, Cambridge University Press, 1992.

Rosenau, J., "Governance in the twenty-first century" in *Global governance: A review of multilateralism and international organizations*, Vol. 1, No. 1, 1995: 13-43.

Rosenau, J.N., "Governance in a new global order" in Held, D. & McGrew, A. (eds.), *Governing globalization: Power, authority and global governance*, Polity Press, Cambridge, 2002: 70-86.

Rosovsky, H., "Some thoughts about university governance" in Hirsch, W. & Weber, L. (eds.), *Governance in higher education: The university in flux*, Economica, London, 2001: 94-104.

Salmi, J. & Verspoor, A.M. (eds.), *Revitalizing higher education*, IAU Press, Oxford, 1994.

Salter, B. & Tapper, T., "The politics of governance in higher education: The case of quality assurance" in *Political Studies*, 48(1), 2000: 66-87.

Schedler, K. & Proeller, I., *New public management*, Bern/Stuttgart/Vienna, 2000.

Schimank, U., Kehm, B. & Enders, J., "Institutional mechanisms of problem processing of the German university system: Status quo and new developments" in Braun, D. & Merrien, F.-X. (eds.), *Towards a new model of governance for universities? A comparative view*, Jessica Kingsley Publishers, London/Philadelphia, 1999: 179-194.

Schneider, V. & Kenis, P., "Verteilte Kontrolle: Institutionelle Steuerung in modernen Gesellschaften" in Kenis, P. & Schneider, V. (eds.), *Organisation und Netzwerk. Institutionelle Steuerung in Wirtschaft und Politik*, Campus Verlag, Frankfurt a.M., 1996: 9-44.

Scott, C. "Regulation in the age of governance: The rise of the post-regulatory state" in Jordana, J. & Levi-Faur, D. (eds.), *The Politics of Regulation*, Edward Elgar Publishing, Cheltenham, 2003.

Scott, P., "University governance and management: An analysis of the system and institutional level changes in western Europe" in Maassen, P. & van Vught, F. (eds.), *Inside academia. New challenges for the academic profession*, Elsevier/De Tijdstroom, Utrecht, 1996: 113-133.

Scott, P., *Higher education re-formed*, Falmer Press, London/New York, 2000.

Scott, P., "Universities as organizations and their governance" in Hirsch, W.Z. & Weber, L. (eds.), *Governance in higher education. The university in a state of flux*, Economica, London, 2001: 125-142.

Simonis, U.E., "Defining good governance – The conceptional competition is on", (WZB Discussion Papers), Berlin, 2004.

Slaughter, S. & Leslie, L., *Academic capitalism: Politics, policies, and the entrepreneurial university*, The Johns Hopkins University Press, Baltimore/London, 1997.

Sporn, B., *Adaptive university structures: An analysis of adaptation of socioeconomic environments of US and European universities*, Jessica Kingsley Publishers, London, 1999.

Stichweh, R., *Wissenschaft, Universität, Profession – Soziologische Analysen*, Suhrkamp, Frankfurt a.M, 1994.

Taylor, J. & Miroiu, A., "Policy-making, strategic planning and management of higher education", UNESCO-CEPES (Papers on Higher Education), Bucharest, 2002.

Tierney, W.G., "Organizational culture in higher education: Defining the essentials" in *Journal of Higher Education* 59(1), 1988b: 2-21.

Tierney, W.G. (ed.), *The responsive university. Restructuring for high performance*, The Johns Hopkins University Press, Baltimore/London, 1998.

Tierney, W.G., "Why committees don't work: Creating a structure for change", in *Academe*, 87(3), AAUP (American Association of University Professors), 2001.

Titscher, S., Winckler, G. & Biedermann, H., *Universitäten im Wettbewerb – Zur Neustrukturierung österreichischer Universitäten*, Rainer Hampp, München und Mering, 2000.

Tomusk, V., *The blinding darkness of the enlightenment. Towards the understanding of post state-socialist higher education in east Europe*, University of Turku Press, 2000.

Trow, W., *Managerialism and the academic profession: Quality and control*, Open University Quality Control Centre, London, 1994.

Van Ginkel, H., "Variety and impact: Differences that matter. Some thoughts on the variety of university governance systems and their impact on university policies and strategies" in Hirsch, W.Z. & Weber, L. (eds.), *Governance in higher education. The university in a state of flux*, Economica, London, 2001: 155-166.

Van Kersbergen, K. & van Waarden, F. (2004) "'Governance' as a bridge between disciplines: Cross-disciplinary inspiration regarding shifts in governance and problems of governability, accountability and legitimacy", *European Journal of Political Research* 43, 2004: 143-171.

Van Vught, F.A., van der Wende, M. & Westerheijden, D., "Globalisation and internationalisation: Policy agendas compared" in Enders, J. & Fulton, O. (eds.), *Higher education in a globalising world. International trends and mutual observations*, Kluwer Academic Publishers, Dordrecht, 2002: 103-121.

Vlasceanu, L. & Purser, L., "From words to action. Changing higher education governance and management structures in certain south-eastern European countries/entities", Papers on Higher Education, UNESCO-CEPES, Bucharest, 2002.

Weick, K.E., "Educational organizations as loosely coupled systems" in *Administrative Science Quarterly*, 21, 1976: 1-19.

Wolverton, M. & Gmelch, W.H., *College Deans: Leading from within*, American Council on Education and Oryx Press, Phoenix, 2002.

Wood, M. & Meek, L., "Higher education governance and management: Australia" in *Higher Education Research*, 11(2-3), 1998.

Zechlin, L., "No Public Management. Die österreichische Politik verabschiedet sich von der strategischen Steuerung ihrer Universitäten", in *Zeitschrift fuer Hochschulrecht, Hochschulmanagement und Hochschulpolitik Heft*, 4, Springer, Graz-Vienna, 2002: 139-143

Ziegele, F., "Reformansätze und Perspektiven der Hochschulsteuerung in Deutschland", in *Beiträge zur Hochschulforschung*, 24(3), 2002: 106-121.

Appendix 1

Ministry of Education, Finland, Management and Steering of Higher Education in Finland, Publications of the Ministry of Education, Finland, 2004.

Ministry of education
22 December 2003

Performance agreement between the Ministry of Education and the University of Joensuu for the period 2004–2006 and resources for 2004

AIMS

The operations of universities are governed by the Universities Act and the Development Plan for education and research adopted by the Government on 4 December 2004.

> The mission of the University of Joensuu, as part of the international and national academic community, is to conduct research and supply education in response to needs in eastern Finland in particular and provide relevant services to the community in its fields.
> The University's knowledge fields are multidisciplinary, broad-based teacher training, educational research and life course studies; forests, other renewable resources and the environment; specialised high technology; and social development and cultural interaction in border regions and fringe areas.

> The University shall enhance its strategic work in support of its profile definition.

The aim of the universities is to contribute through their own work to cultural, social and economic welfare in Finnish society. Universities shall take the principle of sustainable development into account in all their activities. The universities shall aim at a high international level and quality in research, researcher training, education and artistic activity.

The universities shall carry on the development of comprehensive quality management and its methods. The findings of evaluations shall be used in quality enhancement.

The universities shall improve conditions for research and education by developing their library and information services and the ICT infrastructure in support of these services. The universities shall develop the provision of virtual teaching as part of the overall educational development.

The universities shall develop their work communities in order to improve their competitiveness as employers as well as take care of the work capacity and satisfaction of their personnel.

Research and researcher training

In their research activity, the universities shall focus on high-quality, internationally competitive and ethically sustainable research.

The universities shall enhance prerequisites for professional researcher careers and pay special attention to promoting equal opportunity in the academic community. Graduate schools shall be developed as the principal track to a doctorate, which is the primary goal of postgraduate education. The universities shall step up researcher training with a view to lowering the mean age of new PhDs to 32 by the end of the contract period. The

19

graduate schools shall actively recruit foreign students and researchers. The aim is that in 2006 ten per cent of the graduate school students are foreigners.

In the University of Joensuu, the average annual number of doctorates in the period 2004–2006 shall be 68, with the following breakdown:

Theology	2
Humanities	10
Education science	9
Social sciences[1]	7
Psychology	2
Natural sciences	27
Agriculture-forestry	11

[1] The target for doctorates in the Business Administration field at the Lappeenranta University of technology includes 1 post-graduate student studying at the University of Joensuu.

Undergraduate education

Each university shall draw up an admissions strategy with a view to developing the student selection system. The strategy must determine measures for stepping up student placement, reducing the number of selection units and streamlining the selection procedures at the national level and in each university. The aim will be that by the end of the performance agreement period 2004–2006, at least 50 per cent of new students are the same year's matriculated students.

The quality of teaching and the systems for planning, guiding and monitoring studies shall be developed with a view to intensifying graduation and shortening study times especially in the humanities, mathematics and natural science, and technology fields. Universities shall introduce personal study plans devised together with students in all fields by 2006. The universities shall prepare and put in place the two-cycle degree system and determine the extent of studies as outlined in the report of the Ministry of Education committee for the development of university degree structure (OPM:n muistioita 39:2002) in order to enable the new structure to be adopted flexibly from the autumn term 2005–2006 onwards.

In the targeting of their education provision, the universities shall especially cater for the changing needs of the national health project, teacher training and information industries. In the targeting of the education supply, universities must avail themselves of the possibilities of structural development.

The target annual number of entrants for the University of Joensuu in the period 2004–2006 shall be 1,280.

The average target for the annual number of Masters' degrees in the period 2004–2006 shall be 760, of which 184 in subject teacher training with the following distribution:

	Master's degrees	Of which subject teachers
Theology	35	10
Humanities	170	70
Education science	245	25
Social science[2]	100	7
Psychology	15	2
Natural sciences	150	70
Agriculture-forestry	45	

[2] The target for Master's degrees in economics at Lappeenranta University of Technology includes 25 students studying at Joensuu.

Internationalisation

Universities shall intensify and increase international cooperation and networking with a view to making Finnish universities active and competitive players and valued partners especially in the European Higher Education and Research Area. Universities shall increase cooperation with Russia and strengthen Russia know-how in Finland.

Universities shall increase their supply of English-language education in their respective

26

strength areas and pay special attention to the quality of teaching and teaching methods. Universities shall recruit foreign degree students primarily to Master's programmes and postgraduate education. Student guidance shall take the special needs of foreign students into account. The supply of instruction in Finnish/Swedish language and Finnish culture shall be increased.

Annually 260 students in Master's programmes shall study abroad for three months or longer.

Societal services

Universities shall boost the vitality of their regions by networking with the foremost players in the region. New university units shall not be established, but regional university centres and universities' other regional activities shall be concentrated into sufficiently large entities which have potential to achieve a high quality and effectiveness in their operations. Universities shall cooperate with polytechnics as outlined in jointly devised strategies.

Universities shall enhance their contacts with business and industry by strengthening their business know-how, their innovation services and the commercialisation of their research findings. The prerequisites of universities to support entrepreneurship shall be improved.

Universities shall promote employment and equal opportunity in education by means of their adult education provision. Adults' opportunities to study for university degrees shall be improved by means of Master's programmes and open university supply (Bachelor's degrees).

The annual target for students coming via the open university track to the University shall be 115.

The annual target for open university instruction shall be 1,150 full-time equivalent student places.

Supplementary funding

Universities shall widen their funding base by supplementing the direct budgetary appropriations with other financing. The supplementary funding must support the universities' basic mission and relevant targets.

The aim shall be to achieve a high standard in the procedures, administration and monitoring of the supplementary funding as part of university quality management.

Construction

The aim is that the Aurora II building will be completed during the agreement period.

Practice schools

The aim of the practice schools shall be a high level of activities in support of teacher training and close interaction with the University. Practice schools shall ensure the quality of curriculum design and teaching and develop diversified practice teaching and the use of educational technology.

Resources in 2004

Operational expenditure

With a view to achieving the targets determined in the performance agreement of 2004–2006 it is proposed that the Government include in its 2004 budget proposal to Parliament the following appropriations in the university sub-item (29.10.21)

21

	€ in 2002	€ in 2003	€ in 2004
Core funding	42,172,000	45,087,000	**50,874,000**
For national societal tasks	1,985,000	1,985,000	
For national programmes	3,048,000	3,203,000	**2,381,000**
Project funding	959,000	582,000	**870,000**
Performance-based funding	1,059,000	675,000	**764,000**
Total	49,223,000	51,532,000	**54,889,000**
Transfers from the previous years	7,743,000	8,068,000	
Add. budget		900,000	

The target income from university business activities in 2004 shall be 2,000,000 euros and the target profit 100,000 euros (5% of income). The target income from research cooperation shall be 3,500,000 euros. The estimated amount of endowments is 100,000 euros.

Core funding

The core funding includes

* 729,000 euros for open university provision
* 3,141,000 euros for graduate school salary costs
* 1,873,000 euros for other societal tasks, the remainder of the funding needed to be provided by the University from its operational expenditure.

The core funding includes extra 1,995,000 euros to cover the pay raises agreed in the collective agreement of 30 November 2002 (in 2003 and 2004).

The core funding includes an additional 31,000 euros as a transfer of one person-year from sub-item 31.24.21.

National financing

A total of 2,381,000 euros for national programmes as follows:

* Information industry programme 498,000 euros, of which
  - 189,000 euros for graduate entry education (based on intakes agreed upon earlier)
  - 309,000 euros for improving the prerequisites of education and research in information industry fields.
* Virtual University projects, 636,000 euros, of which
  - payable to the coordinating university
    - 300,000 euros for the Eastern Finland Virtual University
    - 168,000 euros for the OVI project and
  - 168,000 euros for virtual teaching projects prioritised by the University and to relevant staff-development training.
* Teacher training as specified in the Appendix, 460,000 euros (775,000 euros in 2005 and 745,000 euros in 2006).
* Business know-how development (2004–2006), 300,000 euros
* Border Research, EU & Russia, 120,000 euros, (150,000 euros in 2005 and 180,000 euros in 2006)
* Development of the study process (Graduation in five years, 2004–2006), 100,000 euros
* Regional development in higher education, 200,000 euros, for enhancing the mathematics, physics and chemistry knowledge base in teacher training (70 persons /year, 150,000 euros in 2005–2006)
* Language technology (2004–2005), 67,000 euros

Projects

The University's projects

* 500,000 euros for the development of the tourism education network and other Savonlinna operations (2004–2006)
* 70,000 euros for the development education relating to cultural content in the media (2004–2006)

22

- 100,000 euros for the development of learning environments (2004–2006)

Equipment
- 200,000 euros for a physics clean room

Performance-based funds
- A total of 764,000 euros of performance funding is proposed to be payable to the University's operational expenditure sub-item on the basis of the centre of excellence in research, the centres of excellence in teaching, students' progress, Academy of Finland funding and other external financing.

Practice schools
- Resources proposed for the practice school sub-item:

	€ in 2002	€ in 2003	€ in 2004
Core funding	9,720,000	9,823,000	10,294,000
Project funding	117,000	12,000	14,000
Performance funding	17,000	15,000	15,000
Total	9,854,000	9,850,000	10,323,000
Transfers from previous year	1,353,000	1,326,000	
Add. budget	175,000		

The netting income from the practice schools is estimated at 120,000 euros of which 80,000 euros from business activities and 40,000 euros from co-financed activities.

The core funding includes an extra 387,000 euros to cover the pay raises (in 2003 and 2004) agreed in the collective agreement of 30 November 2002.

The core funding includes 15,000 euros of performance-based funding.

The core funding includes 14,000 euros for the project Information strategy for and research.

The renovation of the Joensuu normal school will mean an increase of 151,000 euros in facilities expenditure: 34,000 in 2002 and 84,000 in 2003. The extension of the Länsikatu school (year-classes 1–2 and special-needs classes) shall be carried out.

Monitoring and reporting
The achievement of the targets and other implementation of this agreement shall be reviewed annually in connection with the performance negotiations. Apart from the oral feedback in the negotiations, the Ministry of Education will give feedback in writing concerning the quality of reporting, the effectiveness of operations, and development needs in strategic priority areas.

The University shall supply the requested data to the KOTA database by the dates specified and prepare for changes in its own monitoring and reporting systems owing to the development of KOTA.

Arvo Jäppinen
Director General

Perttu Vartiainen
Rector

Markku Mattila
Director

Petri Lintunen
Director of Administration

Appendices
Appendix 1. European Structural Fund programmes
Appendix 2. Financing of societal services included in the core funding 2004–2006
Appendix 3. Teacher training development programme 2004–2006

23

Ministry of education
Department for Education and Science Policy

Structural Fund programmes

* M.A. (Educ.) E-learning master (Savonlinna)
* M.A. (Soc. Sc.) social geography, leisure and recreational service (Savonlinna)
* M.A. (Soc. Sc.) regional and community development
* M.A., German, English, Russian, translation technology (Savonlinna)
* M.A. (Educ.) arts and crafts, design and technology (Savonlinna)
* International Master's Programme for Tourism Studies (Savonlinna)
* Construction: reservation for additional costs incurring from the construction of the Savonlinna tourism cluster

The condition for the projects is that they otherwise fulfil general requirements set in the programme document /policy /the overall action. The Ministry of Education reserves its opinion on the adequacy of project funding.

Ministry of Education
Department for Education and Science Policy

Financing of societal tasks included in the core funding (excluding open university instruction), 1 000 euros/year

University of Joensuu

Societal service tasks included in the core funding

Orthodox theology	200
Training of student counsellors, special education teachers and kindergarten teachers	450
Development of services relating to the utilisation of research findings and strengthening of regional impact	1,223
including	

* Karelian Institute
* Development of the Savonlinna unit and the science park

24

Appendix 3 (Joensuu)

Ministry of Education
Department for Education and Science Policy

Teacher training development programme 2004–2006

The target for subject teacher training at the University of Joensuu shall be a minimum of 184 graduates annually. The annual target for the humanities shall be at least 70 subject teachers. In the humanities, the University shall focus on subject teacher education, especially English teachers, and take note of current small need for history teachers. In the natural sciences, the target shall be at least 70 subject teachers, especially in response to the need for in mathematics, physics and chemistry teachers. In education science, the University shall focus provision on class teacher training at least to the present extent and take note of the growing need for pedagogical qualification studies. The annual target in special education shall be a minimum of 36 special-needs teachers and in pupil/student guidance a minimum of 25 graduates.

The University of Joensuu shall implement the programme for increasing teacher training in 2004–2006 as follows:

Project	2004 (1 000 €)	2005	2006
Teachers' pedagogical qualification studies in Eastern Finland (50)	100	100	100
English teachers (- major 10/year - minor 10/year - graduate entry 12/year) The project is proposed start in 2005.		120	140
Arts and crafts teaching network KÄSNET	30	35	35
Mother tongue and literature teachers (- major 10/year - minor 16/year - supplementary studies 4/year) The project is proposed start in 2005.		200	200
Swedish and German teachers (- major 5/year - minor 4/year - graduate entry 7/year)	80	70	70
Special-needs kindergarten teachers (30/year)	250	250	200
Total	460	775	745

25

133

The governance of higher education institutions

Dijana Tiplič

1. Introduction

Over the last three decades, the field of higher education research has developed significantly. However, it is seen as a rather young field where some of the fundamental questions still beg for further investigation. One example is the question of the most effective institutional governance structure for higher education institutions. Some argue that institutional governance has become an international issue in higher education, and ought to be addressed through comparative research by sharing research findings across national systems, which in turn would lead towards identifying common themes and important differences (Reed, Meek & Jones, 2002: xv). That said, a central question in higher education governance research becomes a dilemma on how we should treat the university: as a distinctive institution with core authority structures that survived over the centuries or as any other modern organisation (Reed et al., 2002, xxvi). The point of departure in addressing the issue of institutional governance in higher education is seen in the changed relationship between higher education and the state. This changed relationship has frequently involved reforms of governance arrangements imposed by the state. Consequently, a number of complex relationships between various stakeholder groups (for example, academics, students, other civic and commercial groups) have evolved.

This paper attempts at better understanding how institutions of higher education are governed. In what follows, I will briefly review some of the models of higher education governance, as well as the corporate trends that tend to have an impact on the internal management of higher education institutions. Then I will shed some light on existing empirical evidence of the described trends with regard to both the European and non-European situation. The subsequent section will provide an insight into emerging issues in higher education governance. Finally, some concluding remarks will be presented.

2. Codes of governance in higher education

Depending on the level of analysis (for example, national, local, institutional, or subunit), we can distinguish between various meanings of governance in higher education. Clark (1983: 205-206) draws our attention to three primary authority levels: the understructure (i.e. basic academic or disciplinary units), the middle or enterprise structure (i.e. individual organisations in their entirety), and the superstructure (i.e. government and other regulatory mechanisms that relate organisations to one another). All three levels must be considered when trying to understand what is happening within particular higher education institutions and systems (Meek, 2003: 3). At the same time, the interaction between levels, as well as the dynamics within each level will be determined by the relevant context. The context, as argued by Clark, will depend on where higher education institutions are placed within the triangle of governance/co-ordination constituted by the forces of academic oligarchy, state authority and the market.[60] The three forces are dynamic and 'pull' institutions and systems in different directions. Due to its robustness, Clark's triangle has been widely applied by scholars in the field.

a. Governance at the system level

With regard to the superstructure level, national systems differ substantially in the ways they have organised the governance of higher education. In practice, two broad and distinctive pressures can be identified: the European Continental[61] model and the Anglo-Saxon model. The former is characterised by government increasingly stepping back from the direct control of higher education institutions, resulting in strengthened institutional autonomy; the latter, in contrast, is characterised by governments introducing various quality control and accountability mechanisms to better define educational outputs (Meek, 2003). This in turn can be seen as a loss of some institutional autonomy. However, governments in Europe have also been highly interested in the accountability issues, especially the quality assurance issue (Meek, 2003: 3).

In more general terms, the ability of higher education institutions to exercise initiative in the context of system- or nation-wide authority structures will depend on the type of higher education system that is in place. For instance, in the 'bottom-heavy' type of system characterised by high institutional autonomy, government policy will follow a change process initiated at the departmental, faculty or institutional level. On the contrary, in the 'top-down' type of system, higher education institutions will act in order to respond to the policy initiatives that are enforced upon them by the power of state. Consequently, higher education institutions will tend to redefine themselves in relation to transformations in the control and co-ordination occurring in the external environment. As Clark (2000: 36) puts it:

> The institutions have trajectories of their own; they have policies of their own, of which governmental dictates are only a part. It is important analytically to pursue the ways that higher education operates as a 'self-guiding society' as well as to see it as composed of institutions dependent on certain main patrons.

It is seen as important to keep this feature of higher education as a self-guiding society when examining the response and adaptation of higher education institutions to their respective increasingly complex and turbulent environments. In so doing, our focus shifts towards the questions of *governance* and *management* at the institutional level. The two subsequent sections intend to shed more light on these issues.

---

60. A parallel can be drawn to the title of the conference which resulted in the present publication: higher education governance between democratic culture, academic aspirations and market forces.
61. Empirical evidence seen as collected mainly in the "western" European countries.

b. Institutional governance in higher education

The literature on higher education provides a number of different traditional conceptual models of governance: bureaucratic (Stroup, 1966), political (Baldridge, 1971), organised anarchy (Cohen & March, 1974), collegial (Millett, 1978), and professional (Mintzberg, 1979). The more recent literature, however, reveals other types, such as the service university (Tjeldvoll, 1997), the entrepreneurial university (Clark, 1998), and the enterprise university (Marginson & Considine, 2000), to name but a few. It is beyond the scope of the present paper to provide more detail about each of these organisational types. However, in order to provide a clear cut comparison among some of the distinctive types of university organisation and governance, it is considered as useful to have a closer look at Olsen's (2005) typology of four university visions: a community of scholars, an instrument for national purposes, a representative democracy, and a service enterprise embedded in competitive markets. This typology is seen as relevant since it encompasses both the traditional and corporate trends of university organisation. *Firstly*, the author claims that the university as a community of scholars is organised around the universal criteria of, *inter alia*, free inquiry and intellectual freedom, rationality, intelligence, learning, academic competence and expertise. The university's identity originates from a shared commitment to search for the truth, rather than to search for political or economic benefits. The essence of this vision is seen in the university's collegial organisation and governance. *Secondly*, the university as an instrument for national purposes finds its rationale in implementing policies created by elected leaders. One of the key features of this perspective is applicability of research for practical problem solving, and the university's specialisation in order to achieve excellence (Olsen, 2005). *Thirdly*, the university as a representative democracy, as argued by the author, is a governance model focused on internal stakeholders (i.e. employees and students), whereas the university's performance is improved by empowering administrative and technical staff. *Fourthly*, the university as a service enterprise embedded in competitive markets operates as an enterprise within regional or global markets with a main objective to be competitive and profitable, whereby research and higher education are treated as commodities. The university is deliberated from the state and political authorities, and government's role is to provide incentive mechanisms. University leaders become entrepreneurs within a wider environment (Olsen, 2005). Hence New Public Management (NPM)[62] ideas prevail in this perspective.

In light of the ideas mentioned above, it is important to keep in mind that the various models and conceptualisations of higher education governance should be treated mainly as 'ideal types'. Some scholars see the university moving towards corporate enterprise, where the challenges facing it are "broadly similar to those of a range of public service agencies in the late twentieth century" (Askling & Henkel, 2000: 113). Others are not quite convinced in what direction these 'new' movements in the university's organisation and governance are heading. As Reed et al. (2002: xxvii) put it:

---

62. NPM rests on neo-liberal ideology, emphasises efficiency, downsizing and decentralisation, excellence and service orientation, and introduces quasi markets into the public sector.

> While much of the current writing on higher education assumes a movement away from traditional models of governance (themselves varied and complex), the direction of this movement is far from clear and varies considerably in both content and intensity from country to country and over time.

This is supported by some empirical research, which points to the resilience of higher education institutions and questions whether the present changes tend to be the codification of existing practices (de Boer, Goedegebuure & Meek, 1998).

To bring the issue of institutional governance a step further, there is an underlying assumption that government introduces the regulatory, policy and funding frameworks within which the higher education institutions are expected to adapt or strengthen their management structure (Maassen, 2003: 49). According to the author, management structures in higher education institutions have been identified as specific governance arrangements that can be influenced by external actors such as governments.

c. Institutional management in higher education

Over centuries, a widely accepted myth has developed that academics are able to manage their own affairs. As late as the 1980s, this model of collegial organisation and governance came under attack through requests for more efficiency and, not least, profitability. These new concepts, introduced along with the notions of managerialism, have created a tension with the former long-lasting academic values, such as scientific excellence and academic freedom.

Prior to engaging in further discussion about managerialism, it is important to distinguish between the terms of 'governance' and 'management' that are often used interchangeably, and yet, there are important distinctions between them (Middlehurst, 1999: 311-312):

> In simplistic terms, leadership and governance are concerned with overall direction and strategy within a framework determined by regulatory requirements on the one hand and purpose, values, culture, history and mission on the other. Management and administration involve processes of implementation, control and co-ordination with particular emphasis on resource frameworks and structures: human (individuals and groups), physical and technological infrastructures, finance, materials and time.

When it comes to the notion of managerialism, the key question becomes: what happens to institutional dynamics when management thinking and practice penetrate higher education? Or in other words, what are the effects of management and managerialism on the basic institutional functions of higher education teaching, research, relations with students, generation of knowledge, and relationships with external stakeholders? Answers to these and similar questions vary across the various contexts, yet there are some common trends and issues that may be discerned (Meek, 2003: 2). Here our focus shifts towards the issues of institutional autonomy, academic freedom, 'de-professionalisation', academic loyalty, and leadership. The following account will briefly reflect upon these important issues.

Taking Europe as an example, we can note that the 'rolling' back of public authorities in many European countries from direct control and detailed regulation has created a vacuum to which institutions have been forced to respond. As already mentioned, this trend is generally linked to a shift in focus from input to output in governmental steering of higher education. Consequently, an increased but more conditional institutional autonomy emerged. This said, academic freedom and institutional autonomy are frequently confused with each other; however, they are two quite distinct concepts (Ashby, 1966: 293). Indeed, academic freedom is defined as an individual scholar's freedom to pursue truth in teaching and research wherever it seems to lead, without fear of punishment or termination of employment for having offended some political, religious or social orthodoxy (Ashby: 1966). On the other hand, the ingredients of institutional autonomy, as analysed by Ashby (1966: 293-296) have the following dimensions: (i) freedom to recruit staff; (ii) freedom to select students; (iii) freedom to set standards; (iv) freedom to decide to whom to award degrees; (v) freedom to design curricula; and (vi) freedom to decide how to allocate income. Hence a natural question arises as to what extent institutional autonomy and academic freedom are interrelated. Assuming that this question is of high interest for all those involved in higher education, this relationship and its implications are seen as important empirical issues. One research path may be to study these issues with respect to the different degrees of importance attached to the contextual factors such as academic aspirations, market forces, and democratic cultures.

Another tension brought about by processes of massification, changes in the nature and value of knowledge and, not least, new management processes, is a tension between academics and administrators. This dualism in a university's organisational structure has a long history. It is a general trend that the academic profession, which used to enjoy prestige and indulgency, has come under strong attack. In extreme cases, this trend resulted in the perceived de-professionalisation of academics. Leicht and Fenell (2001) described the present situation by claiming that "elite managers are becoming the 'new professionals', while professionals are being captured by organisational stakeholders that consume and pay for professional services" (cited in Reed, 2002: 179). Or in other words, academics have become 'managed professionals' and administrators have become 'professional managers'. In addition, the loyalty of academics started to be questioned. For centuries academics used to be disciplined, loyal and professionally oriented. That kind of loyalty has been challenged, since demands upon loyalty to the institution score high on the managerial agenda (Meek, 2003). Needless to say, all these issues are empirical issues and beg for further investigation.

Finally, a key element in the emerging models of institutional governance is the strengthening of institutional leadership. Indeed, the increase in institutional responsibilities calls for measures to strengthen the central executive capacity. As Middlehurst (1999: 326-327) puts it:

> The function of leadership is to assist the institution (and particular parts of the institution) to identify and evaluate emerging realities, to assess the options available and to prepare strategies for moving towards one or more scenarios... The kind of leadership called for is beyond the scope of one individual, however visionary; it requires the creative and expert input of many individuals both to identify future directions and to take forward the organizational transformation that will be necessary.

To sum up, in some countries the above-mentioned processes have been relatively gradual and, by now, rather well established. In others, the decision-making apparatus at the institutional level has been historically weak. Thus neither their structure nor cultures appear to have been prepared for the change. Comparative work, which will analyse institutional responses to the new expectations, should reveal whether it makes sense to draw general conclusions about the emergence of managerialism across national borders (Amaral, Jones & Karseth, 2002: 296). The account that follows will shed light on some of the existing empirical evidence that is seen to be relevant to this discussion.

3. Management reform: empirical evidence

Empirical evidence on the impact of managerialism within higher education institutional governance varies in different national settings. For instance, at one end of the continuum are countries such as Portugal and France. Namely, Amaral, Magalhaes and Santiago (2003) did not find empirical evidence about the emergence of managerialism in Portuguese higher education, whereas de Boer (2003) claims that in the case of France, many of his respondents perceived collegiality as the main feature. Some countries, such as Norway, tend to be placed somewhere in between the two poles of the continuum, since, according to de Boer (2003), the majority of respondents claimed that "there remains a strong culture of democracy and collegiality", although a number of respondents perceived a shift towards managerialism. On the other end of the continuum, there are countries such as Finland, the Netherlands, and the UK. The UK case is an example where managerialism has emerged in its strongest form (Fulton, 2003). The Dutch case is another example of penetration of managerialism into university governance (de Boer, 2003). Not least, the Finnish case, according to Salminen (2003), is an example of relatively successful implementation of managerial reforms. Of non-European countries, Australia is the one in which managerialism seems to have made a remarkable impact. Moving to Latin America, some of the recent empirical evidence (Leite, 2003) points towards the emergence of policies of 'good' administration aimed at increased efficiency and effectiveness. Last, but not least, there is the case of the US, with its long tradition of strong central administration and control by 'boards of trustees', and lack of a strong tradition of the university as a self-governing community of academics and students.

In general terms, the above mentioned empirical evidence implies that some similarities and differences among the different governance models can still be drawn. For instance, it seems that the academic authority structures of European Continental universities, on the one hand, and Anglo-Saxon universities, on the other, do not differ to a high degree. Namely, there is a similar hierarchy of committee decision making flow between departments, faculty academic boards, and university senates. However, the question of appointing or electing academic staff is the one that brings about the main difference. Taking Australia and the UK as examples, the vice-chancellor, who is the equivalent of the rector, tends to be appointed by the institution and has greater executive authority. Needless to say, there may be some exceptions to this tendency.

4. University's governance: current and emerging issues?

The dilemma of the future of higher education, as outlined at the outset of this paper, still remains. This dilemma is related to a question of whether the traditional university has been replaced by entirely new organisational types or whether it is still traditional at its core, albeit though some modifications and mutations have taken place. The former has been addressed earlier in this paper; the latter is, to a certain extent, elaborated in the work of Bargh, Scott and Smith (1996) with reference to the UK higher education institutions. The account that follows will provide a brief look into the Bargh et al. (1996) approach.

With regard to the future of higher education, Scott (1995) distinguishes between the 'core' and the 'distributed' university. The 'core' university, according to the author, is the equivalent to the traditional university, implying that it consists of the activities determined by the university's traditional mission. The 'distributed' university, on the other hand, is mainly preoccupied by the role of higher education in the domains of lifelong education, distance learning, and industrial collaboration. Institutions of higher education are not expected to be split on the basis of these two elements, core and distributed, but will rather encompass both of them. This would in turn imply the increased significance of the governing bodies, whose key role is anticipated as threefold: firstly, as "gate-keepers policing the flow between core and distributed activities"; secondly, as "both-ways interpreters between the university and its stakeholders"; and thirdly, as "guardians of institutional integrity" (Bargh et al., 1996: 178). These three functions, according to the authors, cannot be performed merely by senior management or by the academic guild, implying that the governance of higher education institutions will become a central concern for the twenty-first century university. Here, the three key changes are discerned (Bargh et al., 1996: 179): (a) governing bodies should be more representative of both their civic and commercial stakeholders; (b) university governance's democracy deficit must be addressed by, for instance, requiring vacancies for independent members on governing bodies to be publicly advertised; and (c) the principle of open government should be applied.

There is little doubt that the last account leads to questions of democratic culture, academic aspirations and market forces in higher education. It raises the important issue of institutional governance in higher education with regard to these three dimensions. The challenge for higher education institutional governance in the twenty-first century is seen in 'deliberative partnerships' (Kennedy, 2003), whereby there is a need for defining the decision-making structures that will allow the academic guild, the 'new' managers and governing bodies, to work as partners committed to communication, debate and public interest.

5. Concluding remarks

In light of the above, drawing some strong conclusions is considered to be rather difficult. The field and existing empirical evidence appear as rather chaotic. For the purpose of illustration, two paradoxes follow.

As late as 1962, some claimed that universities "have apparently chronic and irremediable problems of internal organisation, yet they manage to be in some important ways extremely efficient in accomplishing their tasks; and in spite of the constant flow of criticism directed against them, there is a general belief in their necessity even among their critics" (Ben-David & Zloczower, 1962: 46). In similar vein, Birnbaum (1988: 3) with reference to the US situation put forward provocatively that "colleges and universities are poorly run but highly effective". If we assume that this is true, at least two conclusions may be allowed: (a) leadership or management and institutional performance are not closely related; and (b) they are successful because they are poorly led or managed.

In summation, what can be said with certainty is that the empirical evidence tends to show a variety of ways to distribute authority within institutions across national systems and between higher education sectors. One hypothesis may be that the increased external complexity will lead to increased internal complexity. Another hypothesis may be that managerialism probably makes less difference than commonly presumed. A point here is that all these and interrelated issues become empirical issues. Therefore, what we need is far more research on the questions of the governance and management of such a complex social organisation as a university.

References

Amaral, A., Jones, G.A. & B. Karseth, "Governing higher education: Comparing national perspectives" in Amaral, A., Jones, G.A. & Karseth, B. (eds.), *Governing higher education: National perspectives on institutional governance*, Kluwer Academic Publishers, Dordrecht, 2002, 279-298.

Amaral, A., Magalhaes, A. & R. Santiago. 2003, "The rise of academic managerialism in Portugal" in Amaral, A., Meek, V.L. & Larsen, I.M. (eds.), *The Higher Education Managerial Revolution?*, Kluwer Academic Publishers, Dordrecht, 2003, 131-154.

Ashby, E., *Universities: British, Indian and African*, Harvard University Press, Massachusetts, 1966.

Askling, B. & Henkel, M., "Higher education institutions" in Kogan, M., Bauer, M., Bleiklie, I. & Henkel, M. (eds.), *Transforming higher education: A comparative study*. London: Jessica Kingsley Publishers , 2000: 109-127.

Baldridge, J.V., *Power and conflict in the university*, John Wiley and Sons, Inc., New York, 1971.

Bargh, C., Scott, P. & Smith, D., *Governing universities: Changing the culture?* Buckingham: SRHE/Open University Press, Buckingham, 1996.

Ben-David, J. & Zloczower, A., "Universities and academic systems in modern societies", *Archives Européennes de Sociologie*, 3(1), 1962: 45-76.

Birnbaum, R., *How colleges work: The cybernetics of academic organisation and leadership*, Jossey-Bass, San Francisco, 1988.

Clark, B.R., *The higher education system: Academic organisation in cross-national perspective*, University of California Press, Los Angeles, 1983.

Clark, B.R., *Creating entrepreneurial universities: Organisational pathways of transformation*, Pergamon Press, Guildford, 1998.

Clark, B.R., "Developing a career in the study of higher education" in Smart, J. (ed.) *Higher education: Handbook of Theory and Research*. Vol. XV, Agathon Press, New York, 2000: 36-38.

Cohen, M.D. & March, J.G., *Leadership and ambiguity*, McGraw-Hill, New York, 1974.

De Boer, H., Goedegebuure, L. & Meek, V.L. (eds.), "New perspectives on governance", *Special issue of Higher Education Policy*, 11(2/3), 1998: 103-235.

De Boer, H., "Who's afraid of red, yellow and blue? The colourful world of management reforms" in Amaral, A., Meek, V.L. & Larsen, I.M. (eds.), *The Higher Education Managerial Revolution?* Kluwer Academic Publishers, Dordrecht, 2003: 89-108.

Fulton, O., "Managerialism in UK universities: Unstable hybridity and the complications of implementation" in Amaral, A., Meek, V.L. & Larsen, I.M. (eds.), *The Higher Education Managerial Revolution?* Kluwer Academic Publishers, Dordrecht, 2003: 155-178.

Kennedy, K., "Higher education governance as a key policy issue in the 21st century", *Educational research for policy and practice*, 2, 2003: 55-70.

Leicht, K. & Fenell, M., *Professional work: A sociological approach*, Blackwell Publishing, London, 2001.

Leite, D., "Institutional evaluation, management practices and capitalist redesign of the university: A case study" in Amaral, A., Meek, V.L. & Larsen, I.M. (eds.), *The Higher Education Managerial Revolution?*, Kluwer Academic Publishers, Dordrecht, 2003: 253-274.

Maasen, P., "Shifts in governance arrangements: An interpretation of the introduction of new management structures in higher education" in Amaral, A., Meek, V.L. & Larsen, I.M. (eds.), *The Higher Education Managerial Revolution?*, Kluwer Academic Publishers, Dordrecht, 2003: 31-54.

Marginson, S. & Considine, M., *The enterprise university*, Cambridge University Press, Melbourne, 2000.

Meek, V.L., "Introduction" in Amaral, A., Meek, V.L. & Larsen, I.M. (eds.), *The Higher Education Managerial Revolution?*, Kluwer Academic Publishers, Dordrecht, 2003: 1-30.

Middlehurst, R., "New realities for leadership and governance in higher education?", *Tertiary education and management*, 5, 1999: 307-329.

Millett, J.D., *New structures of campus power: Success and failure of emerging forms of institutional governance*, Jossey-Bass, San Francisco, 1978.

Mintzberg, H., *The structuring of organisations*, Prentice Hall, Englewood Cliffs, NJ, 1979.

Olsen, J.P., "The institutional dynamics of the (European) university", Working paper No. 15, University of Oslo, Centre for European Studies (ARENA), Oslo, 2005.

Reed, M.I., Meek, V.L. & Jones, G.A., "Introduction" in Amaral, A., Jones, G.A. & Karseth, B. (eds.), *Governing higher education: National perspectives on institutional governance*, Kluwer Academic Publishers, 2002: xv-xxxi.

Reed, M.I., "New managerialism, professional power and organisational governance in UK universities: A review and assessment" in Amaral, A., Jones, G.A. & Karseth, B. (eds.), *Governing higher education: National perspectives on institutional governance*, Kluwer Academic Publishers, Dordrecht, 2002: 163-186.

Salminen, A., "New public management and Finnish public sector organisations: The case of universities" in Amaral, A., Meek, V.L. & Larsen, I.M. (eds.), *The Higher Education Managerial Revolution?*, Kluwer Academic Publishers, Dordrecht, 2003: 55-70.

Scott, P., *The meanings of mass higher education*, Open University Press, Buckingham, 1995.

Stroup, H., *Bureaucracy in higher education*, The Free Press, New York, 1966.

Tjeldvoll, A., *A service university in Scandinavia?*, University of Oslo, Institute for Educational Research, Oslo, 1997.

The actors in higher education governance

Robin Farquhar

In principle, the range of actors who could play roles in the governance of higher education is virtually limitless (particularly for public institutions). The number of people who are both willing and able to do so, however, is considerably smaller. Some would like to participate but have little of value to contribute, while others could make worthwhile contributions but do not want to become involved; and those who *are* both willing and able include some for whom no opportunities are available and others who are not aware of the opportunities that *do* exist. An important challenge in university policy and management, then, is to identify persons who will contribute well to governance, convince them to act in this capacity, provide them with meaningful opportunities to do so, and enable them to play the role effectively. In confronting this challenge, several issues arise which must be addressed – and it is the purpose of this paper to discuss some of them.

Because higher education governance is situation-dependent, it is important to recognise the writer's context since my comments derive necessarily from my own experience as president of two Canadian universities. Our institutions in North America have been characterised by quite democratic forms of governance for many decades, enhanced by considerable autonomy from government authorities (even in the case of public universities). But higher education in Canada is distinct from that in the US and Europe in certain respects that are relevant to this discussion; for example:

1. we share with our American counterparts a "communitarian" conception of "ownership" (wherein participants have a common commitment to the institution, for which they feel primarily responsible), as distinct from the "stakeholder" approach found in some parts of Europe (wherein participants' principal role is to represent the interests of their respective constituencies [some of them quite political], to which they feel primarily responsible); but

2. our Canadian universities (all of which are "state" institutions) are more like the private American universities than the public ones in terms of freedom from government intervention, enjoying considerably more autonomy.

These distinctions inevitably shape the nature of higher education governance with which I am familiar, and so they must be acknowledged as contributory to what follows.

In this paper it is assumed that the potential "actors in higher education governance" have already been identified as comprising the various internal and external constituencies outlined in Jochen Fried's comprehensive review (with the addition of support staff). So attention here will focus on certain of the issues involved in engaging their participation, as encountered in my own experience:

consideration will be given first to how their different forms of participation can be structured; some approaches to stimulating their effective involvement will then be explored; and finally, various operational matters that must be managed in order to enable actors' contributions to good governance will be noted. The main contextual reference, given my experience, will be to the institutional (rather than the systemic or suprastate) level.

Organisation

At the most authoritative level, higher education governance where I come from features a "bi-cameral" structure in which university policy formulation and decision making are shared between two statutory bodies: (1) a senate (or academic council) which is comprised mainly of internal constituency representatives like faculty, students, staff and administrators, and is responsible for policies and decisions of an academic nature like admission requirements, programme curricula, graduation standards and quality assurance; and (2) a board of governors (or trustees) which consists mainly of external representatives like community leaders from the business and professional sectors, alumni representatives and government appointees, and is responsible for policies and decisions of a corporate nature like legal contracts, personnel practices, financial affairs and property management. There is obviously a possibility of conflict between these two bodies; for example, the senate may approve creating a new academic programme but the board may not have (or be unwilling to allocate) the resources and facilities necessary to implement that programme. Thus, mechanisms must be in place to reduce or eliminate such conflicts – and there are typically three means of doing this: (1) cross-membership through which the board includes some members appointed to it from the senate, and vice versa; (2) joint committees on which representatives from both bodies work through common issues together; and (3) the president (or rector) who often serves as both chair of the senate and executive officer of the board. Such "bridging" provisions are essential to effective university governance and, if they fail to produce the necessary resolution of differences, there must be a clearly recognised final arbiter with jurisdiction over all university affairs (in Canada this power is sometimes lodged with an external personage – such as a distinguished senior judge – but more usually it resides with the board itself as the ultimate institutional authority).

Care must be taken as well, of course, to clearly delineate the relationships among these statutory governing bodies, the state or national government, and the rector or president; ultimately, the crucial question is who can appoint and/or terminate whom – which boils down to which powers the government has ceded and where it has lodged them. In Canada our provincial governments (which have constitutional authority for education) have vested "ownership" of the universities in their governing boards, and only the latter can appoint or terminate a president. A subsequent issue that must be resolved is who speaks publicly for the university – the board's chair or the institution's president. We often share it, with a crude division giving primarily policy-related subjects to the former and management-oriented statements to the latter.

The participation of various actors in higher education governance, however, need not be restricted to the exercise of authority through statutory bodies (and their various committees). Indeed, governance tends to be more participatory, substantial, and influential when it is channelled through a variety of less formal structures whose mandate is advisory rather than determinative. Typical examples from my experience include:

1. curriculum development committees comprised of faculty, student, employer and professional representatives convened to review academic programme content in their areas of expertise and propose revisions in it;

2. Faculty advisory boards (especially for professional schools) through which a dean can solicit the counsel of distinguished practitioners in the field concerned on matters related to the school's mission, priorities, and programme policy;

3. presidential advisory councils, like we established in a dozen cities across Canada (with local professional and community leaders as members) to meet semi-annually and provide me with thoughtful commentary on major institutional policy and management decisions that were pending on my desk; and

4. various other established bodies that can play a role in "steering" certain elements of the organisation's operation (for example, alumni associations, women's auxiliaries, athletic "booster" clubs, etc.).

In addition to these fairly regularised avenues for input, numerous ad hoc opportunities arise continually for engaging "stakeholders" in helping to "steer" a university. These include task forces and focus groups on various topics, consultations associated with strategic planning and quality assurance, well-organised social and ceremonial events, etc.

My main point here is that the actors in higher education governance can participate in many different ways with varying degrees of authority, responsibility, accountability, scope, expertise, and effort. University leaders need to organise "menus" of such opportunities so that people in different circumstances can select those that suit them best – and these opportunities must then be made known to the constituencies that one wants to engage.

Motivation

Once the structures for engaging in higher education governance are in place, attention turns naturally to people's reasons for participating. This is important both to encouraging the involvement of those whose expertise and support are wanted, and to discouraging those who may wish to become involved for unhelpful purposes. In my experience, the typical reasons for which one seeks to participate in higher education governance include: to advance a particular cause, to pursue a special interest, to perform a civic duty, to satisfy a personal curiosity, to nurture one's own career, to do somebody a favour – or to help an institution one cares for. Obviously, some of these (especially the last) hold more potential for constructive contribution to the university's advancement than others; but it is essential to recognise that these different motivations exist, to try and identify the primary motive(s) of each individual concerned, and to keep that in mind when deciding whom to involve and how to engage them.

I believe there are two main criteria that should be applied in recruiting the actors in higher education governance: (1) representation – in order to ensure that the views of those who have a legitimate interest in a category of decisions are considered in making them; and (2) competence – in order to ensure that the kinds of knowledge required for sound decisions in a particular area are available in making them. Transcending these criteria, however, is the desirability of finding (or "training") participants whose primary loyalty is to the progress of the institution (or programme) in whose governance one is engaged. Whether appointed by an authority (for example, the ministry), elected by a constituency (for example, the students) or designated by the governing body itself (in a self-perpetuating arrangement), all those involved in a particular governance endeavour must share a principal commitment to the object of their mutual efforts – and there need to be clearly articulated and fully understood guidelines in place to resolve any conflicts of interest in this regard.

Having determined whom an institution wishes to attract and retain as actors in higher education governance, the issue of incentives to foster this arises. Participation in the leadership of university affairs has certain inherent attractions for many people – including the opportunities it provides for networking with significant fellow participants, for adding a respectable line to one's curriculum vitae, and for contributing to deliberations that are generally deemed to be important and possibly interesting. But greater inducements may be called for. At the very least, the contribution of one's time and talent to university governance activities should not result in out-of-pocket costs to that person; direct expenses incurred in the "line of duty" (such as for parking, entertainment, travel, etc.) should be reimbursed. However, one should not be financially compensated for doing the job; to do so would be inappropriate in a non-profit organisation, it might lead to awkward conflicts of interest, and it could add another reason to the list of unhelpful purposes for which people serve that I outlined previously.

There are some more positive incentives that a university can offer to governance actors. Beyond ensuring that one's participation is not an uncomfortable experience (through attention to room temperature and lighting, refreshment [free] and bathroom breaks, seating and other furnishings, etc.), the institution could provide such rewards as access to its library and fitness facilities, reduced rates for purchases at its book store and cafeteria, invitations to major athletic and cultural performances as well as to special social and ceremonial events, and the like. Also, the simple act of publicly acknowledging an actor's governance service and expressing appreciation for it on the part of senior management can go a long way toward stimulating participation.

Ultimately, however, the strongest motivator is one's genuine affection and concern for higher education in general and for a given university in particular. This inducement can be engendered and strengthened through generating a sense of shared commitment (or *esprit de corps*) among governance participants, and there are several common approaches to stimulating this. With governing boards, for example, they include such activities as:

1. day-long orientation workshops for new members each year at which questions are raised and answered and information is provided about the institution's history, mission, functions, priorities, plans, problems (current and anticipated), financial status, organisational structure, academic programmes, campus facilities (sometimes including a tour), distinctive features, key personnel, etc. – and at which the role, responsibilities, organisation and procedures of the board itself (as well as the expectations and duties of individual members) are explained;

2. annual "retreats" at which board members gather (typically at some off-campus location) for a day of discussions on such subjects as updated information about finances, enrolment and other management data, present plans and pending problems, recent trends with policy implications, and contemporary success stories that can serve as "talking points" for promoting the university publicly; these sessions can also engage governance participants in the strategic planning process, and they often include some "state-of-the-board" deliberations to assess and improve the functioning of the governing body itself; and

3. social events to encourage "bonding" among governance participants – some intended for board members only (fostering a "club" mentality) and others for significant non-participant "stakeholders" at which board members represent the institution's governing authority (fostering an "ownership" mentality).

An intended result of such activities is increased solidarity, comfort and pride in the participation of higher education governance actors, which should strengthen their motivation to serve.

Facilitation

Good governance in higher education requires more than organisational structures to accommodate it and people who are able and willing to conduct it. Certain operational norms and procedures are needed to facilitate its successful practice by the actors involved. Among them are the following:

1. Relevant, accurate, and full information is essential to wise decision making (whether advisory or determinative) by the participants in university governance. Managers must not only compile such information and make it accessible in as palatable a form as possible, but they also need to "train" the governance actors to seek and study it.

2. Included with the information that participants need to know is a clear indication of their obligations and liabilities in performing their governance roles. This is especially important for those serving a stewardship function on statutory governing bodies: they have a fiduciary duty that requires them to act honestly, with good faith and in the best interests of the organisation; and

they have a legal responsibility to ensure that the institution complies with all applicable laws and legislation, regulations and collective agreements. Those who fail in the discharge of these obligations could be held liable for damages, and they need to know this from the outset of their engagement.

3. Governance actors should understand that their work entails transmitting information as well as receiving it. In particular, those whose participation is by virtue of representing a given group of "stakeholders" (for example, students) must ensure that they inform their fellow actors of the predominant views of their constituency on the issue at hand – and no less importantly, they should make every effort to communicate back to their constituency about the governance deliberations and decisions in which they are engaged.

4. The most fundamental distinguishing value in higher education is academic freedom, so it is natural to expect that those engaged in its governance will conduct their work in a democratic fashion, welcoming legitimate differences of opinion and spirited open debate, in order that all relevant and sincere alternative positions are heard fully before reaching a decision. Meetings should be open to interested observers except in clearly confidential cases (as with sensitive personnel or contractual issues), and the decisions should be determined democratically – either by consensus (which works well with advisory bodies) or by simple majority vote (probably desirable when exercising statutory powers) – with secret ballots being rare.

5. Such deliberations should be carried out according to certain accepted norms of civil behaviour – most notably mutual courtesy, tolerance, and fairness. It is also legitimate to expect that participants will take their work seriously, will prepare in advance for governance meetings and then show up and participate genuinely in the debates, and will not publicly complain about or criticise decisions which are arrived at democratically but with which they personally disagree (as long as there has been a reasonable opportunity for their contrary views to be heard during the deliberative process).

6. Participation in higher education governance should not be a permanent engagement. While a reasonable amount of continuity among actors is desirable, there need to be clearly understood provisions – such as specified terms of office – to enable turnover among participants; this is important to expand opportunities for participation and to inject fresh views into deliberations – and it also provides graceful means to end the engagement of less productive actors. Moreover, explicit conditions should be established to terminate the participation of those whose performance is demonstrably unsatisfactory.

Operational understandings and arrangements such as the above have proven to be constructively instrumental in facilitating the engagement of actors in higher education governance.

The foregoing exposition draws on the writer's own experience to suggest some ways in which opportunities can be structured to extend the range and amount of participation by various actors in higher education governance, some approaches to rendering such participation attractive so that actors with desirable attributes will be motivated to become engaged, and certain operational arrangements that can facilitate the effectiveness of their engagement. Underlying all of this is an assumption which I have not questioned: that it is in a university's best interest to include in its governance as many of its "stakeholders" as it is possible to involve meaningfully, constructively, and productively. This assumption reflects the Canadian context from which I come, and its validity has been confirmed in that setting over many years.

However, my work during the past decade with the Salzburg Seminar and the European University Association has led me to the observation that there are certainly jurisdictions in Europe which are not ready for Canada's approach to university governance and it would be inappropriate and unwise to urge them in that direction. I stated at the beginning of this paper that higher education governance is situation-specific, and the situation in much of Europe is not suitable to the importation of a North American model. Each jurisdiction (and to some extent, every institution) needs to determine the governance arrangement that is most compatible with its own traditions and aspirations. There seems to be a trend across Europe toward expanded participation by various actors in higher education governance; I find this commendable, and I hope that our Canadian experience may be of some value as this development progresses. But I look forward to the emergence of a distinctively "made in Europe" approach, from which we in Canada will be able to learn much that is worthwhile.

What does it really mean? – The language of governance

Josef Huber

> "If you desire to see, learn to act!"
> *Heinz von Foerster*[63]

Migrating concepts

Dictionaries usually give the following definition of a concept: "a concept is an abstract or general idea inferred or derived from specific instances". As such it is a human construct and cannot be conceived of as independent of the cultural, social and economic context from which it originates. This is particularly true when a concept or a lead idea is transported by means of a simple phrase or even just a catchword. However, concepts have always travelled from one place to another, whether exported or imported, and the necessary cultural information for understanding them is neither always readily available nor consciously sought. We may adopt concepts because they seem better fit to support us in our quest to maintain or to change a status quo, we may adopt them almost osmosis-like from cultural activities/phenomena surrounding us or because they seem to represent modernity. They may, however, also be forced upon us by the presence and discourse of an economically and politically stronger power.

Concepts change, mix with the cultures that they meet, and finally might end up representing something fairly different from the original meaning they transported.

In a world of increasing international and intercultural exchange we are led to use them, discuss them, argue against and for them, take a political position for or against, negotiate their meaning, yet there will always remain a doubt whether we are talking about the same thing.

This opens up another dimension: can we really say that a concept belongs to a particular language and culture or a group of languages and cultures? At first sight one would be tempted to give a positive answer to this question, thinking of the many examples which often defy straightforward translation and may be used in other languages in their original form, like German "*Gemütlichkeit*" or "*Leitmotif*", French "*savoir vivre*", English "pub" or "soap opera".

Or to put it differently, does English "public service" evoke the same connotations as French "*service publique*" or German "*öffentlicher Dienst*"? And does everyone outside the English speaking countries fully grasp the difference between "public service" and "service to the public"? Do the terms "I love you", "*Ich hab*

---

63. Foerster, H. von, "On constructing a reality", in Preiser, F.E. (ed.), *Environmental Design and Research*, 2, Dowden Hutchinson and Ross, Stroudsburg, 1973: 35-46.

dich gern", *"Je t'aime"*, *"te quiero"* evoke the same palette of feelings? And what about complex terms like "human rights" and "democracy"?

This is not the place to attempt finding an answer to these questions, but rather to indicate their complexity. At second sight, we probably also have to consider the possibility that same or similar concepts and states of affairs might be expressed in different ways but still carry the same meaning. And translators will have to go beyond the nearest or most similar word in search for the most appropriate and fitting concept in the target language and culture if they want to avoid the criticism implied in the expression *"traduttore – traditore"*.

One obvious example of a term that has almost entirely lost its original meaning and has acquired an entirely new one is "gay", which has gone from describing a state of mind or mood to denoting sexual orientation. The English word has then migrated and been adopted in many languages in its new meaning, even where other, more native sounding words are available (cf. Spanish, which has the neutral "homosexual" and the pejorative *"maricón"*).

We will come back to the issue of translatability later on.

Governance of higher education

The Council of Europe forum on the governance of higher education presented an excellent opportunity to discuss and to clarify the concept itself and its implications for higher education systems, institutions and the different actors involved. The diversity of participants from over 40 countries coming from different backgrounds – ministerial, academic, transnational institutions, non-governmental organisations – also entails a diversity of cultures, contexts, world views and positions.

Together with the complexity of the concept, this gave rise to questions of meaning, in particular, to the question whether the term "governance" has an equivalent in the different languages represented at the forum, whether the term is used as a loan word or whether it can be translated. These questions initiated an on-the-spot collection of possible translations/ transpositions in a large number of languages.

We are aware that the translations thus collected do not constitute a valid body of data: they are more of an anecdotal nature. However, they can be seen as a first approach to the language of governance, and could serve as a starting point for reflection. In addition they could point towards the potential of future research into the implications of the migration of concepts, in particular but not only, concepts of governance, and their implications for successful international co-operation. In this context "successful" would tentatively have to be defined both as reaching the aims it sets out to do and as being accepted by all concerned.

Globalisation leads to increased contacts between different ways of doing things and going about one's business, there are cultural differences and there are language differences. A common way to show one's departure from the respective traditional codes and ways of thinking and acting lies in the adoption of a new terminology, often from "outside", from abroad, from a different language. Given the fact that language use and language change also reflect relative power gradients, these will often be taken from the language of a dominant player, in our present days very often from English.

Another factor influencing the formation and transformation of concepts and thus language change can be located in international treaties, conventions, agreements, declarations and similar documents which are the basis of international co-operation. It would be interesting to study the effect of official communiqués like for example the communiqués of the successive summits of ministers of education in the framework of the Bologna Process on the languages, the discourse and by extension the realities of the countries participating in the process.

Such a study/research would further have to address:

- the relative influence of new terminology not only on the language (through loaning and/adaptation) but also on conceptual thinking, culture and realities;

- the reciprocal influence i.e. how existing concepts in one language act upon the newly introduced concepts from outside and change their meaning (at least in a given area) and how important these departures from the original can become;

- the extent to which concepts used in international discourse transport (openly or masked) ideological bias;

- what the impact of concepts on realities really is;

- the differences between the specialist's use of a concept and the (mis)use of it by the wider public and politicians.

Furthermore, there is the question of how all these factors determine the exportability/importability of concepts which by definition consist of a diversity of constituent factors and can only 'work' when all the key constituents are united. If, for example, concept A is made up of five constituent factors, and after migration only four of them are present, it would be reasonable to assume that either the concept will not 'work' in the new context or that it will 'work' but as something which doesn't necessarily bear any major resemblance to the original. A thorough analysis of the sociocultural framework and set of interrelated factors is necessary to answer this question.

Governance in many languages

Let us now have a brief look at the translations offered in the framework of the conference.

Participants of the conference were asked to indicate the language, offer one or several translations or equivalents of the term governance and also to indicate briefly the connotations which the translated term carries in their country on the basis of their personal impression.[64]

---

64. The full list of terms and comments can be consulted in the web pages of the Council of Europe's Higher Education and Research Division at: www.coe.int/higher-education

Karavarum, kiravanne, upravljanje, upravlenie, upravljanje, řízení, proces rozhodova'ní, rozhodovací proces, vedení, vla'dnutí, management, bestuur/bestuurskunde, governance, gouvernance, mmartvelova, Steuerung, strategische Führung, Kunst der Leitung, Regelung, Organisation, Lenkung/Steuerung, Leitung, Aufsicht, diakinvernisi, kivernisi, dioikisi, diikisi, igesia, ira'nyíta's, korma'nyza's, vezete's, governo, gestione, direzione, administrazione, guida, governanza, governo allongato, governo dell' universita', párvaldíba, valdymas, upravuvanje, rakovodenje, vladeenje, tmexxija, styring, ledelse, styring, zarzadzanie, kierowanie, reprezentowanie, governanca, governo, governança, guvernação, guvernare, administrare, conducere, upravlenije, upravljanje, upravkjanje, usmerjanje, krmarjenje, gobierno, ¿gobernanza?, ledning, yönetişim, upravlinnje, pravlinnje, kerivnitstvo

In looking at these terms we need to keep in mind that these sample data were collected in a random fashion i.e. the participants' profile was relevant to the conference on higher education governance and not necessarily to a linguistic survey, and that the instructions were not very detailed. Some respondents offered just one term with or without an explanation of the connotations of the term or how this term fits into the semantic field surrounding different approaches to governing higher education, while others replied quite extensively commenting on a number of terms and their different connotations.

It is certainly true that there exists an overlap between the different connotations and that it is never easy to clearly separate the meaning of each. However, it can be noted that at a general level a majority of the connotations revolve around notions of government, control and regulation, quite often also interchangeable with management, implying top-down often also centralised processes of governance.

Language	Translation	Connotations/comments
Polish	**ZARZĄDZANIE KIEROWANIE REPREZENTOWANIE**	All are synonyms of RZĄDZENIE (RZĄD=government)
Macedonian	**UPRAVUVANJE RAKOVODENJE VLADEENJE**	No real difference of meaning between the first two terms: management and governance; governing in the sense of government
Belarusian	**KIRAVANNE**	General term (subsumes management and control)
Romanian	**GUVERNARE**	Restricted to use with central/national government
Spanish	**GOBIERNO**	Government, no specific term for "governance"
Hungarian	**IRA'NYÍTA'S**	Command, control, direction

A second set takes up the idea of 'steering' which is nearer to the meaning of the word of Greek origin '*kybernaein*' (to steer a vessel), as Pavel Zgaga explains in his article (p. 33), but does not necessarily point towards any specific form of steering be it centralised or decentralised, top-down or bottom-up.

156

Language	Translation	Connotations/comments
Norwegian	**STYRING**	Steering, but not only
Croatian	**UPRAVLJANJE**	To control direction, to navigate, to make steps with amplified effects; the same word would be used for management
Slovenian	**UPRAVLJANJE**	"prav" = right; give right course, direction
Swedish	**LEDNING**	Steering[65]
Ukrainian	**UPRAVLINNJE**	Polysemic term: steering, direction
German	**STEUERUNG LENKUNG/ STEUERUNG LEITUNG**	Technocratic/managerial Both with the "steering wheel" connotation of the term "governance"
Dutch	**BESTUUR/ BESTUURSKUNDE**	Related with steering

There is a third set that refers more to 'leadership' or 'taking the lead' thus putting the accents more on the actors than on structures and processes.

Language	Translation	Connotations/comments
Norwegian	**LEDELSE**	Leadership, management
German	**STRATEGISCHE FÜHRUNG**	Task-oriented
Hungarian	**VEZETE'S**	Lead, control
Italian	**GUIDA**	Steering
Greek	**IGESIA**	Leadership

There are a number of examples which deserve special attention be it by their brevity, the imagery implied or by the comprehensiveness of the explanation given.

The *'process of decision-making'* in Czech will be called *'proces rozhodova'ní'*, while in Georgian *'mmartvelova'* implies *'ruling'* (with connotations of "driving" a car for example). The English definition of governance offered goes well beyond the processes and includes the relationship of these processes to agreed values and preferences by stating "the processes and institutions by which revealed values and preferences translate into collective actions that enhance the security, prosperity and moral development of a group and its individual membership".

---

65. Norwegian and Danish "*ledelse*" would be the same, but all three have elements of governing, leading, setting the course for others to follow. Swedish and Danish have "*styrelse*", which is the same word as Norwegian "*styring*", but may be used more to denote bodies than action.

The Maltese term '*tmexxija*' (pronounced 'tmeshiya') seems to put the focus on purposeful action aimed at advancing '*mexa* = to walk; *mexxa* = to make/ cause to walk or proceed; *tmexxija* = an abstract noun implying leadership and administration', although, due to the fact that English is an official language in Malta, the English term governance is mainly used in the higher education community even when speaking Maltese.

Greek offers an example of ongoing language change. A new term, '*diakin-vernisi*', has recently appeared to take its due place amidst words referring to government, leadership, steering and control. It expresses 'the way one governs, the system of parameters affecting the act of governing, the results of governing'. Dionyssis Kladis offered a more extensive explanation which I would like to quote in its entirety:

THE TERM "GOVERNANCE" IN THE GREEK LANGUAGE

In general, the term "GOVERNANCE" is used as the noun derived from the verb "TO GOVERN". Until recently in Greece, the term "GOVERNANCE" had the same meaning with the terms "MANAGEMENT" and "GOVERNMENT". Even now, the confusion still exists and, in many cases the term "GOVERNANCE" is still used with the same meaning. However recently, a new Greek term has appeared, aiming at expressing the meaning of the term "GOVERNANCE". This is the word "ΔΙΑΚΥΒΕΡΝΗΣΗ" ("DIAKIVERNISI") and has the following meanings:

1. The act of governing itself.

2. The results that are derived from governing.

3. The principles and values that affect the act of governing.

4. The manners used in governing or the way in which one governs.

As we can see from this brief glance at the collected sample data from different linguistic, cultural and sociopolitical contexts, the semantic and lexical field surrounding the concept of governance spans a wide array of connotations which would deserve further study and research.

The results of such a research, based on distinctive features analysis, could offer what could be called an intercultural mind map of the meaning of governance highlighting distinctive as well as shared features along central markers such as *control, centralisation, top-down, autonomy, accountability, transparency, inclusiveness, efficiency, legitimacy*, etc., indicating their presence or absence and scaling their relative importance.

Such a study would not only be an interesting contribution to comparative semantics and semiotics, but it would also contribute to intercultural understanding and allow an appreciation of potential obstacles and resistances.

From buzzwords to shared understanding of actions

Between the dictionary meaning, with or without recourse to etymology, the acquired meaning in a given context and the particular and very diverse meanings individuals may attach to a concept, there might be a world of difference.

Perhaps, for understanding's sake we have to turn to another alternative and this is the point to come back to the quotation at the beginning of this article "If you desire to see, learn to act". This 'imperative of learning', as Heinz von Foerster calls it, can be understood as implying that the meaning of a concept can only be seen and understood through the actions that follow and exemplify it. It is in the nature, orientation, content and impact of the actions that we enact our understanding of the concept and thus bring it to life.

Focusing on the concrete actions has the added advantage of facilitating a shared understanding of the meaning and of being easier to translate.

The current publication may well be a step towards such an action-oriented approach to the definition of governance and help to find a common language.

In the end it may prove less important what we call it than what we actually do, whether we are doing the right things and whether we are doing these things right.

Case studies

Educational reforms in Georgia – A case study

Aleksander Lomaia

> "Good policy begins with sound diagnosis"
> *Aoki et al., 2002*

1. Introduction

For about 70 years, Georgia as a republic of the Soviet Union was seldom associated with a separate country and the international community on the opposite side of the Iron Curtain knew almost nothing about its long-standing history and culture. Awareness of and interest in Georgia was particularly intensified since the Rose Revolution in November 2003. After this peaceful revolution the reform process was introduced and the new government with the incumbent president, Mikheil Saakashvili, embarked on a large-scale project of radical restructuring, encompassing every sphere of public activity, including political, economic, social and cultural areas. The strategy of contemporary Georgia is clear-cut and straightforward i.e. *smoother integration with Europe*.

2. Educational reforms in post-Soviet Georgia 1990-2003

Reforms in the educational system of Georgia were launched immediately after gaining independence in 1991. It was self-evident that with the arrival of the new regime fresh policies had to be implemented. Policies are usually implemented by the decision makers whilst the aftermath of the Soviet Union was marked and marred by the extreme dearth of qualified professionals. Even though the European experience was taken as a role model, still there were neither human nor financial resources to implement the policies effectively and efficiently.

The soviet regime was notorious for its extreme centralism and *ideologically driven policies* that were dictated from above. The whole machinery was designed according to the pyramid principle, where the top was the Kremlin and the republics were acting like marionettes i.e. they were extremely vulnerable without instructions from above. Education and science policy was one of the major instruments maintaining the status quo. A high rate of employment was ensured by a stiff employment policy elaborated well in advance. The private sector was non-existent and economic stagnation was artificially preserved. The learning process was extremely teacher-centred and academic achievement was associated with the mechanical memorisation of texts without questioning or challenging their content or volume. In most cases the taught subjects were divorced from reality and they were useless on the labour market. Even though the general education was free and mandatory and the literacy rate was quite high, access to the advanced knowledge was still elitist and it was open only to the highest strata of society. The borders of the Soviet Union were closed and access to any information was strongly controlled. All information was first filtered and then channelled to specific layers of society. In such circumstances gaining independence was like sunstroke, paralysing the whole country. The people did not have adequate skills, knowledge and experience in taking independent decisions and thus mismanagement problems cropped up in every field.

Despite the myriad of problems in education a lot of changes have occurred since 1991, for example:

- in 1991 by decree of the Supreme Council a private sector was introduced;

- in 1992 the Cabinet of Ministers adopted a decree on granting a limited autonomy to higher education institutions;

- in 1993 the two-cycle degree system based on 4+2 formulae was formally established;

- tuition fees were also introduced for some sectors of state institutions.

Despite these novelties, in reality these shifts were quite superficial. Instead of resource optimisation and cost-effectiveness of operations, institutional autonomy entailed anarchy and professional incompetence. It became common practice to open new degree programmes without any approval by professional groups. The shadow economy was flourishing and was provoking *rampant corruption*. In 1995-2000 the average salary of a university teacher possessing advanced scientific degrees constituted around €20 (equivalent in Georgian laris (GEL)), 10 times less than it was in 1990. Paradoxically, the official income of a professor was less than that of a watchman or an office cleaner. Besides, public universities still used the Soviet system of remuneration, which was based on an individual's formal qualifications and length of service rather than on performance and achievement, thus providing few incentives for improved performance and professional growth. Moreover, frequently the salaries were *frozen* for months and people were not paid at all. Thus the system itself was the prime instigator of corruption and society was implicitly or explicitly forced to engage in illegal activities.

In terms of corruption, the worst cases were detectable at the *admission exams* where even the least-qualified candidates could easily gain entry to higher education institutions using backdoor means, such as bribery, political or personal connections and influence. According to some estimates most slots at public institutions were sold outright to prospective students. Only 15% to 20% of the students who entered the Tbilisi State University, did so without paying bribes. According to a survey published by the Transnational Crime and Corruption Centre (TRAC-CC) based at the American University in Washington, DC, students applying to Tbilisi State University faced fees from US$5 000 to US$15 000 for entrance exam preparation classes taught by the same professors administering the tests. According to a survey conducted by the Georgian government in 2001, families spent at least GEL12 million (approx. US$6 700 000) every year on so-called private tutors for university entrance exams. But in addition to the millions spent on tutors, the government found that another GEL6.4 million (approx. US$3 600 000) was being paid every year directly as bribes. These figures alone total 18.4 million, a sum greater than the 2004 budgets of Georgia's five leading universities.

As for the *private sector*, the Ministry of Education was authorised to issue licences and over about three years 294 higher educational institutions were licensed. The private institutions acted like diploma mills without paying due attention to quality and academic excellence. As a result, the number of higher education diploma holders was skyrocketing whereas the state could not provide jobs even to half of them. The problem was particularly exacerbated because of the so-called prestigious professions. The majority of people obtained diplomas in medicine and law whereas the country did not need so many doctors and lawyers. For example, each year, the system of medical schools granted medical diplomas to about 3 000 youths, whereas the Georgian medical system needs no more than 300 new young medical doctors per year.[66] Deteriorating educational quality, mushrooming higher education institutions, overproduction of diploma holders all together provoked an alarming situation on the local labour market.

Another problem was related to introduction of the two-cycle degree system. The majority of higher education institutions in Georgia moved to this system without first adjusting the management system, content of the programmes as well as the material-technical basis. To be more specific, in most cases the Soviet-type one-cycle study programmes were merely split into two cycles and the methodology, curriculum and the reading literature remained the same.

The hidden crisis[67] was first and foremost predetermined by the decreasing share of education in the budget of the country. Besides in 1997-2003 the state debt, to ministry staff only, reached GEL22 500 879 00.[68]

In the early 1990s there were several attempts to introduce an *accreditation* system in Georgia that was also reflected in the N 435 decree of the parliament adopted in March 1994. In January 1995 the Cabinet of Ministers established the first national council of accreditation the so-called "Attestation and Accreditation Commission of Non-state Higher Education Institutions". However, the commission ceased its work in 1995. The first attempts of accreditation were designed for the medical programmes. On the basis of the N379 Order of the president on the Complementary Measures for the Improvement of Higher Medical Education of Georgia, and by the joint Order (402/387) of the Ministry of Education and the Ministry of Health Care in 1996, the State Commission of Attestation and

---

66. UNDP, 2000.
67. According to Barnett and Cnobloch (2003) "the crisis among CIS-7 countries (Armenia, Azerbaijan, Georgia, Kyrgyz Republic, Moldova, Tajikistan and Uzbekistan) is hidden for three reasons. First, [...] the education systems continue to function and have not collapsed. Second, the crisis has been somewhat masked by more successful reform efforts in transition countries with higher per capita incomes, such as those seeking European Union accession. Third, the hidden crisis has not provoked any visible human or fiscal crises, as has happened with attempts to shore up deteriorating health and social protection programs. The medium- and long-term effects of the hidden crises in education among the CIS-7 countries are likely to be very serious indeed, however, if deep reforms are not urgently undertaken. Fortunately it is not too late, and there are some encouraging signs of a growing realization that reform is necessary".
68. To date the exchange rate between the euro and the Georgian lari is approx. 1:2.25.

Accreditation was set up. The commission elaborated a self-evaluation question-naire and started an accreditation process that consisted of two phases – internal evaluation and peer review. The commission elaborated a recommendation about the integration of medical institutions; however, the number of private medical institutes did not diminish. There were several additional attempts aimed at devel-oping the accreditation system in the following years, but the comprehensive accreditation process was not organised until this year.

Despite the above mentioned shortcomings there were several important meas-ures that significantly contributed to the harmonisation of the Georgian education system with European standards. For example, Georgia had already joined the ENIC network in 1994 and in 1997, it signed the Lisbon Recognition Convention that was ratified by Parliament in 1999. Besides, Georgia had been involved in the Council of Europe project "Education for Democratic Citizenship" (EDC) since it was launched in 1997. Georgia was also actively involved in the UNESCO project "Education for All" and. the Tempus-Tacis projects, etc. In 1997, Georgia signed the "Partnership and Cooperation Agreement" with the EU of which Articles 53-54 dealt with issues of co-operation in science, technology, education and training respectively.

3. Educational restructuring since the Rose Revolution

After the Rose Revolution, educational restructuring became one of the major pri-orities of the present government. The strategy for change is comprehensive and multifaceted; it envisages all levels and forms of formal and informal education such as pre-primary, primary, secondary, vocational and higher. The course of change is explicitly European but local needs, strengths and peculiarities are taken into consideration to the maximum.

More specifically the *educational reforms* envisaged introducing novelties in the following areas:

- governance
- legislation
- financing formulae
- civic integration
- curricula and textbooks
- teachers' professional development
- child care

The first steps taken were the complete reorganisation of the Ministry of Education including human resources and its structure. In March 2004, by Decree No. 81 of the president, the ministry was renamed and it became the Ministry of Education and Science of Georgia. The reorganisation included recruitment of new staff through open competition where everyone meeting the minimum qual-ification requirements could participate. Consequently, the number of ministry staff dropped from 289 to 155 (65% women, 35% men), their average age also decreased from 51 to 38 and the minimum salary increased from GEL37 to at least GEL115.[69]

At present *the mission* of the Ministry of Education and Science of Georgia is to:

- assure growing welfare and well-being of citizens via the reforms in education and science;
- create a solid basis for developing a knowledge-based society;
- assure equal access to education;
- foster lifelong and life-wide learning opportunities;
- initiate civic integration processes and implement the official language policy;
- facilitate freedom of choice in education;
- safeguard creativity, innovation, academic freedom and institutional autonomy;
- develop an education system that meets the local and international labour market demands, etc.

In addition, the *aims and objectives* of the ongoing reforms include:

- to democratise and decentralise the education and science administration system;
- to introduce a needs- and performance-based financing system.

Joining the Bologna Process was the top priority from the very beginning of educational restructuring and therefore it was essential to meet the minimum international requirements in a very limited period of time. The Bologna Process is an attractive initiative for Georgia since:

- it is a voluntary initiative and not legally binding;
- it focuses on quality and excellence;
- it advocates co-operation versus competition;
- it encourages public-private partnership;
- it envisages wider social engagement and public accountability of universities;
- it combats unemployment via competence-building, internationalisation, recognition, etc.

To meet the minimum requirements for joining the Bologna Process three major reform directions were identified:

- harmonisation of the legislative basis with European standards;
- elimination of corruption at the systemic level;
- introduction of a new model of financing;
- introduction of the up-to-date study programmes curricula, syllabi at HEIs;
- introduction of ECTS and the three cycle degree system, etc.

---

69. Recently, the minimum salary increased to GEL250.

To date, substantial measures in all the directions have already been taken. On 21 December 2004, the Parliament of Georgia adopted the Law of Georgia on Higher Education.[70] Work on the law commenced in 2004 and around 12 000 people participated in the discussions at a series of meetings throughout the country. The law fundamentally alters the existing system of higher education and is compatible with the contemporary international requirements. Specifically, the law regulates the structure of higher education institutions, its management, financing, licensing, accreditation, the rules of student admission, etc. It also responds to all the major action lines set forth at the ministerial conferences of the Bologna Process such as quality assurance, public accountability, and self-governance by elected bodies. More specifically it includes:

- adoption of a system of easily readable and comparable degrees through the standardised diploma supplement issued in one of the internationally spoken languages and free of charge (Chapter I, Article 2, Point "p" also the Order N 149 of the Minister of Education and Science);

- adoption of the European Credit Transfer and Accumulation System (Chapter XV, Point 8);

- award of state grants to students with the highest scores at the Unified National University Entry Examinations (Chapter XIII, Article 80);

- reservation of a third of the seats for students in the representative bodies known as the senates at state universities (Chapter IV, Article 17, Point 4);

- provisions for the autonomy of and academic freedom at higher education institutions (Chapter IV);

- assurance of quality through the accreditation procedures (Chapter X);

- assurance of synergy between higher education and research (Chapter VII);

- adoption of a three-cycle degree system (Chapter VII, Article 46, Point 2, Subpoints "a", "b", "c"):

  ✔ *Bachelor's Degree (at least 3 years)*[71]

  ✔ *Master's Degree (at least 2 years)*

  ✔ *Doctoral Degree (at least 3 years) (Chapter VII), etc.*

In addition to the law, according to the N 13 Decree of the Government of Georgia released on 25 January 2005, 250 grants are to be allocated from a special fund to socially or economically vulnerable students, internally displaced persons and ethnic minorities for the academic year 2005-06.

According to the N 470 Order of the President of Georgia released on 24 October 2004, the Accreditation Council of Higher Education Institutions was set up and institutional accreditation was conducted in January 2005. The following criteria

---

70. The law can be downloaded from the Ministry of Education and Science web page at: www.mes.gov.ge or from the Bologna Secretariat web page at: www.dfes.gov.uk/bologna/
71. Duration of the programmes will soon be substituted by the number of credits.

were used during the accreditation process: (1) the percentage of professors with scientific/academic degrees; (2) student/class size ratio; (3) access to books in libraries; (4) number of personal computers; (5) number of foreign students, and (6) the existence of a web page. The *institutional accreditation* was completed in February 2005. Consequently, out of 237 higher education institutions applying for accreditation less than half of them (48%) were accredited. Non-accredited higher education institutions were not allowed to admit students this year, as the state would not recognise the diplomas of such students. Those higher education institutions that could not gain accreditation this year are allowed to reapply during the following two years.

Another major reform priority was to eliminate corruption in higher education especially at admission exams. The challenge was taken up with the introduction of a completely new model of admission exams. According to the Law of Georgia on Higher Education (Article 89, p.4), in 2005-06 Unified National University Entry Examinations were held throughout Georgia starting on 11 July and finishing on 22 July 2005. This system implies that all the citizens of Georgia who wish to advance their studies at a higher level will have to pass this centralised form of test-based admission exams. This model of exams was elaborated by the National Assessment and Examination Centre (NAEC). The Unified National University Entry Examinations' tests were based on the secondary school study programme. The aim of the Unified National University Entry Examinations is to assess knowledge and skills of entrants objectively, fairly and in a unified manner, to assure maximum transparency and to reveal the best and the brightest. The examination scores were calculated according to the method of *scaling* that is well established in psychometrics. This method enables evaluators to compare the scores received in different subjects with scientific precision.

The admission exams were held simultaneously in all the major cities of Georgia within the 14 admission centres. Up to 76 registration points had been open since February 2005 and served as information and registration centres. In order to better disseminate the information about dates, procedures, rules and the methodology of the exams, a large media campaign had been launched including radio, TV and printing media. Interested persons could also get updated information on the web pages of the NAEC and the Ministry of Education and Science of Georgia. Besides, special manuals and guidelines were published and distributed in all the secondary schools of Georgia. The exams were held in the following subjects:

• Georgian language and literature;

• foreign language (English, French, German or Russian);

• general aptitudes;

• mathematics.

At least two and at most three assessors scored each test independently from each other. This mechanism was elaborated in order to ensure maximum impartiality and fairness. Out of 31 171 registered entrants, 16 507 were admitted and 4 198 of them received state grants that fully cover tuition costs at state-run HEIs. Accordingly, the number of admitted students has been significantly diminished from 35 000 to 16 507 as compared with 2004.

This new model of admission exams is innovative because of a number of reasons:

1. The entrants had the possibility to choose up to five specialties according to their preference at the same or various higher education institutions; thus the chance to gain entrance at least to one of the HEIs was increased.

2. Exams in general aptitudes were included to check the critical-analytical reasoning skills of entrants.

3. The top-scoring entrants received state grants ranging from GEL1 000 to GEL1 500. This new "money follows the student" formula radically changes the former lump sum allocation model of financing education.

4. Students receiving the highest marks on the entrance exams received a grant they could redeem as tuition at any state institution or accredited private college of their own choosing, meaning that instead of throngs of students competing for one university, numerous universities were competing for students. The previous system restricted students by forcing them to take an *all-or-nothing* approach. That is, every university had its own distinct entrance exam and with testing periods overlapping, it was logistically unfeasible for students to apply to more than one institute.

In order to avoid any falsification of results, all the tests were printed in England at the Cambridge University Printing House. Hundreds of test versions were sent electronically to the printing house and with the help of special software programmes only randomly selected tests were printed. The safely sealed tests were sent back to Georgia under tight security guidance and the sealed packages were opened in front of the entrants. To secure anonymity of entrants unique bar codes had been attached to the tests and thus the assessors could not know the identity of entrants. The assessors were selected from all around the country based on their merit and competence. Video cameras were installed at all the examination centres and everybody could watch the examination process from screens fixed outside the examination buildings. The recorded tapes of all the exams were kept in a special safe. The examination processes were monitored by specially trained observers, who did not know in advance to which centre they would be assigned. For example, 30 observers from Transparency International Georgia attended the 14 examination centres during all four sessions and at each centre there were two insiders observing the process of the examination and two outsiders observing the exams from outside. The representatives of the organisation interviewed 973 entrants, 764 parents and 340 examination administrators. About 91% of entrants, 80% of parents and 93% of the examination administrators evaluated the new admission system highly positively.[72]

The president of Georgia commented that the new model of Unified National University Entry Examinations is the beginning of a new era where corruption is no longer possible and where one has to work very hard in order to succeed. It is

---

72. A full report of the first Unified National University Entry Examinations held in Georgia can be downloaded from the NAEC web page at: www.naec.ge

expected that through the new system of admission exams the vicious circle of systemic corruption will be transformed into the virtuous circle of meritocracy and a new generation of students who truly earn their places at the higher education institutions of Georgia will turn into constructive partners and consumers of knowledge and services offered at the modernised higher education institutions.

4. Final remarks

The radical reforms in Georgia entailed the following substantial changes:

- National Aims of General Education were approved by the Government (Decree N84; 18 October 2004);

- the Law on Higher Education was adopted (21 December 2004);

- the Law on General Education was adopted (8 April 2005);

- university and school teachers' salary and stipend arrears comprising GEL49 million were paid;

- the first institutional accreditation of higher education institutions were completed (10 February 2005);

- Georgia joined the Bologna Process (19 May 2005);

- the Concept on Vocational Education of Georgia has been approved by the Government (Decree N150; 31 August 2005) and the draft law will be submitted to the Parliament in 2006.

The following projects are still to be implemented:

- the concept on teachers professional development is being prepared;

- the programme "Deer Leap" of complete computerisation and internet connection of schools absorbing GEL3.3 m (approx.US$1.8m) from the budget for the year 2005 and GEL8 m (approx. US$4.4m) in 2006[73] was launched.

The criteria for assessing the outcome of the reforms are based on the indicators elaborated by the Organisation for Economic Co-operation and Development (OECD), such as:

- quality of education and science;

- accessibility of education;

- student achievements in international assessment systems;

- increasing the volume of financing including the financial normative calculated per student and the salaries of scientists, researchers and teachers;

- approximating the material-technical basis to international standards;

- contemporary IT policy (coefficient – a computer per student);

- international recognition of higher education, science and research;

---

73. In addition to the budget allocations, US$2.8 m is allocated by the British Petroleum Co plc (BP).

• enhanced inflow of foreign students;

• compatibility of student achievements with the benchmarks of the educational programme;

• reduced number of children and adolescents left behind in the study processes;

• increased enrolment ratio of students at vocational institutions;

• reduced brain drain in science and research;

• lower average age of scientific personnel;

• increased employability of graduates.

Despite the tangible results, the education reform in Georgia is still at the inception phase. The real success can be celebrated once the adopted laws are effectively established within the education system of Georgia, and their efficiency is positively reflected in the daily life of the people of Georgia.

5. Suggestions for recommendations

• In the contemporary market-driven environment where academic aspirations and market forces are closely interconnected and education is increasingly considered as a service industry in international trade agreements, students are viewed as consumers and customers. Students expect that the time and money spent at an institution is an investment in their capacities and competences. In this sense HEIs are expected to offer a product that will be profitable both individually and socially.

• In the rapidly changing environment, there is no time for gradual transition; radical decisions and actions are to be taken, causing dissatisfaction, public distrust and fear. One has to be prepared from the very beginning that reforms are not there to be loved by the whole society and sometimes you have to take some very painful steps. But it's like curing people – you may have to inflict some pain to cure the patient.

• To meet the societal expectations and market demands HEIs should have adequate human, material and financial resources and efficient strategic policies envisaging continuous fund-raising through liaising with the business sector and networking with international partners.

• The majority of HEIs now lack the necessary human resources such as qualified managers and specialists in social restructuring. In such situations the optimal solution is to make an in-depth study of the existing human, material and financial resources and initiate mobility schemes for students and staff. Assistance from the public sector as well as international organisations can play a vital role.

• The prerequisite for successful reforms is the incremental financial provision both from public and private sources. Scarce financial resources may become the reason for failure of the reform. The reform implementation is also connected with the readiness of higher education institutions to implement the changes envisaged by the process. Success significantly depends on the position of the governing bodies and on active public engagement in the process of reform implementation.

• The issue of corruption is not only about the system but also about the perception. Transition from the centralised, ideologically-driven, bureaucratic system towards the democratic, decentralised model is a radical shift and entails a number of factors obstructing the smooth flow of the process. The principal bottleneck is the cynicism and distrust of society and a vehement opposition of the proponents of the old system. The reform process envisages that academic councils composed of university faculty will still retain power over academic issues but with more students involved in administrative and financial oversight, thus universities will become increasingly effective and decreasingly corrupt. Besides, it is very important that universities are autonomous and at the same time accountable to the public, it allows public universities to be democratically governed from inside.

References

Aoki, A. et al., "Education" (Chapter 19, draft 22 July 2002) in The World Bank Group, Poverty Reduction Strategy Plan, Vol. 2, *Macroeconomic and Sectoral Approaches*, The World Bank Group, Washington, DC, 2002.

Barnett, N. & Cnobloch, R., *Public spending on education in the CIS-7 Countries: The hidden crisis*, the paper prepared for the Lucerne Conference of the CIS-7 initiative, 2003. Retrieved from
http://lnweb18.worldbank.org/eca/cis7.nsf/ECADocByUnid/85256C370063EBBE 85256C14005956DF/$FILE/Burnett%20-%20Education%20-E-%2022DEC-I.pdf

Beradze, T., & Sanadze, M., *Saqartvelos Istoria*, Book I, Saqartvelos Matsne, Tbilisi, 2003.

Botkin, J., *Toward a wisdom society: An interview with James Botkin by V. Miller & M. Jain*, 2003. Retrieved from http://.newhorizons.org/trans/botkin.htm

Noah, H.J. & Eckstein, M.A., *Doing comparative education: Three decades of collaboration*, Comparative Education Research Centre, Hong Kong, The University of Hong Kong, 1998, Chapters 1-3.

Janashia, N., *Fighting Corruption in Georgia's Universities*, 2004. Retrieved from http//www.bc.edu/bc_org/avp/soe/cihe/newsletter/News34/text006.htm

Peuch, J.C., "Georgia: Education Minister Determined to Proceed with Controversial Reforms", Radio Free Europe, 2004.

United Nations, "Towards a Knowledge Based Economy. Georgia", *Country Readiness Assessment Report*, United Nations, Geneva, 2002. Retrieved 4 April 2003, from http://www.unece.org/operact/enterp/documents/coverpaggeorgia.pdf

United Nations Development Programme (UNDP), United Nations Human Development Report (2000), "Dimensions of Human Development", Chapter 4. Retrieved 25 March 2002, from http:www.undp.org.ge/nhdr2000/chpt4.htm

The governance of higher education systems – Lessons from Estonia

Jaak Aaviksoo

The university (or universities) as such has (have) proven to be one of the most viable organisations of modern civilisation – the history of which goes back to the late 11th or early 12th century at the start of the Middle Ages. Even individual institutions, in spite of temporary setbacks, have survived through many social, economic and cultural changes. In general, universities are believed to be very conservative organisations and this fits well with both their long history as well as the personal experience of most people that things do not change at too fast a pace in universities. At the same time, the mere fact of surviving all these changes indicates that universities have to be very adaptable organisations. They may well be called the most experienced learning organisations in the world.

In recent years, increasingly more people and different stakeholders are, however, raising and emphasising the need to modernise and reform the universities so as to better serve the stakeholders and respond to the changing needs of society. Usually people mean by this that the changes have to take place first and foremost in the universities themselves. Universities have to start moving (at last!). Why is it then that these organisations of learning do not respond adequately and fast enough to the changing environment? Although I do not believe that universities should react hastily to every external change, however important, it is right to pose this question. In modern societies, universities (hereafter all higher education institutions) do not function as independent players in a more or less regulated market but as elements of (national) higher education systems, which to a large extent defines their mission, rules and modus vivendi and even, sometimes, identity. It is my deep conviction that most of the problems which our nations' different higher education institutions face are much more linked to the bottlenecks in the system rather than at the institutional level. It follows both from horizontal or international comparisons as well as from the historical perspective. Higher education has been under growing pressure over the last ten to fifteen years and it has yet to attain equilibrium despite all the changes that have already been undertaken and are taking place. But in contrast to the last major change in higher education, the expansion of the late 1960s and 1970s when it was possible to respond (to the growing demand for higher education and need for a highly qualified workforce) at the national level, modern pressures are essentially global. What the universities face, governments follow and society grasps at large – increasing competition, more turbulent dynamics of economic and social variables, controversial and even conflicting signals from the stakeholders, unpredictability of the expectations of outcomes, increasing risks of all sorts and related fears and, last but not least, irrational financing patterns – is not due to national

175

developments but more the indirect result of globalisation. Here I use the trifle hackneyed term of globalisation to denote the global dimension of the increasingly free movement of goods, capital, services, information and people (labour).

National higher education systems were established to function within national limits in times when national armies controlled the borders, national steel and coal companies supplied them to do so and self-sufficient sovereign states used national flagship airlines to fly to bilateral trade meetings to agree on protectionist taxes, tariffs and quotas. These times are long gone but national higher education systems still survive and most probably they will also outlive national energy and other utility monopolies now yielding to pressure. Education is a sensitive topic – it touches and is believed to shape the core of every individual and collective identity. Since the 12th century (when the Bologna University was established) universities were founded by giving them an identity or a name and privileges related to them by the Pope, a king (or sometimes a duke) and later (national) governments. In return, they were expected to commit themselves to their mission – to serve the good cause of their founders by increasing their prestige. Alexander von Humboldt reformed the university by exhorting them to serve the Truth and granting them the academic freedom to do so, but the system was already in place. The system (level) was further strengthened after the emergence of the nation state and especially when (European) governments took to funding students' tuition fees. The (national higher education) systems stand strong today and it is most interesting to follow one of the most remarkable developments – the Bologna Process – which poses a fundamental dilemma between a European vision of global appeal – the European Higher Education Area (EHEA) – and the national systems.

I turn to my country/nation Estonia. Ours is a small country with a "long history" – converted to Christianity by the Germans and the Danes in the early 13th century, the Estonians have experienced the rule of the Germans, the Swedes, the Poles and the Russians. Our first university – the University of Tartu – was founded by the Swedish King Gustav II Adolf in 1632. In 1802 it became a Russian Imperial University teaching in German for almost a century. The Russian higher education system, largely thanks to Tartu University, was based on the German (Humboldtian) model as was the case almost everywhere in eastern and central Europe. There was an academic continuity, despite all political changes, which lasted until the time to which the Estonians refer to as 'the singing revolution' of 1988-91. In 1988 we had a Soviet higher education system, based on the German model, which combines the academic ideas of von Humboldt with the systematic objective logic of Hegel and the statesmanship of Bismarck. The Soviets added the totalitarian-bureaucratic organisation under a Ministry of Higher Education (one of more than 120 ministries, which functioned as state monopolies in their respective areas of responsibility). This may be styled a higher education system par excellence. There followed the years 1988-95 and until 2003 when it was replaced by an Estonian system largely built on grass-roots ideas about "a market-oriented democratic western higher education system". Nobody really knew what this meant but it posed no problem. Today to some of the participants of the revolution, myself included, this does not unduly worry us.

Why is this interesting to understand and analyse? Primarily because of the extent of the socio-economic change, which was enormous. In all former changes in Estonia (and there have been very many) most legal, social and even economic institutions were left in place, at least for long periods. In this case, all the laws and other rules and regulations were at least questioned if not at first ignored then later replaced. This was largely the case in all former Soviet dominated countries but the Baltic states had to recreate their statehood from the beginning and the Estonians were probably the most radically minded in doing everything differently and as fast as possible. So we have a unique case of replacing a carefully planned higher education system by a new one, built from scratch from grass-roots ideas under a strongly market-oriented, democratic and very open public sentiment. Even knowing that the terms describing the context differ from their established meaning in more developed European countries, it surely indicates in which direction these ideas push the established system when given a chance.

The first reform ideas (in the years 1988 to 1992) were bottom-up and rather revolutionary or at least did not comply with any rules previously in force. In 1988, after the death of the rector, appointed by the Communist Party, and who had managed the university for seventeen years, the University of Tartu itself decided to elect the new rector and formed an Electoral Assembly composed of university members including students. The authorities, after some very serious consultations, surrendered and recognised the new rector. The next step was to revise the rigid Soviet study programmes by cancelling a number of disciplines, first of all those connected with military training and communist ideology. At the same time the first private universities emerged, although without formal recognition by the Estonian rather reform-minded regional government let alone with the consent of the central government in Moscow. A sufficient number of people trusted the enthusiastic educational entrepreneurs and some of both the entrepreneurs and students are now among the ruling elite of Estonia today. It may sound strange, but technically-speaking most of the private university graduates of the first years still do not have officially recognised diplomas, although this causes no problems in practice. It is also noteworthy that all the founders of the first private universities had some American academic experience and that they started to award bachelor and master degrees from the very beginning when these degrees had no official status in the Soviet system which was still in place.

In these years, the Senate of the then so-named Tartu State University decided to restore its former name Tartu University. Other higher educational institutions like the Tallinn Polytechnic Institute and the Tallinn Teacher Training Institute "upgraded" themselves into universities. Next, a semi-official decision was taken by the Estonian government – they gave universities (note: all institutions which called themselves universities) the right to award academic degrees (until that point only the Higher Attestation Committee in Moscow had the right to do so). Let me summarise. What did people (it was very important to have wide public support for these revolutionary steps, otherwise the authorities would surely have intervened by legal means) and academic institutions consider as important in these initial times of change? Firstly, institutional autonomy or rather the legal right to act on our own behalf (or to decide our own destiny). Secondly, the right to establish our identity. Thirdly, the understanding that higher education has to be a free (from outside interference) trade. Lastly, the understanding that academic programmes, including their objectives and outcomes, and not only the ways to achieve these, are an institutional responsibility. These ideas are fundamental to the present debate about the possible ways ahead in higher education in a number of countries worldwide and especially in Europe. This is also the reason why the development of these ideas in Estonia and the lessons, which we have sometimes painfully learnt, may be useful.

In 1992, four months before the Estonian Parliament adopted the new constitution, the Act on Education became law, which, although being very declarative in general, fixed the basic "democratic" principles of higher education. This law is still in force despite several recent efforts to replace it with a "constitutional law". It has become evident that the broad although superficial consensus on several educational issues that allowed us to adopt the first liberal framework law has, to some extent, disappeared.

The radical ideas of the Law on Education were further developed in the Law on Universities passed in 1995. The most important ideas may be divided into five categories: firstly, legal status and economic and related financial rights of universities; secondly, academic autonomy; thirdly, the status of the academic staff; fourthly, the structure of the higher education organisation, and lastly, financing of the universities. Let us analyse these ideas separately.

Legal status and economic and financial rights of universities

The public universities were constituted as independent public legal entities (much like the chartered institutions in the Anglo-Saxon tradition) with far-reaching financial and economic rights including owning their real-estate and other property, the right to buy and sell their property as they felt fit, the right to take loans from the bank, the right to establish profit and non-profit making companies. One of the most important rights of the public universities is the right to admit, in addition to the fixed number of students which are funded by the government, fee-paying students on the same terms as the private universities (including the right to set fees). In a way, this law made public and private (both for-profit and non-profit) universities equal in legal and economic terms and paved the way for real competition, which was also one of the main considerations in the political debate that took place in parliament. It was well understood that this legal autonomy, which also entails great risks of mis- and mal-management by the largely self-governing public institutions, and experience over the last ten years, has shown that indeed the institutions have had very *different practices* (mixed results). Let it be said that the larger, stronger, and most visionary institutions with strong leadership have largely profited from these freedoms to decide their future and shape their identity whereas others have been less successful.

In order to better understand the Estonian context, let me offer some statistics. In 1988 there was one state university and five state polytechnics in Estonia. In 2003, there were more than 50(!) higher education institutions – 6 public universities, 7 private universities, 23 polytechnics and some 15 vocational educational institutions offering short-term tertiary programs. Despite a large number of private universities and polytechnics, some 60% of all students still study at the 6 public universities. It is true that most people (including policy-makers) believe that there are far too many higher education institutions (the smallest having only 23 students) but most of them are reluctant to solve the problem by administrative means. It seems that public and political reaction to these developments is still positive and even in the case of difficulties (including potential bankruptcy), self-regulatory mechanisms are preferred to administrative interference. It must be noted that there has been only one case of bankruptcy and a number of forced mergers and liquidations among private universities. Some private universities have also been absorbed into public institutions.

We can conclude that the liberalisation of the higher education market and opening up of public universities to competition has been accepted by society. It has brought about extremely strong differentiation and diversification between the institutions and, indeed, a wide differential in quality of the courses (not necessarily in favour of the public institutions). It has also become clear that market mechanisms function in a very complicated manner and usually very slowly and that quality issues are a very serious problem in some cases. On the other hand, liberalisation of the market has solved the problem of meeting the increasing demand (the total number of students in Estonia has grown two and a half times in ten years) in spite of only a modest increase in public funding. One important, if not the most important conclusion, is that public universities have been very effective and flexible in reacting to these changing conditions. This ability, however, is fundamentally linked to their extensive legal and financial autonomy, which has made it possible to rearrange institutional structures and resources to respond to the new challenges.

Academic autonomy

The most important right is the right to select our students and staff. Selection rights, coupled with the right freely to negotiate salaries of staff, enable universities to build their specific academic profiles. As a result, some of the universities strive to become more research orientated, some try to cater for the specific needs of more vocationally orientated students. Some define themselves as internationally visible, others address first and foremost local needs. There are extremely few formal requirements in the Law on Universities, the only one being that potential students must have secondary education, and that docents and professors must hold a PhD. The same flexibility holds true for academic programmes. The one and only physics diploma programme, standardised for the entire Soviet Union, has been replaced by four to six physics programmes of different orientation for Estonia. They all have merit and it may be that all of them are not viable in the long run, but on the whole, they most probably respond better to the different needs of the labour market and to the individual preferences of the students compared with the standardised Soviet model. The law stipulates, however, that the government shall establish the general requirements for any higher education programme category in a document called "the higher education standard" and that all programmes shall correspond to its requirements. This approach is very close to the idea of establishing a general European reference framework – a general framework of qualifications (for higher education). In Estonia one conflict has become apparent and has yet to be resolved. If universities are given extensive rights (and through competition also the need) to develop (flexible) academic programmes, the dual nature of the higher education structure, namely the academic and vocational split, may not be adequate in many cases. This causes us to modify artificially the programme structure in order to meet the formal requirements of the higher education standard. This is increasingly evident in the case of regional colleges of public universities (former state-run polytechnic higher education institutions), which can only function in close co-operation with local employers with their special needs and requirements.

Employment of academic staff

In the early days of higher education reform there was a strong belief that universities and other academic institutions were too closed and stagnant institutions with meagre career opportunities for younger staff. The dominating idea was that academic positions would only be filled on a competitive basis (or by open competitions after the posts were advertised) and on temporary three to five year contracts. This is still the legal situation. In addition, a compulsory retirement age (65) was introduced by Tartu University. It is true that in Soviet days the average age of the academic staff was high and there was too little mobility between and within institutions. The new rules increased academic mobility and lowered the average age. This resulted also in a considerable increase of productivity but the positive trend soon stopped. In a small country with high language barriers there are simply not enough candidates to fill the vacant positions every three to five years and in reality this rule of temporary contracts only has caused 'inflexibility' and unnecessary instability in a number of cases. This policy is currently under review. A much more positive step was to give the universities the right to set salary levels and staff numbers. It has allowed us to enhance staff motivation and avoided, or at least alleviated, the otherwise serious problem present in a number of developing countries with under-funded universities – "moonlighting" to cover one's living costs. The right to determine the number of academic staff, with rather lax rules for academic appointments (depending very much on institutional policy) has considerably increased the number of professors in Estonia bringing with it a clear devaluation of the job and its social status. At the same time, the reputation of a professor depends very much on the university and hence also on the individual. I believe that formal titles play less of a role whereas the reputation of the institution and the individual matter much more now than in the old system. It is also noteworthy, that people who complain most about these changes are the academics themselves, many of whom have lost the security of tenure and now have to prove themselves constantly both inside and outside academia.

Organisation of higher education

I have emphasised already that the Soviet university system was essentially modelled on the German model, involving a long diploma cycle, followed by a candidate of sciences study *(aspirantura)* and finally the habilitation or the Doctor of Sciences degree. In 1995 this structure was replaced by what was thought to be "the democratic western model" consisting of a bachelor-master-PhD sequence. It took universities seven years to adapt to this new "theoretical" structure and as a result we ended up not with a "western" but with an incompatible Estonian system that we are now replacing with the Bologna model. The lesson learned from this reform was that it is not very productive to try to introduce artificial (and rigid) structures into higher education but rather to try to follow the internal logic of both the academia and the labour market. This, in turn, is only possible if the legal frameworks are sufficiently flexible. The situation is similar to the academic/vocational split as is the case in some other countries. It seems that all the different formal classifications of the body of higher education, which might have made life easier for both employers and students in the industrial era, are gradually becoming obsolete since they do not allow for the necessary flexibility required by modern dynamic economies.

Last but not least let us analyse the newly introduced financing patterns of universities. The most fundamental change is conceptual – the Estonian public universities are not funded by the state in the usual meaning of the term funding. Instead, the government, through the Ministry of Education and Research (but including other ministries), purchases certain educational services from the university on a contractual basis. In simple terms – a university (be it public or private) receives, for example, 1 million kroons from the state and in return offers five student-years of medical training (or, in a modified version, has to award three degrees in medicine to non-fee-paying students). In addition to educational services, the government also purchases other services from the university. There are at least two important aspects of this conceptual change – the price of the services is not directly cost-related but rather a result of negotiations and if the university does not deliver what is agreed upon direct financial sanctions shall follow.

Let us conclude. My main statement is that the pressure on universities to change may have only limited, and even counterproductive results, if we do not loosen the grip of the national systems, which largely belong to a past era. Secondly, don't be afraid of your universities provided they trust their students – young people deserve to be trusted and good universities are good enough to understand it. Thirdly, don't be afraid of drawbacks – be patient in observing the balance of interests to emerge. Fourthly, take time and think about the price. Estonian liberal radicalism has shown a way ahead but also warned of the overshooting phenomena, which have heavy price tags on them. And last but not least – if you really wish to contribute, insist on quality and promote quality culture. Be wary of starting at the systems level and moving downwards in a good dialogue with all stakeholders.

181

Universities in Serbia

Radmila Marinković-Nedučin

1. Initial remarks – defining the starting-point for reforms

With the positive social and political changes in our country since 2000, new energy for change has appeared in the universities, but still under a burden of additional circumstantial factors. Ten years of international isolation had caused the deterioration of academic structures and standards. Being formally autonomous and independent institutions, universities were nevertheless under strong political pressures, but the majority of the academic community (professors and students) retained their integrity and contributed to a considerable extent to the articulation of democratic notions in the country during this extremely difficult time. The University Law passed in 1998 cancelled the autonomy of the university and brought universities under full political control, which caused the suspension of Serbian universities from the CRE (European Rectors' Conferences, now EUA). After political changes in October 2000 and the election of a democratic government in 2001, a consensus was reached between universities and the government (Ministry of Education and Sports) that universities could practice different forms of democratic procedures in the election of their governing bodies as well as the election of their professors. This enabled universities to re-establish the principles of basic autonomy even before the official changes of the legal system and the University Law.

From this point on, Serbian universities face the serious challenges of the Europeanisation (Bologna Process, 1999) and globalisation of the Higher Education Area (EHEA), provoking the need for serious reforms, both of the higher education system and of university practices and standards. The re-establishment of international and regional co-operation, and incorporation of Serbian universities in international/European associations were recognised as top priorities. The political context of the planned transformation of the university system was and still is turbulent, due to political, economic and social transition, coupled with the exhausted economy of the country and limited financial support available for the renovation of the university infrastructure (equipment, laboratories, etc.).

The university structure is characterised by a weak confederation of highly autonomous faculties, each having its own independent institutional development and policies, building its own educational, research and administrative infrastructure. The fragmented management emerging from such a structure places considerable constraints on strategic planning of the university as an autonomous institution, offering only a very limited possibility for rapid and successful changes in line with the objectives of the Bologna Process.[74]

---

74. Institutional Evaluation of Universities in Serbia 2001/2002, European University Association (EUA).

2. Reform strategy

Being aware of the gap between current university practice in Serbia and those of the modern European universities, in 2001 the Serbian academic community started to develop its reform strategy. At that point the perception of the existing gap, based on the initial knowledge of the processes in Europe, was quite fuzzy and the main issues were not well defined and understood, but left no doubt that "something has to be done".

Self-evaluation of the Serbian universities was performed for the first time based on common European procedures (EUA, 2001), giving a first insight into the overall performances of universities and highlighting some critical issues necessary in defining the starting point for the reforms. Low efficiency, overloaded curricula, lack of quality management systems were recognised as general weak points in university practice, while showing a considerable potential, based on the overall results in both teaching and research, for further development in line with European and global trends in the higher education area. Many additional questions emerged such as university management and structure, the relation between autonomous universities and the state, and the influence of stakeholders on university policies.

Additional knowledge, gained through intensified international co-operation and through participation in various programmes and projects, has contributed to an awareness of the necessity to follow the current trends in and the goals of the EHEA. The first conference on the major aspects of the Bologna Process "Serbian higher education on the road to Europe", organised in March 2001 by the Council of Europe, CRE, Serbian Ministry of Education and the Alternative Academic Educational Network (AAEN), was followed by a number of seminars and conferences with the help of the Council of Europe and the following organisations: EUA, HRK, DAAD and Konrad Adenauer Stiftung. The Student Union of Serbia organised a series of seminars and workshops on the Bologna Process and student participation (2002-05). The universities of Novi Sad and Niš took part, as pilot institutions, in the "Regional University Network on Governance and Management of Higher Education in Albania, Bosnia and Herzegovina, Croatia, FYROM and FRY" financed by the EC and co-ordinated by UNESCO-CEPES (2002-04). The external evaluation of Serbian universities by EUA (2002), in addition to previously mentioned activities, helped considerably in initiating the reform processes on different levels (universities, faculties, departments, pilot projects) even before Serbia joined the Bologna Process (2003). The Ministry of Education and Sports of Serbia prepared the analysis "Higher Education in Serbia and Bologna Process" (2003), outlining the state strategy in the reforms.

In defining the strategy of change and adopting the standards of the EHEA, universities in Serbia have faced *three major challenges*:[75]

　　1. how to *organise* and *manage* universities to become equal partners for other European universities on all playing fields;

---

75. University of Novi Sad, Self-Evaluation Report, 2002.

2. how to develop a *quality management* system that matches European trends;

3. how to cope with wider social and political reforms in our country, specifically with the move from predominant but insufficient state funding of universities to a more market-orientated system which provides *more* financial
freedom, but *also lowers revenues from the state.*

The current management and governance structure of state universities – having
a weak and mainly administrative role of university and fully autonomous faculties as independent legal entities, restrains the efforts for reforms. Internal integration of the university could be considered as a top priority in establishing a
university according to European standards. Only integrated universities, which
speak with one voice will be able to develop their own strategy and policies and
take the responsibility towards the state and society for their own development.

3. The process of reforms

January 2002 activities started on a national level with the analysis of the
European HE systems, the analysis of the current state of the Serbian HE and consequently, with the outline of the reform strategy of the Serbian HE system. The
strategy outlined the legal context for reforms together with the issues to be
addressed at the institutional/university level.

The provisional University Law, approved in May 2002 and considered as temporary and transitional legislation, restored university autonomy including provisions for:

• autonomy in defining curricula (approved at university level);

• autonomy to appoint professors (approved at university level);

• governance and management autonomy (17% of university/faculty council to
be appointed by government);

• financial autonomy, to some extent, (bulk sum of salaries and operating costs
distributed to faculties, ownership of acquisitions gained from faculty's income).

This provisional University Law established the National HE Council in charge of
the evaluation and accreditation procedures and strategic issues related to HE. The
National HE Council appointed the Accreditation Committee in January 2003. In
this way the initial form of quality control system was established at national level
as an important focal point for the development of a future quality management
system as a new approach with no equivalent in former university practice.

The provisional law did not change the basic university structure of autonomous
faculties (legal entities, almost highly specialised "universities" in themselves),
but introduced a certain level of supervision over the faculties (promotion of professors, PhD thesis). The faculties have their own statutes, governing and executive bodies, educational and employment policies and budgets (accountable
directly to the ministry).

There is still a misbalance between the authority of the rector (mostly honorary) and the dean (executive), with very limited space for strategic planning at university level. The relationship between the honorary-academic function of the key personnel and the actual institutional management is still not clarified. There are no common funds at university level, the rector's office (representing "the university") being state-financed with a limited number of administrative staff. The Educational/Research Council (all academics), in charge of curricula, promotions, elections, institutional development and policy, has the major role in management at university/faculty level. The status of the student is strictly faculty-orientated in all relevant aspects, with consecutive difficulties in organising multidisciplinary and interdisciplinary studies and research.

The external evaluation of Serbian universities[76] underlined university integration processes as the priority in reaching current European standards, based on the fact that "the sum of the faculties" developing behind closed doors is very much in contrast to an efficient university able to manage its overall potential. The mobility of students and staff within universities is restricted in such a structure, limiting the flexibility of the curricula and interdisciplinary approach to both education and research. Information flow between "units" is very limited, common services are hard to organise and administrative staff are inefficiently used (with duplicated "units" at all the faculties).

Even if the provisional University Law did nothing to encourage university integration, it did not forbid it either. It provided some "free" space which could be used to adapt university statutes accordingly if there was enough motivation and energy behind this.[77]

For example, the University of Novi Sad has used the "free space" to initiate its integration processes (Statute of UNS, July 2002) by introducing various university bodies and by promoting common standards, procedures and services. The internal quality management system was outlined, together with the draft strategic plan, which defined objectives, ongoing strategies and an action plan. The agreement on some common funds was reached, with a small but still promising budget for some common activities. Although some results are obvious, particularly in implementing new approaches to curricula reforms, ECTS and teaching quality standards, there are still many obstacles for establishing the university management in the full sense of the word; not to mention the lack of university funds and an undeveloped information system, which limits information flow within the institution. Furthermore, the need for trained and professional administrators capable of providing the core university functions is evident.

A lot of energy has to be spent in order to reach a consensus about integration processes even though awareness of the need to change is high in the academic community. There is still strong opposition from faculties as this not only affects faculty administration but also income channelling. As a heritage of self-

---

76. EUA evaluation report, University of Novi Sad, 2003.
77. The University report on the Salzburg Seminar visiting advisory programme, University of Novi Sad, 2004.

management systems, which existed for a long time in our political system, one has to convince the majority about the advantages of an integrated system, being aware that the small "kingdoms" on different levels mainly do not see beyond their own interest within quite narrow limits. Bringing to the forefront the "broader picture" and developing a vision of the institution as the whole is still a great challenge for university managements.

The conference "Higher education in Serbia on the road to Europe – four years later"[78] held in Belgrade in September 2004, gave an overview of the reform processes at the universities in Serbia. Examples of good practice from all the state universities were presented, together with an analysis of the overall process presented by the former rectors and an outline of the strategy stated by newly elected rectors. Besides curricula reforms, being the focus of most of the presentations, the development of a quality management system, both national and institutional, and a new approach to the university governance and managerial structures were outlined among the priorities. It was underlined that a new legal framework was a prerequisite for further coherent development of the whole higher education system.

4. Development of a new legal framework

At the beginning of 2003, the National HE Council appointed a committee to prepare the concept of the new HE Law, which was finished and accepted in July 2003. The concept offered integration of the university as a prerequisite and a framework for an insight into further institutional development. The new HE Law was drafted in September 2003, initiating broad discussion in the academic sector, especially concerning the degree of integration, the relation between university and faculties, the level of organisational and managerial independence of faculties, the status of students and professors within the university, the financial flow at university level and financial independence of faculties. Gradual functional integration of universities was finally envisioned as a sustainable solution, leaving enough space within the legal framework for individual university management structures for each university. Integrative functions were defined concerning quality assurance, strategic planning, employment and enrolment policy, final decision on curricula, international co-operation, common standards for services, information systems, and capital investments.

The proposal of the HE Law was passed to the National Assembly in May 2005, but then postponed for the later session (more than 100 amendments were submitted) and adopted in September 2005. The basic concept remained, even with some changes brought about by the amendments. The HE Law is generally in accordance with European developments and the intentions of the Bologna Process, as a framework for the whole HE system (state and private institutions; academic and applied studies) introducing:

- the three-tier study system based on ECTS;

---

78. "Higher education in Serbia on the road to Europe – four years later", UNESCO Chair for University Management, AAEN and Association of Serbian Universities, Belgrade, 2005 (digest in English).

- quality assurance and accreditation on a national level (independent Accreditation Committee);

- a national HE expert institution (National Council for HE) developing the overall HE policy and quality standards;

- a student parliament as student representative body and student participation in decision making.

The new approach to the governance and management of universities is promoted by integrative functions of the universities defined by the law, as mentioned before, but still keeping legal entities for the faculties. Financing of the public university sector is only generally outlined (based on public funds and a university's/faculty's own funds derived from revenues from both teaching and research).

The HE Law, defining the overall framework of the system, opens the space for internal regulations within the University Statute in many aspects, offering the possibility for each institution (within the broad spectra of HE institutions differing in size, stage of development and structure) to define its own strategy and search for the optimal specific solutions. The detailed regulations concerning university organisation and internal structure, the institutional governance and the managerial bodies, the study system, the internal quality management standards and procedures, promotion standards and procedures are expected to be determined by the University Statute. The University Statute is defined as a framework for the whole institution, the faculties being obliged to adopt their own regulations/statutes in accordance with the solutions agreed upon at university level. The comprehensive work on a new University Statute has to be finished within the year, since a two-year period has been defined for the overall transformation of the HE system.

5. The University of Novi Sad – some initiatives and experiences

The University of Novi Sad, searching for the optimal organisational and management profile through learning from good practice and experiences, initiated the TEMPUS project "Integration through internal agreement". In co-operation with Serbian state universities, the project is orientated towards shaping the institutional profile, structure and processes, within the new legal framework, towards a modern and efficient scientific-educational framework within and across the fields. The proposal of an overall organisational and managerial structure of the institution is expected to be one of the project outcomes, leaving the more detailed regulations to the university statutes according to the specific needs of each institution.

The University of Novi Sad, at the level of the Autonomous Province of Vojvodina and its government, also initiated work on a strategic paper concerning higher education development. The shift from a state-controlled to a state-supervised model of university is seen as one of the possibilities in establishing a modern, efficient, accountable and probably more entrepreneurial university.[79]

---

79. Initial report on the higher education performances/basis for strategic policy, Government of Autonomous Province of Vojvodina, 2004.

There are many serious policy challenges to the University of Novi Sad which simply cannot be dealt with adequately without some purposive integration of key elements of the university; these were mentioned by external advisers:[77]

- coherent response to the Bologna Process;

- common approaches to quality assurance and accreditation;

- lifelong learning;

- responding to society's needs for R&D, services connected to regional development, etc.;

- providing support for both weak and strong academic areas in a strategic framework.

The wider objective of integration is to support university reforms as a result of an internal agreement in order to strengthen the idea of the university as an integral academic place and to link them with economic and social processes. It includes restoration and permanent maintenance of quality of communication between constituent units, prevention of parallel tracks of evolution and a multiplicity of disciplinary sectional interests and identities, development of the university database and the university management information system, development of a culture of integration and integration of student organisations.[77]

The University of Novi Sad and its leadership attempt to deal creatively with many of the issues mentioned. Results cannot be guaranteed, but so far the developments are promising. The work on the new University Statute has started with the initial consensus to broaden the space for decision making at university level, identifying the areas in which there is high agreement of all the constitutive units/faculties for integration: internal quality standards in both teaching and research, introduction of multidisciplinary and interdisciplinary curricula and research projects, capital investments in research infrastructure, information system, international co-operation and mobility.

.

The actors in higher education governance – The case of Uludağ University

Erdal Emel

1. Introduction

The case study of Uludağ University (UU) starts with a new rector's first term in office beginning in August 2000 in a 25-year-old, rather young and mainly a teaching-focused university with a low profile in research, dispersed institutional goals and poor community relations.

On the eve of a new millennium, when the expectations of a nation towards its institutions to carry it forward into a new competitive era are well above what those institutions can presently offer, naturally the institutions' managers felt the pressure to make every rational move to change their institutions to respond to the needs of a rapidly changing society.

But, how does one change a university with 2 000 academic staff and 40 000 students in just a four-year management term, achieving enough progress to ensure that change for the better will be institutionalised? Thanks to the new rector, answers were provided long before his term commenced and after his appointment by the President of the Republic it was time for action. His appointment was not down to mere luck, but was a reward following a well-designed campaign for selection by academic staff with an overwhelming number of votes. His campaign focused upon the need for UU to change and he asked for the support of staff to respond to this need.

Later, in critical senate meetings, he would recall this campaign focus and the votes he received, in order to smoothly pass the bylaws for the most demanding quality improvement measures at UU. A few months into his office, the new rector's style of management showed itself to be of the leadership type, since he undertook the change process in a reformist way. By 2001, the terminology of educational and research reforms was introduced to internal and external constituents at various meetings. Later, educational reform was split into two: undergraduate (first-tier) degree programmes and graduate (second- and third-tier) degree programmes. On the other hand, research reform was by no coincidence to be intensified in a second stage of educational reforms of graduate degrees.

As the first step of the conceptual basis for UU's self-evaluation and improvement efforts, institutional and departmental vision and mission statements, objectives and outcomes had to be defined. The UU's mission statement has been the most important factor for the crystallisation of the following structure representing a philosophy of continuous improvement.

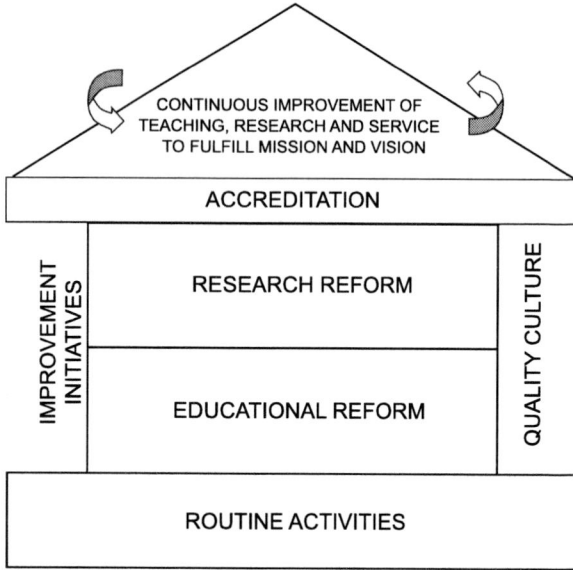

Figure 1 – Conceptual basis of UU activities

How do the "quality culture" and "improvement initiatives" pillars support the building in Figure 1?

- The structure has a base on which all academic and administrative *routine activities* take place and without which the building cannot stand up. These activities have existed since the establishment of UU.

- Above the base, the building consists of two floors. The first floor is made up of activities which fall within the scope of *educational reform*.

- The second floor is where activities regarding the *research reform* take place. The *research reform* is placed on top of *educational reform* due to the priorities set in the mission of UU.

- Both *educational* and *research reforms* can only be supported by a *quality culture* environment and capability *improvement initiatives* within the university. Both these columns of activities need to be continued with strong emphasis as long as the reforms are ongoing.

- The common goal for all the university's programme activities, in finalising their reform efforts, consists of reaching the level of one of the best universities in Turkey as the minimum satisfactory level. This will be proved to all internal and external constituents through the available *accreditation* procedures at the time.

- The accreditation stage will be followed by ongoing work, to continuously improve all activities of UU in order to achieve a level set by the new visions of the university.

In this paper, the main pillar of reformist efforts, namely the *quality culture* setting will be discussed, but from the perspectives of those who are the actors in these reforms. For the sake of clarity, the actors in UU reforms are defined first and then their actions are related as a chronology of events.

2. Definition of actors

a. Governing bodies

The Higher Education Council (HEC) is an autonomous body with juristic personality which governs all higher education and directs the activities of the institutions of higher education. The members of the Council are nominated by the government and the Inter-university Council and finally selected and approved by the President of the Republic.

The Inter-university Council consists of the university rectors and one professor from each university selected by their senates. The Minister of National Education and the President of the Council of Higher Education may preside at the Board's meetings if they deem it necessary; otherwise, the rectors act as the chairperson of the Inter-university Board in turn and consecutively for a term of one year.

b. University senior leadership

Empowered by the Higher Education Act[80] (HEA) of 1981 as the representative of the juristic personality of the university, a rector is invested with the final authority on all financial and human resource related matters. Rectors are appointed for up to two four-year terms by the President of the Republic from among the professor candidates proposed by the HEC after a selection by the academic staff of the university.

As set out in the HEA, three vice-rectors are selected and commissioned by the rector from among the university's salaried professors for five-year terms.

Without being determined by the HEA, the rectors can further select and appoint rector's counsellors from among the university's salaried professors in order to ease off the workload of vice-rectors.

The dean, who is directly responsible to the rector for the rational utilisation and improvement of the first-tier educational potential of a faculty and its units, is appointed by the HEC from among three professors nominated by the rector. The dean can serve for a three-year term. When his/her term of office expires a dean may be re-appointed.

Graduate school directors who are directly appointed by the rector for a three-year term with a possibility for re-appointment, are responsible for regulating the second- and third-tier degree studies run by the departments usually located under faculties.

---

80. http://www.uludag.edu.tr/english/Q1.htm#_Toc39392096

Under the chairmanship of the rector, the senate consists of the vice-rectors, the deans of each faculty, a member of the teaching staff elected for a term of three years by the respective faculty board and the directors of graduate schools and vocational schools attached to the office of the rector. The senate is the university's highest organ responsible for academic activities and for issuing bylaws.

The university has administrative boards of various capacities at the university, faculty and school levels mainly to administer the implementation of the HEA and bylaws of the university.

c. Committees

Compared to the legal framework set forth by the HEA for the previously defined actors, senior leadership may need the involvement of more academic staff into the processes of academic planning and regulation to better utilise the intellectual resources of a university. Based on this reasoning, the following groups have been established at UU as from the year 2000: Deans Council, University Accreditation Committee (UAC) with affiliated accreditation subcommittees at faculty and department levels, University Strategic Planning Committee (USPC) with affiliated strategic planning task committees at faculty or department levels, Student Affairs Executive Committee, Uludağ University-European University Association Relations Committee (UU-EUARC), Graduate Studies Restructuring Committee (GSRC), etc.

d. Academic staff

Assistant professors, associate professors and professors are teaching staff who carry out education and practical studies at three-tier levels in universities in line with the purpose and objectives of the HEA. They also undertake scientific and scholarly research for publication.

Instructors and lecturers are also teaching staff but limited to first-tier studies. Research assistants and specialists are ancillary staff members who assist with research, studies, and experiments in higher education institutions, as well as carrying out other duties assigned by authorised bodies.

e. Students

Higher education, for which a fee is charged, is organised in accordance with the HEA as a three-tier system: beginning with a two-year pre-baccalaureate and/or four-year baccalaureate with some exceptions (for example, medical schools). Students are admitted to institutions of higher education by means of a nationwide examination prepared in accordance with provisions specified by the HEC.

Post-baccalaureate/post-graduate or second- and third-tier degree students are selected by examinations conducted individually by higher education institutions from among those university graduates who wish to study for a master's or doctorate degree, or for a specialisation in a field of medicine, according to principles determined by the Inter-university Board.

f. External constituents (alumni, employers)

As part of the requirement for continuous programme improvement and the understanding of quality management of UU, although not required by the HEA, external (alumni/employers) advisory committees at faculty and/or departmental level were established. The aim of these committees is to evaluate the targets and the outputs of the three-tier educational programmes that the faculty/department runs and to improve the quality of education.

3. Actors in the reforms

a. Stage 1 of educational reforms: undergraduate education

The principle structure established to manage and support the quality framework at UU is based around UAC, USPC, UU-EUARC and GSRC, all of which work closely with the senate. The enormous task of developing and maintaining a quality culture environment together with an effective quality management system has totally occupied the agenda of the UU since 2001.

The greatest strength of UU in this regard is its determined senior leadership joined with enthusiastic academic staff members who are willing to contribute to the quality improvement of education.

As a first stage towards the establishment of a quality management system and the creation of quality consciousness within the university, the rector has first conducted an academic staff survey. The views and comments of staff on academic quality at UU were collected. Since the results of the survey revealed a high level of support for the implementation of a quality management system at UU, the rector then established a steering committee (UAC) in April 2001 to design and facilitate the quality framework as well as to create an awareness of quality culture throughout the institution. UAC prepared the UU Accreditation Handbook as a first task and the rector introduced the requirements contained in the handbook to all academic staff at meetings organised in each faculty. Simultaneously, faculty and department accreditation subcommittees were established as standing programme committees which are responsible for the yearly improvement of the teaching programmes in co-ordination with UAC. Accreditation subcommittees also fulfil the need for an internal feedback channel to ensure two-way communication between UAC and all academic staff within the faculties and departments, and thus involving all the members within the institution into the quality management processes. Furthermore, concerning discussions on some demanding or controversial implementation issues, the rector was invited to UAC meetings to arrive at a final decision. Such decisions by the UAC, with an attached covering letter from the rector, were welcomed by the academic staff.

Usually, the academic staff responded to the demands of the UAC with respect, knowing that the burden of the change process was evenly distributed and that it was for a good cause, namely the improvement of UU. Yet, the senior leadership never forced the staff blindfold beyond the limits of their time and effort. The following steps were part of the overall change process:

- benchmarking Bachelor and Masters programmes at UU with nationally and internationally acknowledged programmes (November 2000-June 2001);

- the introduction of an ECTS-compatible accumulative credit system for all of its undergraduate and graduate curricula (July 2001);

- dual degrees and options are available between programmes (July 2001);

- the introduction of English courses in some programmes (September 2001);

- the introduction of a T-score based Relative Student Assessment Method (September 2001);

- the systematic documentation including curriculum, course contents and ECTS credits in all the departments with undergraduate programmes (March 2002);

- the preparations necessary for providing the diploma supplement for each programme (March 2002);

- the definition of objectives and outcomes for all the programmes and courses, prepared course files including examples of student portfolios and critical reviews of lectures with suggestions for their improvement (March 2003).

UU believes that student feedback is a key, and increasingly important, aspect of the steps taken. Therefore, preparation of Student Course Evaluation Questionnaires were among the first efforts of UAC. A student evaluation process was initiated centrally in 2002 and is regularly applied at the end of each semester in all first-tier educational programmes since then. The qualitative data derived from these questionnaires are circulated to all course organisers with the intention that course organisers can make appropriate changes to their courses and make these changes known to the students so that they can appreciate the value of this feedback process. However, right from the beginning, this process was not fully functional due to the senior leadership's loose attitude based on the fact that the results of student surveys many times revealed that students' action may be biased. UU has seriously discussed other alternatives for feedback such as using student representatives or holding class meetings to identify issues of great concern to students, or request each class to submit reports delineating their problems in a process of continuous quality improvement, together with the involvement of student representatives in the senate after the recent decree of HEC. Student course counselling provided by academic staff is considered to be a further source of feedback for decisions related to curriculum improvement.

UU endeavours to keep in contact with its alumni and representatives of trade, industry, NGOs and ministries as they are a useful source of support and feedback. In this regard, UU has established "external advisory boards" consisting of employers for all of its programmes. Moreover, "alumni boards" were established with a framework of guidelines prepared by UAC that would promote the efficiency of this mutual relationship, and around 500 representatives on two types of boards meet together with academic staff twice a year to contribute to the continuous improvement of undergraduate and graduate programmes.

The second stage of the quality management system focused on strategic planning to all university units and functions, including a top-down and bottom-up approach. Vision, mission, SWOT analysis, objectives, priorities, action plans needed to be prepared for UU as a single institution and also for every academic unit in relation to the university. To handle this multifaceted task USPC was established with 60 members and with subcommittees of at least three members in each academic unit. It was intended that the USPC should act as devil's advocate as well as think-tank for the development of a vision for the university. The proposals formulated by this committee were subject to senate approval. In close connection with UAC and its subcommittees in academic units, almost half the total academic staff of UU was involved in the process. As a first task USPC issued a Strategic Planning Handbook to be followed during the whole process. During the years 2002 to 2003, the institutional planning process took up about six months during which USPC had meetings almost non-stop for days. The meetings were broadcast live on intranet TV in order to get the involvement of all internal constituents. Also, the interim reports, surveys for staff and students were published and distributed for feedback.

During the strategic planning process, the senior management used the EUA Institutional Evaluation Programme and Quality Culture Project as a tool to motivate all constituents to work for a strong institutional image. The rector used many occasions to convey this message to academic councils in a very effective way by also promising his dedication to a long-term prioritised development plan. Therefore, as a member of this institution, it was inevitable that everyone should participate in this process as part of their personal responsibility.

Round I of the EUA Quality Culture Project included UU as a participating institution on a specific theme: "Network 4: Implementing Bologna reforms" (EUA, 2002-03). As a part of the project UU established a special task force, UU-EUARC, to guide and represent the university in the project meetings and also to prepare for the EUA Institutional Review Programme (launched in 1994) . During the course of these EUA-related activities, a young dynamic academic team of five UU-EUARC members provided a great impetus for senior leadership (primarily for the rector) regarding the elaboration of institutional self-evaluation (EUA, 2003a).

In the spring of 2003, educational reform-related activities reached a peak coinciding with visits by the EUA Institutional Review Programme and the final network 4 report of the EUA Quality Culture Project promoting UU as a good example of the implementation of Bologna reforms. It was a memorable series of actions concerning not only staff and students but also all the external constituents, since the requirements of the quality management system forced everybody to become knowledgeable about it and to be active so that a real change could take place. Senior management organised numerous seminars and meetings of all constituents during which the seeds of quality culture were sown.

Stage 1 of educational reform came to an end with the oral report of the findings of the EUA Review Team in June 2003 (EUA, 2003b). Presented before an audience of 300 UU academic staff members, the Review Team leader announced that among the 80 universities all over Europe which had participated over the past ten years in the Institutional Review Programme, comparing the universities with regard to how strong their capacity for change was, the answer for UU was that "there is really a strong performance of this university to be seen in operating this process of change" and the review team would rank the UU in first place, if it were courageous enough. The audience burst into tears of pride; this announcement was a well-deserved prize for all the efforts made by all academic staff over the past three years.

b. Stage 2 of educational reform (graduate education) and research reform

Stage 1 of educational reform came to an end by the summer of 2003, since staff needed a break from the ongoing demands of senior management. Also the rector felt that it was about the right time for staff to absorb the ongoing changes. So, almost a year would pass without any new changes in the educational and research-based activities of the university until the rector's second term of office.

Meanwhile, the review report of the EUA Institutional Review Programme and the final report of the EUA Quality Culture Project were printed and distributed widely, not only in UU but also in the country. Local media covered the positive reviews regarding the university; on several occasions senior leadership used the opportunities to speak on local and nationwide TV channels. All of these had a great impact on other universities in the country. The rector gave presentations at the Higher Education Council and the Inter-university Board and suddenly requests for quality management counselling from other universities were pouring into the senior leadership of UU. UU has responded positively many times to these requests considering the fact that it had already been declared a good example to young universities of Europe anyway.

From summer 2003 to summer 2004, UU shared the pride of these developments with all constituents. Certainly, these brought more responsibility for UU staff to sincerely adapt to already implemented reforms. Meanwhile, student questionnaires, external advisory board meetings, and educational programme improvements were being effectively administered by UAC.

By the summer of 2004, the rector's term was over and the academic staff had to nominate a new rector. After all the high impact profile activities and deeply felt reform processes, academic staff nominated the same rector for a second term with a record number of votes even in this country. The President of the Republic had no difficulty re-appointing him for a second term.

It was already known that the second term would emphasise the reforms in research and graduate programmes. So by September 2004, a Graduate Studies Restructuring Committee consisting of 50 members was established to review the masters level and doctorate level educational programmes. Entry and exit conditions and requirements for supervising diploma theses would be redefined. The rector was very cautious knowing from his first term that UU professors are very sensitive to these issues, since graduate students are the core of their research activities. Any restrictions on graduate studies would be considered to be a direct threat to their interests.

However, for two main reasons the rector decided to impose an improvement process at this stage: firstly, a criticism of the defects of a masters level programme was brought up by a UU student at a national quality congress, right at the moment when the rector was presenting UU's case; secondly, based on the fact that at the beginning of the research reform, when UU senior leadership had increased ten-fold the internal resources for research funding, it was expected that scientific publication performance would also increase. But it is known that for any research activity, it is the quality of the researchers (graduate student and professors) which contributes more to performance than the funding.

From 2004 to 2005, the by-laws of graduate studies, academic staff appointment and graduate supervision rules were changed by the GSRC and approved by the senate. Performance-based appointments were emphasised in every decision made. Certainly, these decisions were hard on many academic staff, involving assistants, and may often have had personal implications.

An important part of UU's understanding of quality control is the monitoring and improvement of individual faculty members. Quality monitoring and assessment is carried out at three different points in time. Firstly, when he/she is recruited; secondly when he/she is promoted to an associate professorial position; and thirdly when he/she is up for promotion to be a full professor. Different sets of criteria are to be used at each step.

Common to many universities, there appears to be a strong sense of 'academic freedom' and 'individualism' in the concept of teaching at UU, which makes it difficult to develop among the academic staff the type of communication, co-ordination, and co-operation required to improve the curricula, teaching methods, and ultimately student learning. The rapid growth of academic knowledge, increased specialisation, and growing competition in research, have inevitably contributed to the making of this academic 'individualism' in teaching. An academic quality assurance mechanism must therefore be designed to provide a starting point that would overcome this predicament and improve the transparency of teaching and research without necessarily undervaluing the academic freedom of teaching staff.

The rector was keen to respect the legitimate demands for minor changes to the by-laws, but many times responded with firm decisiveness to personal interests in the name of institutional interests. It is obvious that the second stage of reforms has created hardships and the positive results of these changes have yet to be seen. The rector considers that hardships can be dissolved during the course of his term. As part of the periodic review process, the implications of these changes will be evaluated in 2007; if the performance indicators are not as expected, there is still one more year to counteract this before the end of his term in 2008.

Rectors can only serve for two terms due to the provisions of the HEA. UU has yet to see its new rector candidates and their campaign slogan. There are only two options available for UU for the next governance term beginning in 2008: the first one is to decisively continue with the reforms, institutionalise the quality management system and stabilise the quality culture; however, the second one would be an environment of uncertainty probably focused on self or group interests.

The future is yet to be resolved.

References

"EUA Report on the Quality Culture Project, Round I (2002-2003): Developing an Internal Quality Culture in European Universities," at: www.eua.be/eua/jsp/en/upload/QC1_full.1111487662479.pdf. Last accessed: 11 November 2005.

"EUA Institutional Evaluation Programme", at: www.eua.be/eua/en/membership_evaluation.jspx. Last accessed: 11 November 2005.

"EUA Institutional Evaluation Programme: Self Evaluation Report of Uludağ University", 2003a, at: http://intoffice.uludag.edu.tr/irp_eng.htm. Last accessed: 11 November 2005.

"EUA Institutional Evaluation Programme: Review Team Report for Uludağ University", 2003b, at: http://intoffice.uludag.edu.tr/irp_rtr_eng.htm. Last accessed: 11 November 2005.

Conclusions and outlook

General report

Martina Vukasović

1. Introduction

It seems that we live in the age of a global quest for better governance. Whether it is the preparation for a possible bird flu pandemic, allocation of resources to a nation's education budget, steering a local company or repairing a street in the town – it is understood that these tasks need to be done in the most efficient and effective way, that decisions need to be legitimate and reached in a democratic and transparent manner. Some would argue that our particular age is marked by the New-Public-Management-speak, while others, less faithful to the managerial approach, would demand a 'New Public Service'.

On the other hand, we might not be doing anything new. It could be argued that, throughout history, mankind has always been, to one extent or the other, troubled by the search for more efficient and more democratic modes of governance, even though the understanding of the terms "efficiency" and "democracy" is continuously developing, together with the understanding of "governance".

Whatever the case may be – higher education cannot escape this trend. Institutions themselves, as well as various actors in higher education governance are discussing whether or not their present modes of higher education governance are suitable for what they are trying to achieve and whether they are an adequate response to the changing conditions in which higher education operates and indeed, if they need to be more proactive. Furthermore, it would be hard to find a country in the world in which everyone is completely satisfied as to how higher education is steered at system level. There are changes being planned or implemented in certain parts of the system almost everywhere in the world. Some countries are on the verge or in the midst of major system restructuring.

However, the issue of governance in higher education has not yet been fully discussed at international level. The topic of governance is usually present as a shadow in the discussions of other changes taking place, such as curriculum development, student mobility, quality assurance, etc. Here it would be relevant to stress that this refers primarily to the so-called political higher education community, or, to put this in other terms, stakeholders in higher education (however they are defined in different national contexts). Educational research has offered some academic insight into the topic, which is presented both in the literature survey and in some of the other contributions to the conference. However, the goal here is not to be either extremely political and interest orientated or extremely academic and theory orientated. The goal is to try to map out at least a part of the intricate fabric of the governance debate, to try to understand how the governance of higher education is related to the changing conditions for higher education and changes in the overall society and to try to agree on some of the basic principles of good governance. Therefore, we should be both academic and political to a certain extent and try to merge the better of the two worlds and discard the interest focus of one and sometimes a very disinterested view of the other.

It also seems that it is a particularly good time to discuss such an issue under the roof of the Council of Europe. The year 2005 is proclaimed "European Year of Citizenship through Education" (EYCE), which provides more visibility to the discussion on higher education governance and puts the topic in the larger context of societal development. One should look into how education as a whole contributes to the establishment of democratic structures, but even more importantly, democratic culture – both in the wider society, as well as within our institutions involved in education. Therefore, the discussion around higher education governance should also bear these questions in mind: What is the role of education in contributing to the development of citizens who take pride in their activities in the civic society and who cherish the values of democracy, human rights and the rule of law? What is the role of higher education in the same endeavour?

Furthermore, it also seems that we have reached a point in the process of the creation of the European Higher Education Area (EHEA) in which it seems that there is a fairly clear idea what changes are necessary to achieve the goals of the Bologna Process. Whether they will be achieved or not in the designated timeframe and in the planned way remains to be seen, but that is yet another aspect of governance of higher education, this time on intergovernmental, supranational and international levels, depending whether the focus is on the role of national ministries, European institutions or international co-operation between higher education institutions. In most cases, although this may differ depending on the depth of the analysis, the planning phase is over. The question no longer is "what" but "how". And this is where the issue of governance comes to the forefront.

2. Complexity of the topic

The topic of governance of higher education is highly complex. The working party of the Council of Europe was faced with this complexity as it tried to establish some borders around the topic and some grid within the topic to facilitate the discussion and ensure the relevance and usefulness of the conference and the conclusions, as well as the recommendations of the project as a whole. It was quite an interesting journey in making the fluffy, intangible and somewhat intimidating topic of higher education governance into something that can be addressed in a short time by numerous participants with diverse professional backgrounds and national contexts.

This complexity is reflected in at least two ways.

The obvious one relates to the term of governance itself. The results of the translation exercise of the term governance in the various languages and cultures reflect this more vividly than could be explained in this report. However, it would be worth pointing out that:

- there are as many as eight different possibilities for translation of the term "governance" in some languages;

- in most languages the translations are closely related to the terms "steering", "management", "government" or "decision making";

- in all these languages it is implicit that the translation does not fully grasp the content of the English term "governance"; and

- it would be interesting to analyse the cultural and societal roots of some of the translations, especially in languages where only one understanding is offered (as is the case in, for example, ex-Yugoslav languages where "governance" is understood as "management" or "steering" and not so much as "democratic decision making").

Even though we will not take the English explanation of governance as the only true one, the exercise of translating the term into the national languages and indeed national contexts showed very clearly that there is an inherent danger of misinterpretation, superfluous or misleading understanding of concepts and we have to be aware of those in the discussions. While a certain ambiguity of terminology may be politically justifiable, as all would be able to interpret it in the way that best suits their needs, too much freedom in interpretation will lead to inconsistencies and incompatibility, which may prove to be detrimental for other aspects of international co-operation in higher education.

We cannot offer a simple, understandable definition of higher education governance, which would be constructed in such a way as to capture different cultural understandings of the notions such as "participation", "democracy", "legitimacy", "transparency", etc. Professor Kohler in his paper offers a definition of the term. But he also makes a note of caution himself by offering "an approximate definition" and using such words as "may be defined as". And the definition is far from simple, it does encompass the various facets of the term, but, as the essence of the concept is not simple, the definition is far from simple. So, is it realistically possible to grasp such a complex topic and present it in one sentence? Is it possible to make sure that this one sentence will be understood properly by actors coming from different fields, different cultural backgrounds and different sources of interest in the topic? The answer seems to be "No".

However, it may be wise to dwell a little on what governance is not and tackle some of the frequent misconceptions of the concept of governance of higher education, which are used and sometimes abused by various stakeholders.

First of all, it is important to stress that governance does not equal management. There are various attempts to reduce governance to only management, and to neglect the fact that management is yet but a part of the governance process, and, in a way, a final stage of a more complex activity. Governance should be understood as a process of setting long-term goals and establishing strategies for reaching these goals. Management refers to the process of implementation of these decisions, the day-to-day activities (not only limited to decision making) ensuring the achievement of the aforementioned strategies and goals. The distinction is illustrated also in the request voiced at the conference for a division of tasks of governance and management between the competent and legitimate governance bodies on the one side and a professional administration on the other.

It is also important to underscore that we should be extra careful to keep in mind that we are not discussing governance per se. We have to remember that we are discussing governance of higher education. And that this means that the governance of higher education should reflect the complexity and multiplicity of purposes and missions of higher education. The multiplicity of purposes: preparation for the labour market, preparation for active citizenship, personal development and advancement of knowledge, is coupled with the multiplicity of values. We have heard different stakeholders focusing on different aspects of higher education and attributing slightly different priorities to the values of:

- competence,

- equality (achieving social cohesion),

- liberty (autonomy and even more so academic freedom – freedom to teach, freedom to learn and freedom to research) and

- what in the literature is sometimes referred to as loyalty – but which includes the demand from higher education to be more responsive to the needs of the society.

Now, having in mind the complexity of purposes and the complexity of values related to higher education, as well as the different national contexts and circumstances in which higher education institutions operate, I believe that Burton Clark in his famous book *The higher education system: Academic organisation in a cross-national perspective* which is also referred to in the literature survey, was right to point out that:

> Any sensible administrator asked to confront directly and to reconcile these ... orientations would undoubtedly seek other employment.

This does not of course mean that most of the people reading the proceedings from the conference should "go seek other employment". This serves to reiterate another point – governance of higher education must take into account the complexity of the tasks of higher education, it must take into account the diversity of contexts in which higher education takes place and it must take into account the diversity of actors in higher education and stakeholders who have an interest in it. This may well be the most important reason for saying that there is no "one-size-fits-all" model of governance, neither at the system nor at the institutional level. The practice of copy-pasting solutions from other countries will not work in higher education, if it actually works anywhere else. Furthermore, copy-pasting from one time to another may not be the best strategy either. Any discussion of higher education governance and policy development connected to this has to take into account "the outer world" – the context in which higher education exists. On the basis of that, the best one can do is to offer some basic principles of good governance.

206

3. Changing context for higher education and impact on governance

Most of the research in higher education stresses that change is seldom fast and linear. Higher education is more an organism that evolves than something inclined towards revolutionary changes. In addition, when change is planned, it very rarely turns out exactly as it was planned. There are interpretations of goals and objectives and there are too many actors to allow for a straightforward implementation. Furthermore, the present higher education institutions bear both old and new marks and it seems that, under the modern structure and terminology lies much of the old traditions, attitudes and understandings. In this respect, some of the presenters and participants in the panel debate were right to point out that the present modes of governance do not reflect entirely the present context of higher education, but are rather a remnant of a time in which higher education was less massive, less diverse and further removed from society. As higher education moves from being a privilege, through being a right, to becoming a necessity for successful life and employment, the spectrum of those interested in how higher education actually operates becomes wider. There are new stakes in higher education and thus new stakeholders. They need new models of learning and new methods of teaching. New patterns of research are being established and likewise new balances between pure and applied, new partnerships between higher education institutions and industry forged. There are new and stronger demands for higher education to become more involved in solving societal problems, whether they refer to industrial development, ecological issues or reconciliation between different ethnic or religious groups. There is, on the other hand, an interest (which may stem from a necessity for additional resources) on the side of higher education institutions to open their doors to society much more, sometimes even more than is necessary or desirable. All these changes then imply discussions on both who should govern higher education, and how, as well as on the notions of autonomy, legitimacy, participation and democracy.

When it comes to the new stakeholders in higher education – they have emerged together with the new demands from higher education. The demand for higher education to be more responsive to the needs of the outside world means that, apart from the internal stakeholders (that is, the usual suspects such as students, teachers, other staff and sometimes the government as a founder and owner of public institutions), there is a need to include external stakeholders in the governance of higher education, including, but not limited to, representatives of the business and civic sector, local and/or regional authorities, etc. Thus, adequate mechanisms of involvement of these external stakeholders, both at the level of the institution and at the level of the whole system, should be put in place. However, the creation of adequate models depends on the contexts, cultures and the rationale of involving the external stakeholders and again there can be no "one-size-fits-all" model.

With the advent of mass higher education and in some countries almost universal higher education, there is an increasing number of those participating in higher education, increasing diversity of their backgrounds and increasing diversity of the ways that the tasks of teaching and research are being conducted in higher education, which is also somewhat changing the roles of those who teach and those who research. The fact that we now have a high number of students from non-traditional backgrounds, non-traditional in age, in origin as well as in education prior to higher education, imposes new challenges on governance structures. The demand for flexible learning paths in itself, clearly stated in the Bergen Communiqué, includes a demand for structures and procedures which will support flexibility in learning. New actors in higher education may also demand a change in admission requirements and procedures, a change in recognition procedures, especially recognition of prior learning, a change in student assessment procedures and internal quality assurance procedures. On the system level, new actors in higher education imply that there are new criteria on which the evaluation of the success of the institutions should be based, new funding mechanisms and new legislative frameworks. It is no longer sufficient, if it ever was, to focus only on research performance of institutions. Different institutions may cater for different needs of society and of economy and it could be that their added value is a more suitable starting point for the evaluation of success.

Given this diversity of both the stakeholders and the actors in higher education, it is important to stress, that, while recognising the necessity for governance to include different stakeholders and take into account the different actors in higher education, those involved in higher education governance should seek to strike a good balance between representing their respective constituencies and working towards achieving the long-term overall purpose of higher education. While it would be naïve to suggest that those representing various stakeholder groups could forget their own interests (if they do, what then is the purpose of having the diversity of stakeholders anyway?), it would also be naïve of the stakeholders to expect that they would not sometimes have to negotiate their own goals and objectives for a greater and more lasting good for all those benefiting from higher education.

This brings us to the basic principles of good governance, which are more succinctly presented in the "Considerations and recommendations" of the conference.

4. Basic principles of good governance

Governance can not be reduced to the decision-making process only or to the organisational structures in the sense that there is more to governance than the skeleton described in the system legislation or statutes of the institution and there is more to governance than the muscles on the skeleton which include additional descriptions of procedures, records of decisions taken and minutes of meetings.

One aspect is that we should not be afraid to admit that in the present situation there is a front stage of governance and also a backstage of governance. Many of those involved in higher education governance refer to the need for "real participation" and participation not in numbers and size but in essence. This seems to be a silent confession that there is more to governance than skeleton and muscles described above.

208

It may be impossible to bring all of the events to the front stage of governance, but what is essential is to diminish the impact of backstage, hidden agendas and power plays as much as possible. This can only be done if one other dimension of governance is added, a sort of mind and soul for the skeleton and the muscles we already have. This is the specific governance culture, values and attitudes understood and shared by those involved in governance, their aspirations towards the respect and development of the basic principles of good governance. The basic principles of good governance would include:

- the demand for transparency of structures and procedures (basically as little backstage as possible);

- the demand for effective mechanisms of accountability of those involved in governance on various levels;

- the ability to reach decisions and ensure their legitimacy;

- the commitment towards implementing these decisions.

This governance culture also means that the atmosphere in which governance takes place should also ensure that the decisions once made, if, and only if, they were made in the spirit of good governance, are to be respected even by those who do not agree with them, understanding that it is more important to ensure "a day in court" for all of the relevant stakeholders than to always have one's own way. Here it should be underlined that this is true only if the decision was indeed taken in the spirit of good governance, meaning with full respect of the set procedures and with appropriate methods of discussion over problematic issues. If this is not the case, then there is substantial justification for the expression of discontent in various ways. And indeed, we can find examples, both at institutional and at national level, that, when full ownership of the decisions was not achieved, reactions ranged from quiet disgruntled murmurs in the far corners of the room, over silent sabotage and impersonation of conformity to open rebellion. And in most of these cases, both the murmurs and the open rebellion are justifiable.

It has to be understood that the principle of legitimacy and the principle of efficiency are not in conflict – can a swift decision reached with seemingly unanimous support be labelled as truly efficient if those to whom the decision is related to do not agree with it and may, as I said, sabotage the implementation? Is a decision efficient if it is not effective, if it does not contribute to the fulfilment of the goals of higher education, in long-term perspective and having in mind the big picture and not immediate narrow interests? We should understand the demand for efficiency as an integral part of the demand for legitimacy of the decision making, so often voiced in the request for full participation and ownership.

We can see here that the basic principles of good governance actually entail what was referred to as "the democratic culture" by the 3rd Summit of the Heads of States and Government of the Council of Europe. In the action plan adopted at the summit it is stated:

The tasks of building a knowledge-based society and promoting a democratic culture among our citizens require increased efforts of the Council of Europe in the field of education aimed at ensuring access to education for all young people across Europe, improving its quality and promoting, *inter alia*, comprehensive human rights education.

5. Governance on the institutional, system and international level

With respect to governance of higher education at various levels, it is important to stress that governance of higher education should not be understood only as governance of HEI or even less only as management of HEI. It should be understood that the basic principles of good governance apply to both the institutional and system level, but also to the international level.

However, there are some specific characteristics of each of these levels.

a. Institutional level

The first issue worth mentioning here is the demand for strengthening the institutional identity, or, to put it more explicitly, strengthening the institutional level of governance. This issue is particularly relevant for some of the regions in Europe, most notably south-east Europe, as the universities[81] there do not exist in the real sense of the term; the rector more often than not has only a ceremonial role and the real focus of power lies at the level of the individual faculties. Recognising the differences between the faculties, it is necessary to strengthen the institutional level of governance, to ensure common sets of standards, to provide for sound and sustainable overall development plans, more effective use of resources and also greater strength for confronting the undue pressures from the outside. This includes both the strengthening of governance in the wider sense on the institutional level, but also the strengthening of central administration, bearing in mind the distinction between management and governance of the institution. The demand for more integration at the level of institution should not be understood as a call for micromanagement and, to answer the very colourful example of some of the deans who are trying to hang on to their present kingdoms – no, this does not mean that the rector shall decide on how much toilet paper the Department of Astrophysics at the Faculty of Mathematics at a particular university needs.

The second important issue is the quest for autonomy. First of all, it should be noted that more autonomy means more accountability and the fact that there seems to be a steady process of deregulation of the authority of the state, as an answer to that there seems also to be a steady process of self-regulation by institutions. The whole discussion on codes of conduct and the role that both national associations of HEI as well as their European counterparts, EUA and EURASHE, are playing is a good illustration of this process. However, it would be worth noting that the disappearance of bureaucracy on one level would, and often does, lead to the appearance of bureaucracy on another, lower, level. Self-regulation should not turn into mere shifting of bureaucracy from the system to the institutional level.

---

81. This refers to universities alone. It does not include other types of higher education institutions.

It is also necessary to further analyse the content and the scope of institutional autonomy with respect to the changed societal contexts. This may be a possible topic of future international higher education fora. Does autonomy refer only to autonomy from the state or is there someone else institutions should be autonomous from? And, what does the demand of autonomy entail – is it only legal autonomy, financial autonomy – and how can these demands be made operational and protected at the level of the system?

b. System level

Concerning the system level, public authorities should seek to provide an adequate legislative framework necessary for the functioning of higher education. This framework should refer both to the private and public higher education institutions which is also reflected in the "Considerations and recommendations" of the conference. Furthermore, it has to be noted that this framework must not be prescriptive, but that it should allow for flexibility in developing concrete solutions to specific problems and situations. It must not suffocate creativity and innovation. Flexibility in the legislative framework is also important to allow for change to take place without the delays caused by preparations of a new or amended legislation and by passing it through the appropriate governmental and parliamentary structures.

In addition to this, it should also be stressed that we should try to see the system level involving not only the government in the narrow sense of the word, presented through the ministries responsible for higher education, research and finance. There are a variety of public authorities which also operate on the system level, such as the judiciary system, quality assurance and accreditation agencies and even buffer structures such as the national councils of (higher) education, all of which are an integral element of the governance of higher education systems.

c. International level

In terms of the international level the basic principles of governance (transparency, legitimacy, flexibility, efficiency and effectiveness) are also valid here.

The increased frequency of cross-border and transnational higher education, through transnational institutions, joint programmes, mobility of students and staff, the GATS negotiations under the WTO, as well as the commitment towards establishing the EHEA and ERA, provide clear proof of the existence of another level of governance in higher education, and also another level where good governance is needed. The success of the ongoing international processes, primarily the Bologna Process, could be seriously jeopardised if they are not steered in such a way as to ensure adequate participation of the relevant stakeholders.

It should be noted that the international actors in higher education should also take upon themselves to facilitate the dialogue and the dissemination of good practice, recognising again that, while we cannot copy models from each other – we can learn from each others' experiences.

6. By way of conclusion

Professor Pavel Zgaga begins his introduction to the issue of governance of higher education by shedding some light on the origin of the word "governance" – *navigation* – the old art of ascertaining the position and directing one's course at sea. Therefore, if governance is navigation, good governance may include:

- an understanding that we are not only sailing the seas and oceans, but also calm rivers as well as turbulent creeks; and
- an understanding that more than one type of vessel is fit to cross the sea, but that each vessel should have sails, ropes and a helm to direct the vessel; otherwise it cannot be called a vessel and sooner or later it will sink.

We also need to have:

- updated maps, reliable compasses and good calculation of the course to take;
- skilled captains and first officers, whose authority is legitimate and based on competence;
- skilled crews, who will keep the decks clean, make sure ropes are not tangled and holes in the sails are repaired, and who, especially during storms and in troubled waters, will not bump into each other or work against each other, but who will complement each other's efforts in bringing the vessel safely to port.

And finally, we need an understanding shared by those who steer the vessel, those who are on the vessel as passengers and those who wait for the vessel in the various ports to make use of the goods the vessel is carrying – that each port is but a stop and that the voyage does not really have a final destination.

Considerations and recommandations

In contributing to the European Year of Citizenship through Education and cele-brating the 50th anniversary of the European Cultural Convention, we, the par-ticipants in the Council of Europe Forum on Higher Education Governance, con-firm the key role of higher education in the development of modern society based on democracy, human rights and the rule of law. The issue of good governance in higher education is crucial not only in the promotion of democratic culture with-in the higher education community but also in society at large; it is also indis-pensable to undertaking the profound reforms needed for creating the European Higher Education Area by 2010.

a. Considerations

i. We see higher education governance as fundamental to achieving the full range of purposes of higher education:

- preparation for the labour market;

- preparation for life as active citizens in a democratic society;

- personal development;

- maintenance and development of a broad, advanced knowledge base.

The range of relevant actors in higher education governance should reflect the multiplicity of purposes of higher education.

ii. It is important to ensure quality in higher education and research. We con-sider governance to be a crucial element of the quality culture of both sys-tems and institutions of higher education. It would not be possible to achieve quality higher education without good governance.

iii. We underline the importance of good governance in promoting social cohe-sion and in affording equal opportunity to higher education for all those qualified.

iv. We further understand good governance to imply, on the one hand, steering the process towards the development of valid objectives and, on the other hand, the development of the instruments needed to achieve these objec-tives – the "fitness *of* purpose" as well as the "fitness *for* purpose".

v. We consider legitimacy to be one of the basic principles of good gover-nance – it should be understood as the heart of the efficiency of gover-nance, and not as its opposite.

vi. Within the basic principles of good governance in higher education it is important to allow sufficient flexibility to take account of the specific con-texts and traditions of given higher education institutions or given systems.

vii. Good governance is not guaranteed by established structures and procedures alone. It is necessary for the actors in governance of higher education to promote democratic culture as another building block of governance and as a basic principle of good governance.

viii. Given the role higher education has for the overall societal and economic development, we see the necessity to ensure the responsiveness of higher education to the changing needs and expectations of society. In this respect, it is important to ensure participation of external actors in the governance of higher education and to allow for flexibility to accommodate the continuous change of the aforementioned needs and expectations.

b. Recommendations

i. The governance of systems and institutions of higher education should be based on the adequate inclusion of all relevant stakeholders. To ensure successful attainment of the agreed set of goals, it should be founded on the principles of:

- transparency in procedures and tasks;

- effective mechanisms of accountability of those involved in governance;

- the ability to reach, win acceptance for and implement decisions;

- participation and the rule of law.

ii. Higher education serves to accommodate the expectations and needs of different groups within society. Those serving on higher education governance bodies, regardless of the capacity in which they serve, should seek to act in accordance with their understanding of the best interest of the higher education system and institutions for which they are responsible, while also paying appropriate attention to the concerns of the constituency from which they originate.

iii. Institutional autonomy is essential for ensuring academic freedom, which constitutes one of the core values of higher education. Public authorities should establish and maintain an appropriate legislative framework that ensures institutional autonomy and provides for adaptability of structures and flexibility of methods within the basic principles of good higher education governance. The legal framework concerning governance should apply equally to both public and private institutions.

iv. It is important to make a distinction between the process of setting long-term goals and developing appropriate strategies for achieving them, and implementing these strategies on a day-to-day basis. The legitimacy and competence of the governing bodies should be complemented with the professionalism of the administration.

v. While avoiding undue micromanagement and leaving reasonable scope for innovation and flexibility, higher education governance systems and practices should facilitate the elaboration and implementation of coherent institutional policies.

vi. International organisations and networks active in higher education should consider promoting good higher education governance by disseminating examples of good governance and fostering dialogue between different systems and institutions on the further elaboration of the basic principles of good governance.

vii. The Bologna Follow-up Group should give explicit consideration to the role of governance in reaching the goal of providing high quality education and mobility of students and staff throughout Europe.

c. Issues for further consideration

We suggest that it is necessary to elaborate on what the autonomy of higher education institutions in the modern society includes, in terms of content (legal, financial, etc.) as well as in terms of bodies and actors. Furthermore, it would be necessary to determine, at both national and institutional level, the sectors of governance of higher education where changes are most needed.

List of contributors

Series editor

Sjur Bergan

Sjur Bergan is Head of the Council of Europe's Department of Higher Education and History Teaching, Secretary to its Steering Committee for Higher Education and Research and a member of the Bologna Follow-up Group and Board. He is a frequent contributor to the debate on higher education policies in Europe, the author of many articles and editor of *The Heritage of European universities* (with Nuria Sanz, 2002), *Recognition issues in the Bologna Process* (2003), *The university as* res publica: *Higher education governance, student participation and the university as a site of citizenship* (2004) and *The public responsibility for higher education and research* (2005).

Editors

Jürgen Kohler

Jürgen Kohler is professor of private law and private litigation at Greifswald University, Germany. He was one of the founders of the re-established faculty of law and business management of Greifswald University after German reunification in 1990. He was rector of Greifswald University between 1994 and 2000. Since then he has represented the German institutions of higher education in the CDESR of the Council of Europe and has been a member of its bureau since 2002. He is active in the Institutional Evaluation Programme of the European University Association, both serving in peer-based evaluations across Europe and in its steering committee. He chairs the German Accreditation Council.

Josef Huber

Josef Huber is administrator at the Division for Higher Education and Research of the Council of Europe and Secretary to the Working Party on Higher Education Governance. From 1998 to 2004, as Head of Programmes and Deputy Executive Director of the European Centre for Modern Languages – an enlarged partial agreement of the Council of Europe – he was, *inter alia*, responsible for the centre's publications series that dealt with a wide range of topics in the area of language learning and teaching, intercultural communication and language education policy.

Authors

Pavel Zgaga

Pavel Zgaga is a professor at the University of Ljubljana and Director of the Centre for Educational Policy Studies at the Faculty of Education. His research is primarily focused on the philosophy of education and on educational policy, particularly in contemporary issues of internationalisation of higher education. He is former Vice-Minister and Minister of Education of Slovenia and a signee at the Bologna Declaration. He was general rapporteur at the Berlin Conference of the Bologna Process.

Virgílio Meira Soares

Full professor at the University of Lisbon, since 1979. Former Secretary of State for Higher Education, former Rector of the University of Lisbon, former Vice-President of the Portuguese Rectors' Conference, and presently member of the Bureau of the CDESR of the Council of Europe, Co-ordinator of the Co-operation of Portuguese HE with East Timor, President of the Evaluation Council of the Portuguese Public Universities and Chairman of the Commission for Access to Higher Education in Portugal. Member of the pool of evaluators of the Institutional Evaluation Programme of the European University Association, since its beginning, and many times expert of the Council of Europe in advisory missions to central and eastern European countries. Present interests: HE policies, member of the Directive Board of CIPES, (Centre for Higher Education and Research Policies, Portugal).

Luc Weber

Educated in the fields of economics and political science, Luc Weber has been Professor of Public Economics at the University of Geneva since 1975. As an economist, he serves as an adviser to Switzerland's federal government, as well as to cantonal governments, and has been a member of the Swiss Council of Economic Advisers for three years. Since 1982, Professor Weber has been deeply involved in university management and higher education policy, first as Vice-Rector, then as Rector of the University of Geneva, as well as Chairman and, subsequently, Consul for international affairs of the Swiss Rectors' Conference. He is also the co-founder, with Werner Hirsch, of the Glion Colloquium and a founding board member of the European University Association (EUA). At present he is Chair of the Steering Committee for Higher Education and Research of the Council of Europe and Vice-President of the International Association of Universities (IAU). He was recently awarded an honorary doctorate degree by the Catholic University of Louvain-la-Neuve for his contribution to higher education.

Jochen Fried

Jochen Fried is the director of education initiatives and academic director of the International Study Program at the Salzburg Seminar. He is the former director of the Universities Project of the Salzburg Seminar. Prior to joining the Seminar in 1998, he worked as head of programmes at the Institute for Human Sciences in Vienna, and as senior officer in the secretariat of the German Science Council in Cologne, Germany. After receiving a doctorate in German literature from Düsseldorf University, Germany in 1984, he was lecturer at Cambridge University, United Kingdom, and at the University of Ljubljana, Slovenia, under the auspices of the German Academic Exchange Service. Dr. Fried's main area of professional interest is higher education and research policy. He serves as an expert for a variety of national and international institutions and agencies (Austrian Federal Ministry for Education, Science and Culture, the European Commission, Council of Europe, the Open Society Institute, among others) and is a member of the editorial board of the UNESCO-CEPES quarterly review *Higher Education in Europe*.

Dijana Tiplič

Dijana Tiplič has studied Business Administration and IT Management in Sandvika (BI Norwegian School of Management) and Comparative and International Education in Oslo (University of Oslo). She holds an MSc in organisational management (2003) (title of thesis: An issue of perceived uncertainty: A case of Bosnia-Herzegovina higher education institutions). She is currently affiliated to the Centre for Education Management Research (www.bi.no/cem) writing her PhD thesis on organisational change in higher education institutions. Her main research interests are within the field of organisation studies and higher education research.

Robin Farquhar

Robin Farquhar, former President of Carleton University and the University of Winnipeg, is now Professor Emeritus of Public Policy and Administration at Carleton. Currently an international consultant on higher education management, he is working with the Association of Universities and Colleges of Canada, the European University Association's Institutional Evaluation Programme, and the Salzburg Seminar. He lives in Ottawa.

Aleksander Lomaia

Aleksander Lomaia is currently the Minister of Education and Science of Georgia. He obtained his PhD from the Moscow Construction Engineering Institute in 1992. From 1989 until 1991 he worked as Vice-Chairman of the Governing Board at the NGO "Georgian Community" in Moscow, Russia where he developed working contacts among NGOs, democratic movements, civic activists, human rights groups, and ethnic communities to mobilise public support for the independence of Georgia and other Soviet republics. In 1991, he was the Acting Ambassador of the Republic of Georgia to Russia, followed by a position as Secretary General of the Christian Democratic Union of Georgia where he managed the institutional and international activities of the Christian Democratic parliamentary political movement, which led to the admission of CDU Georgia as a full member of Christian Democratic International – the first member among the newly independent states of the former Soviet Union.

In 1995, he was the director and editor at the International Affairs Department of the newspaper *Argumenti*. From 1995 to 2000, he acted as a Program Officer, Public Administration/Civil Society at the Eurasia Foundation in Tbilisi, where his duties included developing strategic objectives for the Foundation's regional development; working closely with the three-country Synergy Program designed to promote grass-roots co-operation among the three countries of the South Caucasus. During 1998 he served as a member of the Eurasia Foundation Strategic Planning Committee, participating in development of the Foundation's mission and definition of its priorities. In 2000-02, he was the Country Director of the Eurasia Foundation in Tbilisi, Georgia followed by a position as Regional Director for the former Soviet Union at the Democracy Coalition Project in

Tbilisi. The project facilitated the creation of an international federation of national coalitions which collectively pursued for democratic reforms on the international stage. Subsequently, in 2003-04, he was Executive Director of the Open Society Georgia Foundation (Soros Foundation) in Tbilisi. Dr. Aleksander Lomaia's name is included in *Who's Who in Georgia 2001-2002*, published by the Georgian Biographical Center.

Jaak Aaviksoo

Jaak Aaviksoo has been Rector at the University of Tartu since 1998 and the Chairman of the Board of Estonian Rectors' Conference since 2004. He was Minister of Education of Estonia 1995-1997, before that Vice-Rector of the University of Tartu. He is a physicist, professor of optics and spectroscopy at the University of Tartu. He has been a visiting professor and scholar in Russia, Germany, France, Japan. He is a member of the Estonian Academy of Sciences, Academic Council of the President of Estonia and the Board of the European University Association.

Radmila Marinković-Nedučin

Radmila Marinković-Nedučin is full professor, Faculty of Technology, Physical Chemistry and Catalysis and currently Rector of the University of Novi Sad, Serbia and Montenegro.

Previously, member of the Commission for the new law on higher education of Republic of Serbia, member of Bologna Follow-up Group of the Ministry of Education of the Republic of Serbia and Vice-President and President of the Republic Council on High Education Policy in the period 2003-04/2004 respectively.

Her recent activities in the field of educational policy are as follows: author of *National guide to ECTS* (published by Alternative Academic Network, Belgrade, 2002), co-author of the chapter "Infrastructure/Public research and development in program of economical development of the Province of Vojvodina" (Executive Council of Autonomous Province of Vojvodina, Novi Sad, 2003), co-author of the "Analysis of current state of the development of study program and credit system within the program regional university network on governance and management of higher education", UNESCO-CEPES, 2003.

In the positions held at the University of Novi Sad and the Republic Council on Higher Education Policy, Professor Radmila Marinković-Nedučin has participated in a large number of domestic and international conferencess, debates and workshops and had a crucial role in the process of drafting the new Law on Higher Education in Serbia.

Erdal Emel

Currently the Vice-Rector and the Head of Industrial Engineering Department at Uludağ University. Previously, the rector's counsellor and the Associate Dean of Faculty of Engineering and Architecture of Uludağ University. Graduate of

Istanbul Technical University (BSc 1981) and University of Michigan, Ann Arbor (MSc 1983, PhD 1987) with all degrees in mechanical engineering. Areas of interest range from quality management in higher education to technology and production management in manufacturing industries, in addition to vehicle noise and vibration research.

Martina Vukasović

Martina Vukasović is currently enrolled in the European Masters Programme on Higher Education, organised jointly by the University of Oslo, University of Tampere and University of Aveiro. She worked in the Council of Europe's Division for Higher Education and Research in 2004, was a student representative in Serbia and at European level through ESIB – The National Unions of Students in Europe and, before starting the masters' studies, worked as a project officer in the Alternative Academic Educational Network – an organisation supporting and promoting the reform of higher education in Serbia.

Sales agents for publications of the Council of Europe
Agents de vente des publications du Conseil de l'Europe

BELGIUM/BELGIQUE
La Librairie Européenne -
The European Bookshop
Rue de l'Orme, 1
B-1040 BRUXELLES
Tel.: +32 (0)2 231 04 35
Fax: +32 (0)2 735 08 60
E-mail: order@libeurop.be
http://www.libeurop.be

Jean De Lannoy
Avenue du Roi 202 Koningslaan
B-1190 BRUXELLES
Tel.: +32 (0)2 538 43 08
Fax: +32 (0)2 538 08 41
E-mail: jean.de.lannoy@dl-servi.com
http://www.jean-de-lannoy.be

CANADA
Renouf Publishing Co. Ltd.
1-5369 Canotek Road
OTTAWA, Ontario K1J 9J3, Canada
Tel.: +1 613 745 2665
Fax: +1 613 745 7660
Toll-Free Tel.: (866) 767-6766
E-mail: order.dept@renoufbooks.com
http://www.renoufbooks.com

CZECH REPUBLIC/
RÉPUBLIQUE TCHÈQUE
Suweco CZ, s.r.o.
Klecakova 347
CZ-180 21 PRAHA 9
Tel.: +420 2 424 59 204
Fax: +420 2 848 21 646
E-mail: import@suweco.cz
http://www.suweco.cz

DENMARK/DANEMARK
GAD
Vimmelskaftet 32
DK-1161 KØBENHAVN K
Tel.: +45 77 66 60 00
Fax: +45 77 66 60 01
E-mail: gad@gad.dk
http://www.gad.dk

FINLAND/FINLANDE
Akateeminen Kirjakauppa
PO Box 128
Keskuskatu 1
FIN-00100 HELSINKI
Tel.: +358 (0)9 121 4430
Fax: +358 (0)9 121 4242
E-mail: akatilaus@akateeminen.com
http://www.akateeminen.com

FRANCE
La Documentation française
(diffusion/distribution France entière)
124, rue Henri Barbusse
F-93308 AUBERVILLIERS CEDEX
Tél.: +33 (0)1 40 15 70 00
Fax: +33 (0)1 40 15 68 00
E-mail: commande@ladocumentationfrancaise.fr
http://www.ladocumentationfrancaise.fr

Librairie Kléber
1 rue des Francs Bourgeois
F-67000 STRASBOURG
Tel.: +33 (0)3 88 15 78 88
Fax: +33 (0)3 88 15 78 80
E-mail: francois.wolfermann@librairie-kleber.fr
http://www.librairie-kleber.com

GERMANY/ALLEMAGNE
AUSTRIA/AUTRICHE
UNO Verlag GmbH
August-Bebel-Allee 6
D-53175 BONN
Tel.: +49 (0)228 94 90 20
Fax: +49 (0)228 94 90 222
E-mail: bestellung@uno-verlag.de
http://www.uno-verlag.de

GREECE/GRÈCE
Librairie Kauffmann s.a.
Stadiou 28
GR-105 64 ATHINAI
Tel.: +30 210 32 55 321
Fax: +30 210 32 30 320
E-mail: ord@otenet.gr
http://www.kauffmann.gr

HUNGARY/HONGRIE
Euro Info Service kft.
1137 Bp. Szent István krt. 12.
H-1137 BUDAPEST
Tel.: +36 (06)1 329 2170
Fax: +36 (06)1 349 2053
E-mail: euroinfo@euroinfo.hu
http://www.euroinfo.hu

ITALY/ITALIE
Licosa SpA
Via Duca di Calabria, 1/1
I-50125 FIRENZE
Tel.: +39 0556 483215
Fax: +39 0556 41257
E-mail: licosa@licosa.com
http://www.licosa.com

MEXICO/MEXIQUE
Mundi-Prensa México, S.A. De C.V.
Río Pánuco, 141 Delegacíon Cuauhtémoc
06500 MÉXICO, D.F.
Tel.: +52 (01)55 55 33 56 58
Fax: +52 (01)55 55 14 67 99
E-mail: mundiprensa@mundiprensa.com.mx
http://www.mundiprensa.com.mx

NETHERLANDS/PAYS-BAS
De Lindeboom Internationale Publicaties b.v.
M.A. de Ruyterstraat 20 A
NL-7482 BZ HAAKSBERGEN
Tel.: +31 (0)53 5740004
Fax: +31 (0)53 5729296
E-mail: books@delindeboom.com
http://www.delindeboom.com

NORWAY/NORVÈGE
Akademika
Postboks 84 Blindern
N-0314 OSLO
Tel.: +47 2 218 8100
Fax: +47 2 218 8103
E-mail: support@akademika.no
http://www.akademika.no

POLAND/POLOGNE
Ars Polona JSC
25 Obroncow Street
PL-03-933 WARSZAWA
Tel.: +48 (0)22 509 86 00
Fax: +48 (0)22 509 86 10
E-mail: arspolona@arspolona.com.pl
http://www.arspolona.com.pl

PORTUGAL
Livraria Portugal
(Dias & Andrade, Lda.)
Rua do Carmo, 70
P-1200-094 LISBOA
Tel.: +351 21 347 42 82 / 85
Fax: +351 21 347 02 64
E-mail: info@livrariaportugal.pt
http://www.livrariaportugal.pt

RUSSIAN FEDERATION/
FÉDÉRATION DE RUSSIE
Ves Mir
9a, Kolpacnhyi per.
RU-101000 MOSCOW
Tel.: +7 (8)495 623 6839
Fax: +7 (8)495 625 4269
E-mail: orders@vesmirbooks.ru
http://www.vesmirbooks.ru

SPAIN/ESPAGNE
Mundi-Prensa Libros, s.a.
Castelló, 37
E-28001 MADRID
Tel.: +34 914 36 37 00
Fax: +34 915 75 39 98
E-mail: libreria@mundiprensa.es
http://www.mundiprensa.com

SWITZERLAND/SUISSE
Van Diermen Editions – ADECO
Chemin du Lacuez 41
CH-1807 BLONAY
Tel.: +41 (0)21 943 26 73
Fax: +41 (0)21 943 36 05
E-mail: info@adeco.org
http://www.adeco.org

UNITED KINGDOM/ROYAUME-UNI
The Stationery Office Ltd
PO Box 29
GB-NORWICH NR3 1GN
Tel.: +44 (0)870 600 5522
Fax: +44 (0)870 600 5533
E-mail: book.enquiries@tso.co.uk
http://www.tsoshop.co.uk

UNITED STATES and CANADA/
ÉTATS-UNIS et CANADA
Manhattan Publishing Company
468 Albany Post Road
CROTTON-ON-HUDSON, NY 10520, USA
Tel.: +1 914 271 5194
Fax: +1 914 271 5856
E-mail: Info@manhattanpublishing.com
http://www.manhattanpublishing.com

Council of Europe Publishing/Editions du Conseil de l'Europe
F-67075 Strasbourg Cedex
Tel.: +33 (0)3 88 41 25 81 – Fax: +33 (0)3 88 41 39 10 – E-mail: publishing@coe.int – Website: http://book.coe.int